Betrayal
of an Army

By the same author

The Colonel's Table
Reveille & Retribution
Spit & Polish
Friend & Foe
On Laffan's Plain
'K' Boat Catastrophe
Chitrál Charlie
Valour in the Trenches
Strafer – Desert General
Where Tom Long Roamed

Betrayal of an Army

Mesopotamia 1914–1916

N.S. Nash

Pen & Sword
MILITARY

First published in Great Britain by
PEN AND SWORD MILITARY
an imprint of
Pen and Sword Books Ltd
47 Church Street
Barnsley
South Yorkshire S70 2AS

ISBN 978 1 47384 376 9

Printed and bound in England by
CPI Group (UK) Ltd, Croydon, CR0 4YY

Typeset in Times by CHIC GRAPHICS

Pen & Sword Books Ltd incorporates the imprints of
Pen & Sword Aviation, Pen & Sword Family History, Pen & Sword Maritime,
Pen & Sword Military, Pen & Sword Discovery, Wharncliffe Local History,
Wharncliffe True Crime, Wharncliffe Transport, Pen & Sword Select,
Pen & Sword Military Classics, Leo Cooper, Remember When,
The Praetorian Press, Seaforth Publishing and Frontline Publishing

For a complete list of Pen and Sword titles please contact
Pen and Sword Books Limited
47 Church Street, Barnsley, South Yorkshire, S70 2AS, England
E-mail: enquiries@pen-and-sword.co.uk
Website: www.pen-and-sword.co.uk

Contents

List of Illustrations

Acknowledgements

I am indebted to Lieutenant Colonel W.W.T. Gowans who reviewed the text, suggested corrections, posed me some interesting questions and considered, in particular, my judgments. Similarly, I was fortunate that Professor Peter Liddle, who having read the text, challenged elements of my approach; I enjoyed our debate. Even though they did not necessarily entirely agree with me on all the issues I am enormously grateful to them both. Any errors or omissions are entirely mine.

At Pen and Sword, Brigadier Henry Wilson, my commissioning editor, for the fourth time, eased my path and encouraged my endeavours. Matt Jones was his usual helpful self with all matters technical. My text editor Linne Matthews was not only very skilled and professional but a delight to work with.

Where possible the attribution has been given to photographs and maps but those taken from the Internet do not always identify the original source.

Introduction

In 2009 I was researching the Mesopotamian campaign up to the fall of Kut in April 1916. This was in order to produce my biography of Major General Sir Charles Townshend (*Chitrál Charlie*, Pen and Sword Books, 2010). Townshend was an individual who played a key role during that period and it was he who was, ultimately, surrendered the remnants of the 6th Indian Division to the Turks. Inevitably, he also makes a lengthy appearance in this book. He was a prisoner of war (albeit a comfortable one) when the Mesopotamia Commission sat and so he could not be interviewed, more is the pity.

Much of the research carried out in 2009 has been germane to this book. Facts remain the facts and, over the last century, nothing has happened to change them, although here they are viewed from a different angle and in a wider context.

The far-reaching and abundant military naivety, at a very senior level, that was revealed in *Chitrál Charlie* shocked me. The painful impact that gross mal-administration had upon tens of thousands of British and Indian soldiers made a strong impression and I resolved to return to the subject ere long.

This book is the result and the title is a statement, not a question.

In order to consider the validity of the case against the men who were, allegedly, culpably incompetent it is necessary to visit the battlefields, but it is not my intention to rehash in minute detail the ghastly events that led to so many fruitless deaths.

A hundred years after the events I describe, the soldiers' bones still lie in the desert sand, unvisited in a land once more wracked with extreme violence. One wonders was it all worth it?

The Mesopotamia Commission (MC) was formed to examine a toxic combination of misjudgements, dishonesty and ineptitude. When the MC reported, in June 1917, its findings embarrassed His Majesty's Government (HMG), which was at a loss to see a way forward.

The formation and composition of the Commission was flawed. Although it was empowered to take evidence on oath it had no powers of discipline and its only weapon was that of censure. When the Commission's work was completed its Report became a political football and the tangible benefits were scant. Throughout this text, extracts from the Mesopotamia Commission Report (MC Report) are in italics.

The judgements made in this book are based on my interpretation of the contemporary accounts and the MC Report. My readers must decide if I have struck a fair balance and draw their own conclusions.

Tank Nash
Malmesbury
April 2016

Chapter 1

Hardinge at Bay

'A leader is a dealer in hope.'
(Napoleon)

3 July 1917 was a warm summer day in London and the Chamber of the House of Lords was overcrowded and stuffy. The attendance of so many peers was a clear indication that something of significance was about to happen.

A tall, slim, 59-year-old man in a frock coat entered, stood briefly by the Clerk's table and looked around. On either side of the Chamber he saw four terraces of benches, all completely filled, which rose above the floor of the House. Above them ran a line of galleries, occupied this afternoon by peeresses and members of the lower house.

The chattering voices were stilled and all eyes were focussed on the man at the Clerk's table.

He was Lord Hardinge, latterly Viceroy of India, and one of the most distinguished public servants in the land. He also had the dubious distinction of being the most senior of those subject to severe criticism in the recently published Mesopotamia Commission Report.

This report, now firmly in the public domain, published the result of enquiries into the conduct of the disastrous military campaign of 1914–16. This took place in what was, allegedly, the Garden of Eden but which turned into a version of hell for the British and Indian soldiers engaged there. Of those, 30,000 died and thousands more were still languishing in Turkish prison camps in conditions of extreme privation.

Lord Hardinge was to make a public statement, which his friends all hoped would completely rebut the 'absurd' charges laid at his door. This was a key moment in the career of a distinguished public servant and also of some significance to His Majesty's Government, led by the priapic David Lloyd George.

Hardinge walked briskly up to the table. Exuding self-control and apparently quite unflustered by the situation, he laid his notes down.

1

He tugged at his coat, put on his spectacles, rested his right hand on his notes and allowed his left arm to hang at his side. A journalist who was present observed:

> His body was turned to face diagonally across the Chamber. From this position he rarely moved, and then only to turn one sheet of paper aside as he had finished reading from it.
>
> It was a model of deliverance, clearly enunciated, in well audible, measured tones. There was no impassioned appeal to sentiment, plea for leniency of criticism. Just a plain, well thought out, logically arrayed statement of justification from the point of view of the Indian Government. It was scrupulously free from embittered recrimination.
>
> The performance was really a notable one; the more so seeing that it was the first time he had ever spoken in the House of Lords.
>
> The impression I got was that he had said his say and did not care what the world might choose to think of him.[1]

The MC had formed its conclusions several months before and had published its Report on 20 June 1917. A minority report included the utterly damning observation that Hardinge, as Viceroy, and General Sir Beauchamp Duff, the Commander in Chief of the Indian Army, had shown:

> *little desire to help and some desire to actually obstruct the energetic prosecution of the war.*

This was an accusation that implied malfeasance, bordering on treachery. Little wonder then that the House of Lords was packed and that the Report had stunned the Government. It had sat on the Report for several weeks, but now HMG was in a dilemma as to how to deal with the quite specific charges made against several of the 'great and the good'.

The speech by Hardinge, in which he absolved himself of any culpability for the defeat of Indian Expeditionary Force 'D' (IEF 'D') and of the neglect of the sick and wounded, did not staunch the flow of criticism. His biographer, B.C. Bush, was overly generous in his judgment when he wrote that, 'the general reaction to his defence was favourable.' This was not the case. Busch continued, 'It was his maiden speech in House of Lords and he had not convinced his audience on all the charges, but most recognised his culpability was on a different level to that of the military authorities.'[2] The speech was widely reported in the Press,[3] on 4 July 1917, and the reaction to his performance was generally negative. Hardinge had said nothing to rebut the strictures of the MC and had not helped his cause. He was unduly

1. Lord Hardinge of Penshurst.

verbose, reiterated facts that were not in dispute but, crucially, he did not address the key issues.

The following day the Press commented as follows:

Daily Mail
Lord Hardinge's defence does not rebut   it hardly answers the judgment that the majority of the Commission were compelled to pass on him.

Morning Post
The public in reading Lord Hardinge's speech will no doubt be reminded of a certain unhappy attempt to shift responsibility, of which Mesopotamia was again the scene when the man blamed the woman and the woman blamed the serpent. In the result – if our recollection serves – judgment was pronounced on all three. It is a pity that Lord Hardinge did not resign, for he was condemned by an impartial tribunal.

Daily Telegraph

Thorough reform of the higher command in the administration of India is a proved and pressing necessity. Lord Hardinge was silent on one matter which general common sense seized upon as the most deplorably weak and unbusinesslike of all administrative facilities with which the Commission dealt, namely the practice of governing the Indian Empire, to say nothing of conducting a military effort of unparalleled magnitude from a hill top in the Himalayas.

Daily Chronicle

[We] doubt whether of those who have most carefully studied the reports will be found half a dozen whose judgment is materially modified by what Lord Hardinge said.

Daily News

The impression left by Lord Hardinge's speech in no way diminishes the disquieting effect of the Report.

The Times

Although Lord Hardinge's statement brought to light few new facts, it was accepted as an important addition to the material on which the public and both Houses of Parliament will pronounce final judgment. The debates, for which the Government has promised facilities, can hardly be delayed beyond next week. It is true that the Government have not yet decided on the nature of their disciplinary measures, but when the law officers' opinions and precedents are before them, they cannot long be postponed.

* * *

Clearly this issue, which had aroused public opinion, still had some way to run. The House of Commons would, of necessity, now debate the matter at length. Along the way the performance of some very senior military officers would be questioned and the Government would have cause to regret the manner in which it set up the MC in the first place. A full-on public scandal was underway and to 'the man on the Clapham omnibus' of legend there seemed to be every likelihood that heads would roll.

Chapter notes
1 'Journal' (By special wire) 5 New Bridge St, EC4, 3 July 1917.
2 Busch, B.C., *Hardinge of Penshurst*, p.269.
3 *The Aberdeen Daily News*, 4 July 1917.

Chapter 2

Mesopotamia and its Oil

'Your greatness does not depend upon the size of
your command but in the manner
in which you exercise it.'

(Marshal of France Ferdinand Foch, Major General Sir George Aston,
The Biography of Foch, 1929)

The drama embracing Lord Hardinge in London that summer's day could trace its roots back to 1912 when Admiral Lord 'Jackie' Fisher, now retired, was invited to chair a Royal Commission to enquire into the practicality of using 'Liquid Fuel'. In effect, was it practical or desirable to power the Royal Navy by oil? Fisher's Commission reported, in the affirmative, on 27 November 1912.[4]

At the insistence of the perceptive Fisher,[5] HMS *Queen Elizabeth* and the others of her class now being built would be fuelled by oil – a commodity of which Britain had none. Churchill, First Lord of the Admiralty (1911–15) commented that, 'to change the foundation of the Navy from British coal to foreign oil was a formidable decision in itself.'

Britain may have been resting on a foundation of coal, but the technology had moved on and the limitations of coal had been robustly addressed by a singularly robust and capable personality. There was no doubt that, 'providing the fleet with coal was the greatest logistical headache of the age,'[6] and Fisher judged, correctly, that the future was oil. As a priority the Royal Navy, then the greatest fleet in the world, had to be assured of an ample provision. A major factor in this provision was geography and that of Mesopotamia, in particular, because the head of the Persian Gulf was where oil was available in abundant quantity.

Churchill knew that, if the supply of oil could be secured, 'we should be able to raise the whole power and efficiency of the Navy to a definitely higher level: better ships, better crews, higher economies, more intense forms of war power – in a word, mastery itself was the prize of the venture.'[7]

The principal features of this part of the world are the rivers Tigris and Euphrates. Both rise in the Taurus Mountains of southern Turkey and their sources are only about 20 miles apart. They then flow, broadly north to south, through what was Mesopotamia (now Turkey, Iraq and Syria) and meet to form the Shatt al-Arab waterway at the ill-favoured town of Kurnah (Kurna or al-Qurnah). Kurnah is about 40 miles north of the larger and more important town of Basra.

The Euphrates is 1,900 miles long from its source to the confluence with the Tigris. The latter, to the east of the Euphrates, is about 1,150 miles to that confluence. From time immemorial this river, the only highway, has attracted settlement along its banks. Not the least of these settlements is Baghdad, the capital of what is now called Iraq. Baghdad lies 502 'Tigris miles' north of Basra but only 279 miles as an energetic bird might fly. The two sinuous and relatively shallow rivers were central to military campaigning in that part of the world a hundred years ago, when there was an absolute dearth of roads and railways.

The precise source of that oil provision, so important to Fisher and the Royal Navy, was on the island of Abadan where the Karun River flows into the Shatt al-Arab, about 21 miles south of Basra. This river is more rapid than the Tigris; although shallow in places it is less winding, and easily navigable. In 1914, Messrs Lynch, who had a small fleet of steamers running up the Karun and also plying between Basra and Baghdad, provided steam navigation upon these rivers. The company vessels were of a type specifically designed to cope with the eccentricities of the Tigris and there was a fount of expertise to be found among their captains.

The British Government was a major shareholder in the Anglo-Persian Oil Company and so had an abiding interest in the island of Abadan, where the oil pipelines terminated. The strategic importance of Basra to the north was that it was not only the largest settlement but was also the gateway to Abadan for southbound river traffic coming from the hinterland of Mesopotamia. The Shatt al–Arab, 'regarded technically as Turkish waters',[8] is, hereabouts, about 600 yards wide and from 7–12 feet deep, depending on the season. The Royal Navy had been policing the Shatt, the Gulf and the Indian Ocean beyond, by suppressing piracy for decades with the tacit consent of the Turkish and Arab states along the shores.

Mesopotamia was then, and is now, one of the hottest, most forbidding and hostile places on the planet. In 1914 it was entirely dependent on the two rivers for its water supply and for movement north/south. The country traversed by the two great rivers is a vast plain intersected by swamps and without roads of any description. (Above Kut there was a caravan road to Baghdad.) The soil is a sandy loam, which turns swiftly to tenacious, clinging mud after rain to the degree that, in wet weather and floods, none of the country bordering the Tigris below Kut is fit for wheeled vehicles. *'The climate is exceptionally hot, damp and enervating, with periodical snaps of icy storms in winter. In the heat of the summer a double fly tent is an inadequate protection against sunstroke. Military movements are exceptionally difficult, the rivers being the preferred mode of transport.'*[9]

The other phenomenon that served to make life difficult, especially for soldiers, was the arbitrary appearance of mirages. They are all-pervading and convey a distorted image, and not only of movement, when animals appear to be men. Static objects are subject to similar visual corruption. Trees become hills; bushes and defensive features take on a different and misleading guise.

In the dry season wheeled transport is generally practicable, but the plethora of irrigation canals and creeks that branch out from the river on both sides are wide enough and deep enough to form significant obstacles to riverside movement. Each has to be bridged in turn – this in a country without any material suitable for bridging. An old Arab proverb, much quoted in every book on this campaign, summed it all up by saying, 'When Allah made hell he did not find it bad enough and so he made Mesopotamia – and then, he added flies.'

It was a miserable and uncomfortable place but it was the source of the all-important oil that had to be secured in the face of possible Turkish/German opposition. Hitherto, Britain and Turkey had enjoyed amiable relations, but complacency in the Foreign Office and the casual indifference of His Majesty's Government had allowed an ambitious Germany to move in to fill a gap in Turkish affections. The Germans exercised increasingly greater influence in Turkey and were ensconced in the infrastructure of the Turkish armed forces, usually in command appointments. This, literally, put a German finger on the trigger.

HMG realised, belatedly in 1914, that every effort now had to be made to prevent Turkey taking up arms with Germany against the British Empire because of its interest in the Mesopotamian area.

In the summer of 1914, Britain's relations with Turkey were cool, getting cooler, and they got positively frosty when two warships, the *Reshadieh* and *Sultan Osman 1* that were being built in Britain for the Ottoman Navy, were diverted to the Royal Navy. They duly became HMS *Agincourt* and *Erin*. The Turks were predictably aggrieved, but the pragmatic decision by Churchill, in his role as First Lord of the Admiralty, was entirely sensible. The writing was already on the wall and to supply two ships to a possible or even a probable enemy would have been foolish.

In early October 1914, elements of the Ottoman Navy, under German command and on German initiative, attacked the Russian Black Sea Fleet at Odessa and inflicted heavy casualties. The German finger had squeezed the metaphorical trigger in an event that, in short order, led to hostilities between Britain and Turkey. War was declared on 5 November 1914. In Mesopotamia there were four enemies: the Turkish Army, marauding Arabs, the climate and the geography.[10]

However, in 1921, Talaat Pasha, the wartime Turkish leader in 1914, published his memoirs and clarified the events that finally tied Turkey to Germany. He wrote:

> Our German admiral, Souchon, deliberately took our best Turkish ships [the *Goeben* and others] and bombarded the Russian fleet and some of the Russian cities. We were generally supposed to have sanctioned this; and during the War I let this impression stand, rather than quarrel with the Germans.
>
> Now that I am no longer at the head of affairs, I want it positively known that our Ministry knew nothing of the intended attack. Neither I nor any other official authorised it. On the contrary, we were much upset by it. All the Cabinet members were very angry; we held a hurried meeting, and several of them resigned in protest. The rest of us agreed to try to smooth the matter over.
>
> The Russian ambassador at once sent us a vigorous protest. So did the French and British representatives. The latter two, however, were still hopeful of peace, and proposed that we make our innocence clear by dismissing our German admiral and sailors, and becoming strictly neutral.
>
> We could not prolong this absurd situation. To satisfy the Entente by a public repudiation of Admiral Souchon would have meant the loss of our German alliance forever. We held another anxious Cabinet meeting, the important one at which war was decided on.
>
> My own position was that while much annoyed at the Black Sea affair, I nevertheless continued to believe that we should join with Germany. The Entente could give us nothing but the renewal of promises, so often broken, to preserve to us our present territory. Hence there was nothing to be gained by joining them. Moreover, if we refused aid to our German allies now in the time of their need, they would naturally refuse to help us if they were victorious.
>
> If we stayed neutral, whichever side won would surely punish Turkey for not having joined them, and would satisfy their territorial ambitions at our expense.[11]

From this account it is apparent that the Turks had no desire to fight a war, but as they were drawn in, so too was Britain. In the latter case, and once

NO THOROUGHFARE

BRAVO, BELGIUM!

2. From *Mr Punch's History of the Great War.*

war was declared, things did not go well. Poor diplomatic communications between India and London were the foundation stone of the events that followed. The Indian Government (IG) entertained an unrealistic political aim and under-resourced the military campaign to achieve that aim. In combination and compounded by inept leadership in the field, these factors would lead, inexorably, to a bloody and humiliating military defeat.

In human terms, reputations would be destroyed but of far greater importance was the product of this toxic combination of factors. It was the lives of thousands of British and Indian soldiers. The Turks, tenacious and courageous adversaries that they were, suffered even greater losses.

This book charts the course of military operations from November 1914 to the surrender of Kut in April 1916. It examines the political consequences and the attribution of blame for the debacle overseen by the IG.

However, to put that into context, in Britain from 1914–16 it was events on the continent of Europe that were the centre of attention, as the cartoon on page 9 illustrates.

The Mesopotamia Campaign was always going to be viewed as a sideshow. Indeed, Lieutenant General Sir George Gorringe said, most aptly, 'the Mesopotamia Campaign was nobody's child.'

Chapter notes

4 There were two follow-up reports, on 27 February 1913 and 10 February 1914.

5 Lord Fisher was First Sea Lord 1904–10 and although not back in office until October 1914, he still wielded enormous influence. The First Sea Lords Wilson, Bridgeman and Prince Louis of Battenberg, who were in office from 1910 to 1914, were unable to disregard his interference in naval affairs during this period. He enjoyed the friendship and patronage of King George V.

6 Dahl, E.J., *From Coal to Oil*, p.50.

7 Churchill, W.S., *The World Crisis*, Vol.1, pp.133–6.

8 Barker, A.J., *The Neglected War*, p.18.

9 MC Report, p.10.

10 Dixon, N.E., *On the Philosophy of Military Incompetence*, p.95.

11 Horne, C.F., Ed, *Source Records of the Great War, Vol. III*, National Alumni, 1923.

Chapter 3

Invasion and the Capture of Basra

'Never lose sight of your principal object;
do not act contrary to your orders, do not
be led astray by secondary issues.'

(Lieutenant General Johann von Ewald,
Treatise on the duties of Light Troops, 1790)

The principal and closest British asset to the Mesopotamian oil was the Indian Army. This was a force designed to conduct operations, principally on foot, against dissident tribesmen and to protect the North-West Frontier from Russian invasion.

The Viceroy of India was the heavily decorated and much respected Lord Hardinge. He had taken up the post in November 1910, having been granted a peerage on his appointment. Hardinge was a professional civil servant/diplomat; his previous appointment had been Permanent Under Secretary for Foreign Affairs. There can be no doubt that he was a very capable, experienced and self-confident man. As Viceroy he was a man of massive, unchallengeable power in India and vast influence outside the sub-continent.

In the opinion of Douglas Gould, 'The military operations in Mesopotamia began in a modest and legitimate manner and Lord Hardinge's initial role was cautious and wholly commendable. As early as 17 August 1914 he stressed to the home government that for the sake of Muslim opinion in India, any breach between Britain and Turkey must clearly be seen to be the result of Turkish actions.'[12]

Hardinge was well aware that he had inherited an army with many weaknesses and deficiencies. In his opinion it was run by 'three fairly intelligent old women – Generals Lake, Aylmer and Burbury', and he had a very low opinion of their superior, the Commander-in-Chief, General Sir O'Moore Creagh, whom he described as 'an old man with one foot in the grave'.[13] That was a view shared by Lord Crewe, Secretary of State for India.

There were clearly weaknesses at the top!

Pre-war, the policy of Hardinge, notwithstanding the multiplicity of deficiencies of the Indian Army, was to make it 'more efficient' but at the same time reduce its budget. In these, not necessarily compatible, aims he had the support of Lord Crewe.[14] Neither envisaged the remotest possibility of the Indian Army being engaged outside its borders.

In 1912, Hardinge set up a committee to report on the Army and to decide if reductions were possible. The committee could not agree and so produced two reports. The Majority Report averred that although external threats to India had reduced, the internal dangers had grown. It concluded that the existing military budget of £19.5 million should remain untouched.[15] The Minority Report, on the other hand, emphasised that the external threat should not be underestimated and there was a possibility that troop demands might be made in the future to confront an adversary in Turkish Arabia. It added that the budget should not only be retained at current levels but 'might have to be increased.'[16]

The Minority Report was prescient. The Mesopotamia Commission summed up the capability of the Indian Army in 1914 as follows:

[From 1909] reductions were made on the assumption that the Indian Army need not contemplate the likelihood of a collision outside India with the army of a European power, and the provision for the equipment, organisation and transport of the Indian Army was regulated by the requirements of frontier warfare alone.[17]

In 1914, the Indian Army was capable of engaging in limited operations outside the sub-continent because it had an abundance of volunteer manpower.[18] However, like all British military organisations since time immemorial, it was underfunded and subject to constant calls for economies, or 'savings', in the parlance of the twenty-first century. 'Savings' implies the presence of surplus capacity, readily available for redistribution, without penalty. This is a political myth much favoured by those who have never themselves been asked to 'do the same with less'.

In India, Sir William Meyer[19] was the Finance member of the Government Council that ruled India. In the months that lay ahead he would be accused of being unduly parsimonious and of starving the Army of funds. The fact is that he could not distribute money he did not have.

It will come as no surprise to any reader of military history that stringent economies put in place in peacetime have a direct and deleterious effect on an armed force when, later, that force is required to take military action. A hundred years on, that lesson has still not been learned and the implications

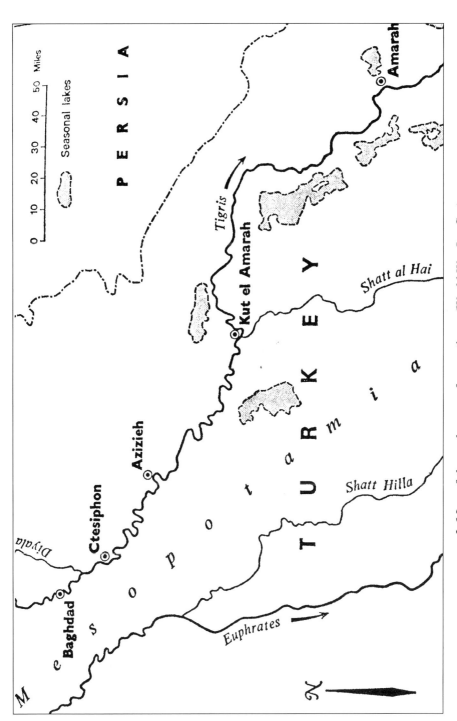

3. Map of the early area of operations. *(World War I at Sea)*

are graver. In 2016, in an increasingly unstable world, Her Majesty's Government is set on the maintenance of the Armed Forces at the absolute minimum level, and by so doing, reducing Britain's capacity to defend itself.

Today, the sophistication of twenty-first-century weapon systems and the increased lead time needed to obtain equipment and train sufficient volunteer personnel to operate that equipment puts the Realm at risk. A call to the colours is not and will not be enough, but the short-term political imperative continues to ignore the hard-learned lesson of history, which, in a nutshell, is: 'disarm at your peril!' The cruel fact of military life, then and now, and for the foreseeable future, is that you cannot have effective defence on the cheap.

The Indian Army in 1914 was made up of indigenous Indian troops led, in the main, by British officers and supplemented by a sizeable leavening of British units.

In London, General Sir Edmund Barrow,[20] the Military Secretary to the India Office, was well aware of the importance of maintaining British prestige among local tribal sheikhs in the British-protected sheikhdoms of the Arabian Peninsula. On this basis, Barrow advised Lord Crewe, the Secretary of State, to negotiate with the Indian Government to arrange the despatch of a significant formation to the Shatt al-Arab waterway at the head of the Persian Gulf. The benefits of such a move were that it would reassure any wavering local allies of continuing British support, whilst at the same time making it clear that Britain was prepared to use force to protect its interest in the Anglo-Persian Oil Company's installations and pipeline terminal at Abadan.

The Viceroy of India's new, very recently appointed, military chief was General Sir Beauchamp Duff,[21] and together they formed an all-powerful team. They were in a position to manipulate the military resources of India as they saw fit, although, notionally, they were part of the Council of Government.[22]

The underfunding of the Indian Army and the lacklustre performance of General Creagh over several years had prompted Hardinge to insist, vigorously, on the appointment of Duff to replace him. The hope was that this officer, renowned for his administrative ability, would somehow revitalise the Army and cure its malaise. The War Office resisted and General Jack Seeley, the Secretary for War, wrote to Lord Crewe that he only acquiesced in the appointment of Duff 'with grief and pain' – powerful words in any context. Seely closed portently, 'You must account this to me for righteousness in time to come.' It was convoluted language but evidently not everyone shared Hardinge's admiration for General Sir Beauchamp Duff.[23]

14

4. General Sir Beauchamp Duff GCB GCSI KCVO CIE KSt.J,
Commander-in-Chief of the Indian Army, 1914–1916.

The Secretary of State for India, Lord Crewe[24] – the political superior of both Hardinge and Duff, but who was many thousands of miles away – was dependent upon both men to advise and inform him on issues of their mutual concern. It follows that 'Command and Control' was ill defined – never a sound basis upon which to operate.

Hardinge and Duff resisted the provision of Indian assets, for the global challenge facing the British Empire as their focus, perhaps admirably, was the security of India. They viewed other issues as secondary to this aim and neither man fully embraced his responsibilities outside the borders of India.

On 29 September 1914, HMS *Espiègle*[25] sailed up the Shatt al-Arab as far as Muhammerah; following her was the armed merchantman HMS *Dalhousie*. The sloop HMS *Odin* patrolled outside the Shatt and beyond the sand bar created over the centuries by the two great rivers. These were all small ships mounting 4-inch guns, adequate for their policing role.

However, times they were a-changin', and so too were attitudes.

Now the Vali of Basra, Colonel Subhi Bey, took exception to the Royal Navy's presence and demanded its withdrawal. His demand fell on deaf ears and Britain made its move on 2 October 1914. Rumours that the German ship *Emden* was en route to the Shatt were countered by the decision to station the old Canopus class battleship, HMS *Ocean*, at the mouth of the Gulf.[26]

As the political temperature rose, so increasing pressure had been brought to bear on the IG. It was eventually cajoled into despatching an infantry brigade, hived off from a force bound for East Africa, to Mesopotamia.

This brigade was the forerunner of what would evolve into Expeditionary Force 'D' to the Persian Gulf.[27] Initially, 16th Infantry Brigade was the formation deployed and it moved to occupy Abadan Island. In a display of poor planning that was to be the pattern for the future, the Brigade was carried by ships that did not have the capability to land troops and equipment other than in the ships' boats, unsuitable for an opposed, cross-beach operation.

Somewhat frustrated, the convoy anchored off Barain (contemporary spelling), from where it could see that the Turkish fort at Fao was under naval gunfire. Some distance away, *Espiègle,* an elegant ship that looked more like a yacht, engaged the Turkish troops opposite Abadan Island and her guns inflicted severe punishment on the opposition. This brief and long-forgotten skirmish became known as the Battle of Abadan. Success allowed 16th Brigade, under the command of Brigadier General W.S. Delamain CB DSO,[28] to pass by the Abadan refinery and its distinctive seven chimneys. The Ottoman troops who had succumbed to Delamain's thrust were no better prepared for twentieth-century warfare than their Indian adversaries. There was an important clause in Delamain's orders, which was 'to show the Arabs that we intend to support them.'

This was the first time in the campaign that British ships had opened fire on the enemy – naval gunfire was to become a feature of the war in

Mesopotamia, as was the reliance of the Army upon the Royal Navy. The Royal Navy was to play an increasingly critical role in all future operations and not least in the advance north up the Tigris. It was HMS *Odin*, a Cadmus class ship, that successfully engaged the Turkish fort to such a degree that it swiftly surrendered.

Basra, with its population of about 60,000, was taken against token resistance. Then 18th Brigade, under the command of Brigadier General C.I. Fry and which was now part of the piecemeal build-up of IEF'D', advanced a further 35 miles up the Shatt al-Arab to threaten Kurnah. Meanwhile, 17th Brigade, commanded by Brigadier General W.H. Dobbie, had joined the formation, bringing the strength of IEF'D' to 15,000, with 1,600 pack camels. Ere long, IEF'D' would be designated 6th Indian Division.

5. Lieutenant General (later Field Marshal) Sir Arthur Barrett KCB KCVO. *(Photo by Russell)*

Leading the force was Lieutenant General Sir Arthur Barrett KCB KCVO. It did not take him long to discover that the grazing opportunities for 1,600 camels were very limited, so he promptly sent half of them back to India. It seemed to be a good idea at the time, but these 800 beasts represented a potent load-carrying asset that would be sorely needed in the months ahead.

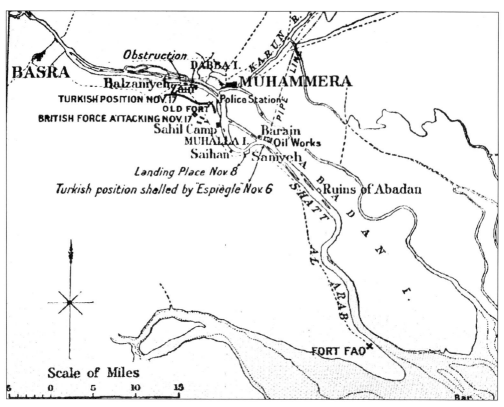

6. The setting for the opening shots in the Mesopotamian Campaign, November 1914. *(World War I at Sea)*

The re-embarkation of 800 camels was not a task to be undertaken lightly as there were no berthing arrangements at Basra. It could not really be described as a 'port' because it was unsatisfactory in every way. However, it was the best on offer and the personnel of IEF'D' had no option but to turn to and make the best of a bad job. The Mesopotamia Commission was stating the obvious when it observed:

> *The provision of adequate and suitable river transport above Basra and of sufficient wharfage and unloading facilities at Basra was a necessity, if effective military operations were to be carried out as an expeditionary force must be sea-borne, sea supported and sea victualled.*[29]

Unfortunately, IEF'D' had to take Basra as it was, warts and all. It was necessary for all personnel, stores and animals to be offloaded into bellums. These were flat-bottomed, ungainly craft with a low freeboard; their design had not changed in a thousand years. They were propelled either by punting or the use of paddles.

Unloading a ship was a slow, frustrating, labour-intensive exercise because the loaded bellums had then to be taken to the bank of the Shatt al-Arab and unloaded. There were no warehouses to accommodate stores and equipment, and very few buildings in which to house the troops. A tented city sprang up. In the meantime the insanitary flies tormented everyone and the smell, filth and squalor repelled those new to this part of the world.

Notwithstanding all of that, to this point all was well and the aim of His Majesty's Government had been achieved. However, two years later, the MC reported:

> *The force, which now amounted to a division, was armed and equipped as for frontier expedition and its medical equipment was even below this scale but the conditions the expedition had to face, both climatic and military, proved to be of a very different character to those which prevail on the frontiers of India.*[30]

The India Office in London agreed that it would be advantageous to press on as far north as Kurnah, if at all possible. The benefits of holding the confluence of the two great rivers, and the control it would provide over the whole of the navigable waterway to the sea, as well as the richly cultivated area around Kurnah, were significant. Supplementary benefits were the effect it would have on the indigenous population and the control of the telegraph to that point.

Kurnah had little else to recommend it. It was every bit as filthy and malodorous as Basra. Its inhabitants fouled the waters of the Tigris and it was prudent to take drinking water only from the middle of the stream. This was because the daily defecation of countless Arabs decorated the banks and the shallows.

One of the aims of IEF'D' was to cement relations with the Arab population, but this was a difficult task as the British and Indian soldiers held the Arabs in the lowest possible regard. They knew them to be masters of larceny who would steal anything, and that included items screwed to the ground. The Norfolks, for example, lost a latrine flag and there was speculation that this might be hung up in the military museum in Constantinople. Soldiers had to sleep on their rifles and despite barbed wire, booby traps and sentries with orders to shoot on sight, the marauders still broke into the lines and stole anything and everything. Tommy Atkins and his Indian comrade were disinterested in making Arab friends who they knew, full well, would cut their throats given the chance. Similarly, the indigenous Arabs were, for the most part, not overly interested in making

7. HMS *Odin* (Nunn)

friends with the Anglo/Indian force now camped in their back yard.

That back yard was not a desert utopia where a man might sit under a palm tree, dabbling his feet in the clear waters of a beautiful river while sipping on something long and cool. It was not like that. It was instead a very deeply unpleasant and repellent place to be. Then there were the flies – uncounted billions, nay trillions, of them.

In this unattractive part of the world there had already been skirmishes with the Turks. Henry Short, a medical officer attached to 33rd Indian Cavalry Regiment, arrived in the theatre in late 1914. He recorded a personal experience during an early engagement with the Turks:

> I saw one Turk firing at us from behind a bush; I jumped off my horse, threw the reins to my orderly and seized hold of this man's rifle. And we had a tug of war: I was only using one hand as I had a revolver in the other! Suddenly a blinding flash in my face and I didn't know what it was. Temporarily blinded, as soon as I could see, I had a hold on the Turk's rifle: he was lying on the ground. I could've shot him but I didn't because he was unarmed. Then we let him go. Major Anderson, when I re-joined the rest, said he was astonished how easily his sword had gone through a Turk. He said it was just like going through butter![31]

On 23 November, after Basra was occupied, a conference was held at the headquarters of IEF'D'. At that meeting, Commander A. Hamilton, an officer of the Royal Indian Marine, recommended to the General Staff that they should, at once, ask for twelve river steamers of the Medjidieh class.

Hamilton had worked on the Tigris for the previous two years and was familiar with the river as far as Baghdad. He was a subject matter expert and eminently qualified to give advice. Hamilton realised that the building of new craft would probably take about twelve months and he counselled that existing ships be diverted from India. The MC commented, '*There is reason to believe that, had Commander Hamilton's foresight, knowledge and advice been acted upon, subsequent difficulties would have been mitigated, if not altogether avoided.*'[32]

As it happens, the Staff was not swayed by Hamilton's expert advice and did not accord that advice any priority, although it conceded that six additional steamers 'might be required.'

Any armed force depends upon the command and administrative organisation that directs and supports it. 'Staff officers', of all ranks and disciplines, people this support organisation. In this case, the Staff in Simla and in Barrett's headquarters was imbued with a strongly entrenched, regulation-driven culture. There was scant room for an officer who dissented from the official line or who initiated any action not fully authorised by existing regulations designed for an army in India. The result was disinterested inertia for the Army serving in Mesopotamia. It was the thousands of soldiers, who depended upon the Staff to meet their needs, who went without. Sir Percy Cox, an Indian civil servant and advisor on civil affairs, was now established in Basra; but he made a poor judgment and did not enhance his reputation when he suggested that an announcement should be made that the occupation should be permanent.

> *This suggestion was peremptorily swept to one side by HM Government on the ground that it would be utterly contrary to the agreement come to between the Allies, if occupation of any conquered country were at once announced as to be permanent, without waiting for the final settlement to be made at the close of the war.*[33]

The Turks who had been defeated in the early exchanges had withdrawn to Kurnah and were in a strong defensive position with wide water barriers on two sides. They could take comfort that any attacking force would have to cross either the Tigris or the Euphrates before they could assault the town.

Colonel P.H. Hehir CB MD FRCS IMS was the Principal Medical Officer up to April 1915. In the opening months of the campaign, his reports to Surgeon General Babtie in India displayed watchfulness and foresight and were in '*refreshing contrast*' with the administration of his successor, Surgeon General Hathaway. Colonel Hehir came out of the MC with great credit and

**8. Honorary Major
General Sir Percy Cox
GCMG GCIE KCSI KBE.**

the Report waxed eloquent on his professional skills and judgment. He was obviously a resourceful and innovative doctor who ducked and dived to care for his patients. However, the desultory operations at the beginning of the campaign, coupled with Colonel Hehir's capacity to improvise and make do and mend, concealed the serious underlying problems besetting the medical establishment in Mesopotamia.

The deficiency covered every aspect of medical care: insufficient medical staff, insufficient medical equipment and insufficient medical accommodation, afloat and ashore. Despite Colonel Hehir's diligence and ability, the MC said of him:[34]

> *It was he who set up the expedients for which he was later on obliged to criticise Surgeon General Hathaway. We think that Colonel Hehir was to blame for failing to requisition India for equipment, which though not indispensible at the time was certain to be indispensible in the future. It was a mistake to risk disaster before taking measures which ordinary foresight would have adopted long before.*

This seems to be an ungenerous judgement on a capable and diligent officer. The Indian Medical Service did not cover itself in glory in Mesopotamia and the serious problems did not manifest themselves until well after Hehir had left his post to serve at the front, incidentally reporting to Hathaway. After the war, Hehir went on to pastures new and to greater glory.[35]

Chapter notes

12 Gould, D., 'Hardinge and the Mesopotamia Commission', *The Historical Journal*, December 1976, p.925.

13 Hardinge to F.A. Maxwell, 18 August 1914, Hardinge papers, Cambridge University Library 93/No. 66.

14 Crewe to Hardinge, 17 February and 3 March 1911, Hardinge papers, 117/Nos. 17 & 19.

15 *Majority Report of the Army in India Committee*, 1912, para. 639.

16 Ibid, paras 112–13 & 705.

17 MC Report, p.10.

18 The strength of the Indian Army at the time was 159,000 Indian troops and 76,000 British troops.

19 Sir William Stevenson Meyer GCIE KCSI ICS (1860–1922). In 1920 he was appointed as the first High Commissioner for India. He died in that post.

20 General Sir Edmund Barrow GCB KCMG (1852–1934).

21 When Lord Kitchener was appointed as Commander-in-Chief, India in November 1902, he ensured the passage of Beauchamp Duff to the highest level and Duff was identified, thereafter, as a 'Kitchener man'. On 8 March 1914, Duff reached the senior position when he replaced General Sir O'Moore Creagh as Commander-in-Chief, India. The Viceroy championed his appointment and, by doing so, set a precedent. It was a departure from the normal practice as previously, a British Army officer always held the post. Beauchamp Duff was an officer of the Indian Army.

22 The Government of the Raj consisted wholly of British officials and was headed by the Viceroy and the appointed members of his council. After the Indian Councils Act was passed in 1861, this executive council acted as a cabinet and also as part of an imperial legislative council.

23 General Jack Seely to Crewe, 15 October 1913, Crewe papers 1/13(9).

24 Lord Crewe KG PC, 1st Marquess of Crewe (1858–1945). Austen Chamberlain replaced him as Secretary of State for India, in 1915.

25 She was a Cadmas class sloop that was launched in 1900.

26 Nunn, W., *Tigris Gunboats*, p.26.

27 The Indian Government sent other expeditionary forces to Egypt (A), East Africa (B and C) and Gallipoli (E).

28 Later, Lieutenant General Sir Walter Delamain KCB KCMG DSO (1862–1932).

29 MC Report, p.9.

30 Ibid, p.13.

31 Podcast, 18 Mesopotamia First World War Centenary, IWM.

32 MC Report, p.44.

33 Ibid, p.15.

34 Ibid, p.70.

35 Later, Major General Sir Patrick Hehir CB CMG KCIE MD DTM FRCPE FRCSE (1857–1937). His medals were sold at auction in September 2006 for £6,200.

Chapter 4

The Capture of Kurnah

'The infantry must ever be valued as the
very foundation and nerve of an army.'
(Niccolo Machiavelli, *Discourses*, 1517)

Operations against Kurnah commenced on 3 December. A landing was made on the *left* bank (looking downstream) and on the British *right* (looking upstream). See the sketch map on page 26, which is worth several hundred words.

Having opted to land on the left bank it was the Tigris that presented the main obstacle to 'a composite force of two Indian battalions [104th Wellesley's Rifles and 110th Mahratta Light Infantry] and a double company of the Norfolks with some sappers and a couple of field guns'.[36]

The soldiers were supported by a small flotilla of five vessels. These ships provided gunfire support once having landed their passengers.

The Tigris at Kurnah, which was 'a stretch of yellow racing water as wide as the Thames at London Bridge', was nevertheless crossed, about 1½ miles north of the town on 8 December. By this time the force had been reinforced and was now 2,300 strong. Thereafter the outcome was not in doubt and the combination of naval gunfire and soldierly aggression was sufficient to win the day.

By 19 December Kurnah was in British hands. The Turks had suffered heavy casualties on the contested left bank, especially around Muzereh. When the town eventually fell, forty-five officers and 989 men were captured. British losses were twenty-nine killed and 302 wounded.

It had been an exemplary operation and all concerned had cause to be satisfied. The scale of the victory, and the relatively small price paid, not only raised morale but must also have raised expectations, most certainly in Simla.

From this point, the aims of His Majesty's Government and the Indian Government started to diverge. Hitherto, responsibility for the direction of Indian Expeditionary Force 'D' had been merely imprecise. Now clear differences started to emerge and the overriding responsibility of HMG for

9. Captain Nunn (right) and Army officers examine a Turkish gun. HMS *Espiègle* at anchor in the background. Turkish arms stacked after capture. *(Nunn)*

the employment of IEF'D' was tacitly questioned. The Secretary of State for India said that whilst he had been content with an advance to Kurnah, he nevertheless *'deprecated any further advance for the present.'*[37] Crewe spoke for HMG in this matter but Hardinge and Duff had a different agenda that, at this stage, they had not shared.

The unvarnished truth is that Hardinge had taken it upon himself to expand the Empire, add Mesopotamia to its assets and administer this addition from India. He had carried General Sir Beauchamp Duff along with his pipe dream. The ambition of both men was entirely beyond the remit of two senior officials whose non-negotiable function was to operate under the direction of HMG.

In mid-April 1915, Hardinge declared that Britain could turn lower Mesopotamia into a 'second Egypt'. Annexation would mean safeguarding, once and for all, all of Britain's traditional interests in the Gulf and would ensure control of the southernmost section of the Baghdad Railway – should it ever be completed. Britain's allies, the sheikhs of Kuwait and Mohammerah, could be protected through permanent occupation, and other Arab chiefs coaxed away from Turkey.[38]

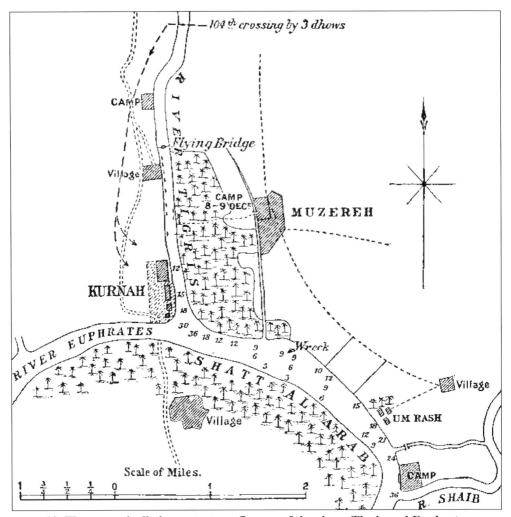

10. The strategically important confluence of the rivers Tigris and Euphrates at Kurnah. *(World War I at Sea)*

However, Hardinge did swither, for example on 9 June 1915, when he wrote to his friend Sir Valentine Chirol saying that with one town taken, 'there is no reason why we should move a yard further upriver.' This rethink did not last long, and on 17 June he restated his enthusiasm for expansion when he wrote to one of his old political colleagues, Lord Morley of Blackburn,[39] and closed by saying, 'I know that you hate expansion, and so do I, but I see no way out of it.'[40] Those were insincere words intended to appease Morley.

Notwithstanding the expansionist ambitions of Hardinge and Duff that were far beyond their remit, they still only allocated the minimum of resources to achieve their aim. They set a task that was impossible for a single division with a fragile line of communication.

Busch observed dryly that, 'Clearly, Hardinge was an early victim of success and Crewe had now to cool his ardour.' Later, when giving evidence to the Mesopotamia Commission, Hardinge made clear that he entertained an aspiration to extend the Empire into Mesopotamia. These personal aspirations, unsupported by HMG, seem to be at the base of his eagerness for a 'forward' policy throughout the campaign.

This campaign gave rise to some unique incidents. One such occurred when, on 12 January, the gunboat HMS *Gadfly* was downstream of a boat bridge by which a column of transport camels was crossing the river. One beast slipped, fell into the river and the 4-knot current swept it downstream towards *Gadfly*. The unfortunate creature was washed under the ship and became wedged under the propeller. At this point a bluejacket made a report to the bridge, probably unique in the long history of the Royal Navy, that there was a 'Camel foul of the screw, Sir'.

All hands of one of HM's ships were called to the scene in order to save a 'ship of the desert' entangled in the screw. A bluejacket dived into the river, secured a line around the beast's neck, but to no avail and it drowned.

Early in 1915, intelligence sources indicated that the Turks were planning to mount an attack on Basra and the pipeline. They would approach by way of the Karun River. This threat had to be confronted and further reinforcement was needed. The IG was asked to provide additional troops and Hardinge and Duff resisted. There was a flurry of terse telegrams and eventually, as the MC commented, '*the Indian Government finally acquiesced.* '[41] Accordingly, on 7 February, a further brigade arrived from India, but this proved to be insufficient and the situation became '*acute*'.

The Viceroy had left India on 25 January to visit the theatre, while these terse negotiations were being conducted, and he arrived in great state on the 31st. 'At Basra Hardinge was greeted with full military honours. He investigated the situation of the sick and wounded and found them cheery, and the hospitals well run, but the Mesopotamian force had not yet suffered the severe losses of later stages of the campaign.'[42]

It was entirely proper for Hardinge to be greeted in a manner befitting his station, with ample ceremony at every turn. It would be an unusual man who was unaffected by the degree of extreme deference that the Viceroy received. Did it generate a feeling of omnipotence? Did that in turn affect his judgement? There is no doubt that Hardinge had a well-developed sense of self-worth. He was a sophisticated gentleman who conducted himself accordingly but he also exhibited a degree of arrogance, probably typical of those of his eminence. His biographer described him as 'cold'.

He received loyal Arab sheikhs and presented them with 'robes of honour'. Bartlett briefed Hardinge and so the Viceroy was fully aware of the current issues. Whatever passed between the two men, it did nothing to curb the Viceroy's ambitions; more importantly, nor did it stir a glimmer of interest in matters logistic.

The future of Baghdad was in his thoughts. He put it to Curzon (at the time Lord Privy Seal), 'I do not want to go to Baghdad unless forced to do so, but when the time comes to make peace with Turkey, Baghdad, Basra and perhaps even Mosel must be lopped off, and while we remain in Basra some kind of protectorate over the rest of Mesopotamia must be established.'[43] There is little doubt that the political vision of Hardinge was interesting, bold and visionary; the difficulty was that his vision owed nothing to the military reality of the day.

The MC Report, at page 103–104, said acidly that:

The control of the expedition ... narrowed down to two high officials ... both permanently stationed in localities which had little, if any, private or personal touch with forces campaigning in Mesopotamia. Although the Viceroy paid a short visit in 1915, yet in the main it is a fact that both he and the Commander-in-Chief, in their management of the expedition, entirely depended upon the official information from that country. The well-being and adequate maintenance of the expedition were therefore dependent upon the requisitions made on Simla by the General Officer Commanding and his subordinates in Mesopotamia.

This is an indictment initially of Barrett, but in far greater measure of the man who would replace him, and his regulation-bound staff. It is also a veiled rebuke to Duff for distancing himself from the activities of his soldiers.

It was still necessary, on 5 March, for HMG to order, peremptorily, the IG to send a further brigade. On what basis this order was given is unclear because the only formal source of intelligence for HMG from this theatre was through the IG. The probability is that Foreign Office assets elsewhere had sounded an alarm, although the possibility exists that HMG had an independent agent in place who, at this time, was able to judge when matters were *'acute'*.

As a sop to the wounded pride of the IG, HMG absolved it of responsibility for any mishaps that might occur in India as a result of the diminution of its domestic military assets.

Business between the two governments was conducted by telegram and there was now growing friction between all the principal players. Interestingly, the MC commented:

It should be noted that practically the whole of the important telegrams ... relating to Imperial demands upon the Indian Government for military expeditions outside India and the replies of India to these demands are 'private' telegrams. A private telegram is the property of the person who sent it, and it is not the practice to record it on file in any public department, although this may be done at the option of the sender. Such telegrams are kept by private secretaries and are, as a rule, taken away at the termination of office by the person who sends or receives them.[44]

On 1 April, the IG, without reference to London, decided to reorganise the force in Mesopotamia into an army corps. Lieutenant General Sir John Nixon was appointed to be the Corps Commander. Hardinge, who saw him as 'a keen hard soldier', admired Nixon.[45] Less so Barrett, who, he complained, 'played too much for safety.'[46] A current description of Nixon was that 'he revelled in responsibility' whereas Barrett 'would take responsibility.'[47]

In the meantime, command still rested with General Barrett and he was conscious of the strategic importance of Shaiba, a modest area about 10 miles to the west of Basra. Shaiba was just above the all-encompassing floods, and relatively defensible. Barrett decided to occupy Shaiba. The decision required Indian and British soldiers to 'march' from Basra. In reality they waded, about 18 miles, through the muddy floodwaters on 5 April 1915. It was an exhausting journey conducted in ferocious heat, with no vestige of shade and with its own unique hazards. The advance was not contested, other than by untold millions of aggressive flies.

Shaiba was occupied and fortified. It was by no means an ideal location. Not the least of its deficiencies was the difficulty of resupply and reinforcement. Barrett's concerns about an attack on Basra from the east were fully justified. The Turks were in considerable strength and concentrating at Nasariyeh, further west, and across the seasonal but very shallow Hammar Lake.

It was at this point that General Barrett left Mesopotamia, ostensibly because he was ill. However, the fact that he was, in effect, being demoted to serve under Nixon might have been a factor. Sir Percy Cox suggested that Barrett 'was probably better fitted to solve the Mesopotamian military problem than his dashing successor.' Whatever the reason, Barrett was

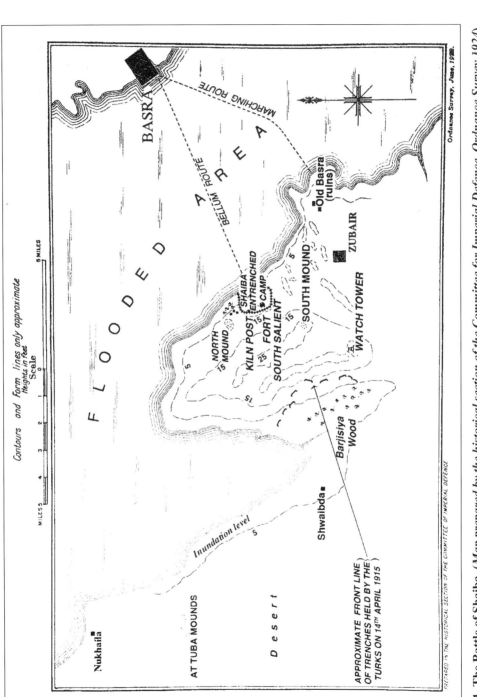

Contours and Form lines only approximate
Heights in Feet
Scale

MILES 5 · · · 0 · · · 5 MILES

FLOODED AREA

BASRA

MARCHING ROUTE

BÉLLUM ROUTE

Old Basra (ruins)

ZUBAIR

SHAIBA ENTRENCHED CAMP
NORTH MOUND
KILN POST
FORT
SOUTH SALIENT
SOUTH MOUND
WATCH TOWER

Barjisiya Wood

Inundation level

Shwaibda

AT TUBA MOUNDS

Desert

Nukhaila

APPROXIMATE FRONT LINE OF TRENCHES HELD BY THE TURKS ON 14TH APRIL 1915

Ordnance Survey, June, 1922.

PREPARED IN THE HISTORICAL SECTION OF THE COMMITTEE OF IMPERIAL DEFENCE

11. The Battle of Shaiba. (Map prepared by the historical section of the Committee for Imperial Defence. Ordnance Survey 1924)

12. Mountain guns at Shaiba, April 1915.

evacuated to India. As it happens, he survived the malady that struck him down and he recovered. This saved him from the blight that affected many of the other generals who served in the theatre.[48]

Later, Lord Crewe, in giving evidence to the MC, remarked that he *'was sorry the change had been made.'* Nixon, clearly not everyone's choice, duly arrived with his Staff in Basra on 9 April. He bore with him his orders from General Sir Beauchamp Duff. The orders were lengthy and specific but, in the interests of brevity, the key elements were that Nixon was ordered to take Sir Percy Cox,[49] the political officer, under his command. He was to *'Report on the requirement for river transport'* and the desirability of building a railway with 137 miles of track. He was, in addition, to *'plan an effective occupation of Basra Vilayet'*[50] and *'plan for a subsequent advance on Baghdad.'*

Percy Cox was in a very influential position. He was, in effect, the Viceroy's personal representative and had a background in colonial administration. His function was to advise Nixon on civilian issues and governance. He ranked alongside Major General Kemble, Nixon's Chief of Staff.

Nixon had no time to play himself in as a reconnaissance in force was being made towards Nukhaila. An Arab force was encountered but the ensuing skirmish was indecisive and unsatisfactory. Major General Sir

Charles Mellis vc, temporarily General Officer Commanding (GOC), 6th Division, was thrust into more serious action on 12 April when about 4,000 Turks attacked his forces, predictably from the west and by way of Barjisiya Wood. For the next three days there was intense and savage fighting, during which Major Wheeler won the first VC of the campaign.[51]

13. Major G.G. Wheeler vc.

The battles were both bloody affairs; British casualties were 1,000 killed and wounded, including eighteen officers killed and forty-two wounded. Usually the proportion of killed to wounded is from 1:3 to 1:4, so the probability was that there were 700–750 or more Indian soldiers needing medical treatment. 'As in all battles, the dead and wounded came chiefly from the best and bravest.'[52] It was ever thus.

The opposition lost about 3,000, and 800 prisoners (who had to be fed, watered, accommodated and guarded). The wounded of both sides were the first test of the Indian Medical Service. The MC Report commented on medical care with the following:

Another defect ... was the failure to supply the expedition with suitable vehicles for carrying the wounded. The only land ambulance transport provided were stretchers and riding mules. Stretchers are not suitable for distances over 2½ miles. Whenever it became necessary to carry the wounded any distance, resorts had to be to the ordinary army transport cart [ATC], which is without springs, has no cover to give protection against rain or the direct rays of the sun; and the bottom of which consists of bars of iron, which, even when liberally covered with mattresses or other paddling, renders the placing of a wounded man, especially cases of fracture, in such a conveyance, a practice which can only be described as barbarous and cruel.[53]

The treatment of the wounded is a topic that will be revisited at regular intervals. As the opposition gained in strength and effectiveness, so there was a commensurate rise in the number of casualties. In the case of the engagements around Shaiba, the distances were relatively short and water transport could be employed across the flooded plain.

Major General Mellis,[54] who had briefly commanded the Division, described Shaiba as 'a real soldier's battle'. He rather hoped that his command would become permanent but it was not to be and he reverted to the command of a brigade – not unusual for a major general at the time. Nevertheless, over the next year Mellis, a notable warrior, would demonstrate that he was not only a physically brave man but that he also had moral courage of a high order. He was one of very few general officers to emerge from the misery of Mesopotamia with his reputation enhanced. The brigade commanded by Mellis now became a component of the 12th Division commanded by Major General George Gorringe.

At the time Duff's orders were given to General Nixon, the home authorities knew nothing about them. As far as 'an advance to Baghdad' was concerned, this was not even a consideration in London and quite what induced Duff to issue such instructions was never satisfactorily explained. He exceeded his remit by a margin – a very wide margin.

It was not until 2 May 1915 that a copy of these instructions reached London, by which time the Battles of Barjisiya and Shaiba had been fought and won against a mixed force of Arabs and Turks, over the period 12–14 April. Suleiman Askeri, who had clearly chosen sides, led the Arabs.

Duff's orders were the first time that 'Baghdad' was mentioned in any official communication and a glance at the map reveals why. Advancing to Baghdad should have been, at best, an aspiration because it was 502 river miles from Basra and that river was the only effective line of communication on offer. It also presented all manner of navigational difficulties, even if appropriate, shallow draft shipping was available. Nixon's orders were quite

14. Major General Sir Charles Mellis VC KCB. He was one of the few generals to return from Mesopotamia with his reputation enhanced.

specific and planning the river transport was high on the list of priorities imposed upon him by General Duff.

> *At Simla Sir Beauchamp Duff, as Commander-in-Chief, was in absolute and untrammelled control of every branch of military administration. The General Staff was in no sense a separate or independent branch.*[55]

The IEF'D' was now composed of two divisions, 6th and 12th, the latter being very weak and without artillery. It has to be said that any division without integral artillery is ineffective. Artillery is the 'Queen of the Battlefield' (as any gunner will tell you, probably at great length) and on the Western Front about 58 per cent of casualties on both sides were inflicted by artillery in its various forms.[56] Thus the new Mesopotamian Corps was, in effect, one and a half divisions at best and deficient in the most effective of modern weaponry.

Major General C.V.F. Townshend CB DSO was appointed to command 6th Indian Division in Barrett's place and arrived in Basra on 22 April 1915. He was to be a very important player in the campaign and it is appropriate to consider him in some detail. The author wrote his biography. They say 'no man is a hero to his valet'; similarly, few men are heroes to their biographers – certainly not in this case.

Chapter notes
36 Barker, A.J., *The Neglected War*, p.34.
37 MC Report, p.15.
38 Hardinge papers, 93/No. 9a, Gould, D., p.930.
39 Lord Morley of Blackburn OM PC (1838–1923). Liberal politician elected MP in 1883. Secretary of State, India Office, 1905–10. Lord President of the Council 1910–14. Resigned from the government in protest at the declaration of war in August 1914.
40 Hardinge papers, 94/No. 33.
41 MC Report, p.15.
42 Busch, B.C., *Hardinge of Penshurst*, p.232.
43 Ibid, p.232.
44 MC Report, p.11.
45 Hardinge to Nicholson, 4 February 1915, HP 93/No. 290.
46 Gould, D., 'Lord Hardinge and the Mesopotamia Commission and Inquiry 1914–17', *The Historical Journal,* December 1976.
47 Wilson, Sir A., *Loyalties: Mesopotamia 1914–1917*, p.33.
48 Barrett went on to greater things. He died in 1926, at the age of 69, as Field Marshal Sir Arthur Barrett GCB GCSI KCVO ADC.
49 (Honorary) Major General Sir Percy Zachariah Cox GCMG GCIE KCSI (1864–1937).
50 Vilayet is an administrative region and, in this case, it included an area that encompassed Amara and Nasariyeh.
51 Major G.G.M. Wheeler VC, 7th Hariana Lancers (1873–1915). He is buried in the Commonwealth War Cemetery in Basra.
52 Field Marshal Lord Carver, *El Alamein,* Batsford, London, 1962.
53 MC Report, p.70.
54 Later, Major General Sir Charles Mellis VC KCB KCMG (1862-1936).
55 MC Report, p.109.
56 Corrigan, G., *Mud, Blood and Poppycock*, p.116.

Chapter 5

Chitrál Charlie, his Regatta and the Capture of Amara

'Leadership is that mixture of example, persuasion and compulsion, which makes men do what you want them to do.'
(FM Viscount Slim, *Courage and Other Broadcasts*, 1957)

Townshend was an interesting character. He was known as 'Chitrál Charlie' as a result of his command of the besieged fort of Chitrál, on the North-West Frontier, in 1895. In that siege he was a captain and he did no more than his duty but, nevertheless, he was appointed a Companion of the Order of the Bath (CB) after the siege was lifted. This was a decoration vastly out of proportion to his rank and, at that time, more normally awarded to general officers (colonel and above). The award had a strong political tinge but it made Townshend something of a celebrity, and for a man who was already an egotist it was very heady wine.

Townshend was a student of the business of arms and he studied his profession avidly. He was an admirer of Napoleon and believed that he shared some of the Emperor's martial characteristics.

Townshend was a gregarious, positive personality. He sang and accompanied himself on the banjo and found most of his friends in the theatre. He was married to a wealthy French woman and spent as much time in Paris as he did in London. He was intelligent, well read, entertaining, quick witted, fluent, capable and inventive. He was also insensitive, utterly selfish, overwhelmingly ambitious and impossibly immodest. One of his other unattractive characteristics was his constant criticism of his superiors. However, his lack of moral courage usually prevented him from challenging them directly.

He was fully aware of his position in the 'Army List'.[57] This is a document few officers will admit to perusing but, at some time, all do. C.V.F. Townshend was at the top end of the Army, which in 1914 was officered by:

15. Major General C.V.F. Townshend CB DSO (later Sir Charles KCB DSO).

11 field marshals (+ 3 Royal)
18 generals (+3 Royal)
28 lieutenant generals
114 major generals

Seniority is really only of academic interest as it was not one of the criteria for promotion. Nevertheless, if Townshend had counted (he probably did) he would have found that he was 66th on the major generals' list. He realised that, with the normal casualties from 'death, disablement or dishonour' among those above him, in the now rapidly expanding army, elevation to lieutenant general and the knighthood that went with it were both firmly on the cards.

Townshend also entertained ambition to succeed to a peerage and become the 7th Lord Townshend. It was a reasonable ambition given that the 6th Marquess was older and unmarried. Charles Townshend was heir apparent. Active service in the bleak wastes of Mesopotamia in command of a division was just what the doctor ordered and Townshend was overjoyed.

His chain of command was through Nixon to Duff and ultimately to Hardinge. It was an unfortunate combination. Lieutenant General Sir John Nixon GCMG KCB, who had been selected to command Indian Expeditionary

16. Lieutenant General Sir John Nixon KCB.

Force 'D', was fifty-seven and had had an exemplary career to date. He had been part of the force that had relieved Chitrál in 1895 and so Townshend was well known to him. He had seen active service in India, Afghanistan and South Africa. He seemed to be just the man for the job. At least his superior, General Sir Beauchamp Duff GCB GCSI KCVO CIE, thought so.

Duff was in a vastly influential post as Chief of the Indian General Staff in Delhi, and he advised the Viceroy on matters military. He had command over and responsibility for hundreds of thousands of lives. Duff was a seasoned soldier and, like most Victorian soldiers, he had a wealth of active service behind him. All of his campaigning had been against irregular or tribal opposition. In 1914 he was exposed to a conflict for which he had direct command responsibility but for which he was ill-equipped. He chose to exercise that responsibility at long range, as noted by the Mesopotamia Commission. To be fair, he had appointed what he believed to be the best senior officers at his disposal and it would have been incorrect for him to breathe down their necks. He could not be too 'hands on' but, Napoleon remarked, 'a general who sees with the eyes of others will never be able to command an army as it should be.' These wise words, from 1817,[58] were extraordinarily prescient when applied to Duff.

The recent victories at Barjisiya and Shaiba had allowed the British to consolidate their position, but the thin cloak of success concealed a serious deficiency. The MC commented:

> *Although the force was doubled the medical equipment sent to the last two brigades was not up to the authorised scale of equipment, and practically two divisions had medical equipment for only one and that on the Indian and not the British scale.*
>
> *Neither was there made such an addition to the river steamer transport as to bring its proportions up to the requirement of the increased forces. These deficiencies do not seem to have had sufficient recognition by the Government of India.*[59]

The oil supply was secure and the original aim of IEF'D', set by His Majesty's Government, had been achieved. At this point the initiative for future operations slipped from the distant hands of Lord Crewe in London and was seized by General Nixon, with the tacit approval of the Indian Government in the persons of Hardinge and Duff.

On 19 April 1915, Nixon asked the IG to furnish him with a further cavalry brigade and a battalion of pioneers but the Viceroy, certainly advised by Duff, rejected the request outright.

It was in April 1915 that Surgeon General (Major General) H.G. Hathaway CB was appointed Principal Medical Officer in Mesopotamia. In this post he answered to Surgeon General Sir William Babtie VC KCMG CB MB KHS, the Director of Medical Services, India, on medical matters but was under the regimental command of Lieutenant General Sir John Nixon. Hathaway was to be a key player in the campaign, with awesome responsibility for the sick and wounded. He was a well-meaning man but, as events showed, he was over promoted and out of his depth. Babtie had wider responsibilities for both the Dardanelles and Mesopotamian theatres and he, too, was later found wanting.

17. Major General William Babtie VC (later Lieutenant General Sir William VC KCB KCMG). He had overall responsibility for medical matters in Mesopotamia and the Dardanelles.

Meanwhile, at Townshend's initial briefing at Corps headquarters in Basra on 23 April, he was told that his orders were not only to drive the enemy from his present position between Pear Drop Bend (see map on page 44) and Kurnah and capture his guns but also to push upriver to attack and occupy Amara (87–90 river miles further north) – the operation to be continuous.[60] The country was under floods and in those conditions movement in any direction was going to be challenging.

On the following day, 24 April, the Secretary of State concurred with the decision made by Hardinge on the matter of the cavalry brigade and added three critical paragraphs to his message, which read:

> *Any advance beyond the present theatre of operations will not be sanctioned by the Government at the moment and I presume Nixon clearly understands this. During the summer we must confine ourselves to the defence of oil interests in Arabistan and of the Basra Vilayet.*
>
> *If an advance to Amara, with a view to establishing an outpost for the purpose of controlling tribesmen between there and Karun, thus adding to the security of the pipe-line, is possible after smashing the enemy in the direction of Karun I should, if such a proposal received your support, be prepared to sanction it. Any proposal involving possible demands for reinforcement or undue extension is to be deprecated, however.*
>
> *Our present position is strategically a sound one and we cannot at present afford to take risks by extending it unduly. In Mesopotamia a safe game must be played.[61]*

On the face of it, that statement of HMG policy appears crystal clear, but it was promulgated in ignorance of the orders Nixon had already been given from India and perhaps in ignorance of the physical extent of the Basra Vilayet. Nixon had already been authorised, in principle, to advance to a position just short of Kut on the Tigris, and to that end, Townshend was actively planning his attack on Amara.

Hitherto, advances north up the Shatt al-Arab had been to consolidate the hold on Abadan but by April 1915 the seizure of Baghdad had become the stated aim of the IG and for that to be achieved the shape and size of the river transport fleet had to be determined and assembled.

By April 1915, the Royal Navy had assembled an extraordinary collection of shallow draft vessels, many of which were 'taken from Trade'. The only feature that the ships had in common was their shallow draught. Civilian ships were adapted for Service use and in many cases they were still commanded by their civilian masters.

The role of this flotilla was ill-defined, initially, and its role developed

41

until eventually it was required to provide gunfire, logistical support and casualty evacuation. The Royal Navy river craft were a combination of floating packhorses, artillery batteries and ambulances. The senior naval officer was Captain Wilfred Nunn.[62] The need for shipping of specific proportions and the delays in their provision was a constant refrain in the later MC Report but, in the meantime, Nunn had to make do with what he had.

On 27 May 1915, Lord Crewe left the India Office. Prime Minister Asquith replaced him with Austen Chamberlain,[63] who at once endorsed his predecessor's policy. Hardinge was relieved at the appointment; as confided to a correspondent, he feared, 'some creature like Winston'[64] might become his new chief.

That same day, Nixon advised the IG that the paddle steamers and tugs sent to him had a draught that precluded them working the river above Kurnah. He said, specifically, that 3 feet 6 inches was the maximum practical draught. As it was, shipping that conformed to the shallow draught criteria had to be carefully tasked in order to use it to best advantage.

Both of the two great rivers had burst their banks, as they did routinely every year. The melt water flowed down from the mountains to the north and the flood covered an area of more than 10,000 square miles. Townshend was faced with the task of taking enemy positions at the far side of a vast lake of uncertain depth. It would involve a painfully slow advance with absolutely no cover from sight or from fire. It was an extraordinary situation that called for an extraordinary solution, and an extraordinary man to put that solution into effect.

Townshend was that man.

His first objectives were 2 miles away and the only way to close with the enemy would be by boat. These could only be the local, unpowered bellums, some of which were 30–40 feet long.

There followed one of the most extraordinary feats of arms in the annals of the British Army. Townshend was separated from enemy positions, which occupied 'dry' ground as opposed to the tactically more desirable 'high' ground by this vast flooded plain. The water could be 3 feet deep in some places but where there was a fold in the ground it might be 15 feet deep. In these conditions any soldier on foot or who was wounded would almost certainly drown.

It is alleged that soldiers said that Mesopotamia had too much water and the Navy said it had too little. Townshend and his troops would have endorsed that in late May 1915. Despite the extensive flooding, the ships were, of course, confined to the deeper water only to be found in the rivers.

18. HMS *Espiègle*. An elegant vessel that played a major role in the river campaign. *(Nunn)*

The difficulty for them was deciding the line of the navigable stream because the river, most inconveniently, did not have raised banks.

Townshend asked that Captain Wilfred Nunn RN, the senior naval officer (SNO), and his ships be placed under command of 6th Division, and when Nixon concurred, Townshend moved to HMS *Espiègle*, which became his mobile advance headquarters.

Captain Nunn later commented that, on meeting Townshend for the first time, he 'found the General, very talkative – indeed loquacious – and he constantly referred to Napoleon's campaigns, maxims and doings … the one thing about Townshend that I did not care for was his rather pompous and boastful style of conversation.'[65] Chitrál Charlie was not everyone's cup of tea for just those reasons.

Townshend trained his troops in the propulsion of the bellums and he assembled 328 of these craft. Townshend's 'fleet' was sufficient to carry one full brigade of 2,560 men. Ninety-six of the bellums were fitted with rudimentary armour as protection from small-arms fire. Seventy-five bellums were allocated to carry the impedimenta of war for this extraordinary operation.

Townshend did not have anything like his entire division for the task as he swiftly discovered that General Nixon had ruthlessly hived off many of

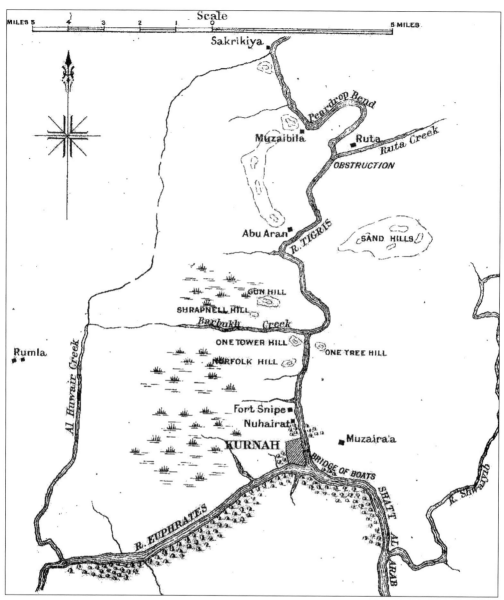

19. The flooded battlefield and the site of Townshend's Regatta, 30–31 May 1915, showing the strategic importance of Kurnah. *(World War I at Sea)*

6th Division's soldiers to staff his headquarters and his messes. Valuable bayonets were being employed as batmen, waiters, clerks, signalmen and a host of other line of communication jobs. In addition, Nixon had withdrawn 18th Brigade and deployed it in defensive positions around Basra. Townshend asked for his soldiers back and got a very dusty answer from

44

Nixon. In effect he had only the weakened 16th and 17th Brigades to carry out the operation. Neither of the brigade commanders relished the prospect of what lay ahead.[66]

The bellums were to carry ten fully armed men, some with machine guns and others with the guns of a mountain battery. One man was to punt the craft and another was deputed as assistant punter, to be employed on the demise of the first. Each bellum carried picks, shovels, ammunition, paddles and caulking material to plug the anticipated bullet holes.

The soldiers had no illusions about the dangers of punting slowly, in reality very slowly, for 2 miles into entrenched enemy positions. This operation, which became known as 'Townshend's Regatta', started on 30 May 1915. Heavy and expensive defeat was on the cards. Even Townshend, who had an overprovision of self-confidence, confided to his batman, Whitmore, that he 'felt anxious'. As well he might, because the whole operation flew in the face of reason.

The bellums with their well-rehearsed crews poled through the reeds, and it was discovered that the armour hung over the side snagged on any vegetation waving in the muddy water. It was a brutally hot day, about 110°F, and clouds of flies tortured the men during their journey.

Townshend, now ensconced in his waterborne headquarters, climbed to the crow's nest on the foremast of *Espiègle* and, from there, he was able to survey the whole battlefield. The Turkish positions showed up as low-lying islands but nevertheless readily discernible targets for the artillery. These targets were named as One Tree Hill, Shrapnel Hill, One Tower Hill, Gun Hill and Norfolk Hill.

Nunn directed matters naval from *Espiègle* and had under command the three sloops, HMS *Clio*, *Odin* and *Lawrence*. In addition were HMS *Miner*, *Shaitan* and *Sumana*, all three of which were 'armed launches'. They all had a part to play and took their place to the rear of the convoy. Nunn also mentions the presence of HMS *Comet*, *Shushan* and *Muzaffari*.[67] It was at the rear of the convoy that the logistic support bellums took station. There was also a collection of barges upon which were installed the mountain guns, machine guns and field ambulances.

This motley force kept pace with the infantry-carrying bellums as the artillery engaged the islands. The point might be made at this stage that although various craft could and would be described as 'His Majesty's Ship', all were small, unarmoured, of shallow draft and, in reality, 'His Majesty's Boat' would be a more accurate nomenclature.

Enemy opposition was ineffective. 22nd Punjabis grounded their bellums on One Tree Island and took the position at the point of their bayonets.

20. The recently promoted Captain Wilfred Nunn DSO RN (later Vice Admiral CB CSI CMG DSO). He commanded a collection of vessels and is, perhaps, unique in fighting naval battles in the middle of a desert. *(Nunn)*

The Oxfordshire and Buckinghamshire Light Infantry (Ox and Bucks) stormed Norfolk Hill, and Captain Brooke, who led, was the first man to die on the position. It is trite to say that there were only 'light casualties'. To the family of Captain Brooke, his was a very heavy loss.

The 'Regatta', thus far, was a crashing success. All the first objectives were taken and Townshend ordered his brigade to bivouac on their captured objectives. The Brigade spent the night among the putrefying enemy corpses. The flies were attracted to the dead but took time out to torment the living.

The following day, 17th Brigade (now commanded by Lieutenant Colonel S.H. Climo) 'continued the movement' and Gun Hill fell to 103rd Mahratta Light Infantry. An aeroplane, the first to be seen in the theatre, overflew Bahran (not on the map) and Maziblah and reported that the enemy had fled from both places. A bag of 300 prisoners had to be evacuated back to Kurnah and dry land.

Townshend's stock was sky high. He had achieved his aim in the most exemplary manner. Nixon, who had played no part in the operation and whose headquarters functioned 'as little more than a post office',[68] embarked in a motorboat and came to share in the success of Townshend and Nunn, his naval subordinate.

Nunn's book chronicling these events makes no criticism of anyone, but having been a participant in a conference with Nixon and Townshend, he wrote later:

> I must confess that the arrangements of the Military High Command in this and other parts of the campaign were – and still are – a puzzle to me. I suppose that having confided this operation to Townshend's division, it would be – or [he] thought that he would be – committing some military discourtesy if he (Nixon) took over and ran the show himself. The force engaged however was very much more than General Townshend's division and further was engaged in an expedition which if successful – as was most likely – would develop into an advance of many miles and would result in the capture of important towns and the acquisition of a great area of Turkish territory. Surely, therefore, it would have been better if he had taken over the direct control of the whole affair.[69]

Although Nixon had no intention of taking command, nevertheless he was bullish and insistent on the advisability of taking advantage of the success already gained. He was anxious that pursuit of the enemy should start immediately. Smoke from their retreating ships could be seen fading away to the north. Nunn recorded that, 'It was General Nixon's energy in urging this course, which decided Townshend after a little hesitation.' Amara, the next significant town on the river, lay 90 miles ahead. The MC took evidence as to the state of the river and noted (at page 9) in its Report:

*Beyond Kurnah the river Tigris narrows rapidly and between Ezra's Tomb
and Kelat Sala, a stretch of 28 miles, the navigation of the river is very
difficult. It twists and turns with sharp bends and hairpin corners leaving
at certain places little or no room for vessels towing a barge on either side
to pass each other. The stream is strong, about 4 knots an hour, and it is
difficult for steamers without independent paddles to avoid striking the
banks when going round corners downstream. Vessels under such
conditions occasionally turn completely round and it is a common
experience to see lighters breaking adrift under the strain.*

Nunn went on ahead to reconnoitre the blockage in the river at Ruta and
found that a large iron lighter had been sunk across the river and mines had
been laid to complete the barrier. *Sumana* cleared the mines and, having
done so, found that there was room for a passage. *Shaitan* and *Sumana* led
the pursuit; *Espiègle* with *Clio* and *Odin* followed in their wake. *Espiègle*
was able to bring her bow guns to bear and engage the two Turkish ships
Mosel and *Marmarice*, which were fleeing north to Amara, but several hits
were not enough to stop either ship.

The river had narrowed from a width of 270 yards to about 70 and
navigation, always difficult, was now very difficult. *Espiègle* could not go
much further and already she was the largest ship to penetrate so far up the

21. *Marmarice* after the pursuit. Photographed on 2 June 1915. *(Nunn)*

river. Darkness fell, with Townshend's force about 20 miles north of their last action. By now it was close to Ezra's Tomb, where three large lighters full of munitions were captured and 300 Turks surrendered without a fight.

Townshend left his General Staff Officer (Grade 1),[70] Colonel Gamble, in command here and, in moonlight, pressed on in *Espiègle*, which grounded several times and on the sharp bends ran into the riverbank. Despite the navigational difficulties, at 0420 hrs *Espiègle's* gunfire hit *Marmarice*, some way further north, and set her on fire. She lost way, stopped and in due course the British force caught up with her.

River conditions were such that it was clear that HMS *Espiègle* could go no further and Townshend transferred to HMS *Comet*, a small paddle-wheel armed steamer. Leaving his force to deal with *Marmarice* and her survivors, he then continued his journey with *Shaitan*, *Samana* and *Lewis Pelly* in company with a handful of soldiers. The party was estimated as being forty-eight strong. That the official arithmetic differed is only of academic interest because the events that followed were either a demonstration of inspired generalship of the very highest order or grotesque and unnecessary folly.

The small flotilla sailed on, and along both banks Arab villages flew white flags and the occupants came out to line the river. It was midday when, at Qalat Salih, a nondescript settlement halfway to Amara, there was a brief flurry of activity. A small mixed force of Turkish cavalry and infantry came into sight. Several well-directed rounds from *Comet's* 12-pounder discouraged any hostile action on the Turks' part and the group headed for the distant shimmering horizon.

At this point a local sheikh came aboard *Comet* and submitted to Townshend. It was an unasked for gesture but indicative of the impact Townshend's excursion was having, not only on the Turks but also on the indigenous population.

Townshend played his trump card when he blustered to the sheikh that he had '15,000 men coming up behind me'. He directed the sheikh to start assembling food for the mythical, oncoming host and generously offered to pay for whatever was provided. Townshend did not hold out much hope of getting the food but he calculated, correctly, that news of the 15,000 men would be widely broadcast.

In warfare, over the ages, deception, bluff and misinformation in their many guises have been used. There never was a better example than this masterly performance by Charles Townshend.

Military wisdom of the previous 2,000 years or so favoured Charlie's unsupported foray to Amara. Sun Tzu,[71] who wrote the *Art of War II* in about 500 BC, opined that, 'if the enemy leaves a door open you must rush in.'

The Emperor Maurice, writing in AD 600, agreed, and said that, 'In war, opportunity is fleeting and cannot be put off at all.'[77]

The consensus is that Townshend was right to press on. He and his small, lightly armed party duly reached Amara without mishap. The MC certainly favoured *'inspired generalship'* and commented briefly:

> *On 3 June Amara was reached and General Townshend with twenty-two sailors and soldiers achieved the surrender of a garrison of 700 Turks. As a military operation this action was audaciously planned and well timed, and it deserves high praise as it achieved great objects with comparatively small loss of life.*[73]

The phrase 'audaciously planned' is ill-chosen because the dash upriver was not planned at all. It was unsupported opportunism. The reality is that Townshend put himself and his party at great risk; nevertheless, his gamble came off in the most spectacular manner. The last word rests with Clausewitz, who wrote, 'Never forget that no military leader has ever become great without audacity.'[74]

For his part, Townshend was aggrieved at the degree of acclaim he received. He wrote, five years later, 'It has always struck me that no one, except the officers and men of 17th Brigade and the naval officers, seems to have recognised the difficulty of the operation and the possibility of disaster.'[75] Clearly, Nixon was insufficiently laudatory, but then the Corps Commander was already looking ahead as he had different fish to fry. However – did he have the means?

Major General Gorringe, one of his senior subordinates, believed that the major factor that determined the outcome of the initial phase of the campaign from 1914 to mid-1916 was the stringent financial constraints imposed by the IG on the conduct of military operations in Mesopotamia.

He had no doubt that officials in Delhi, led by the powerful Finance Member, Sir William Meyer, consistently refused to sanction expenditure on the port facilities or other infrastructural works, such as a proposed railway from Basra to Nasariyeh to take the strain off the river, unless and until it was decided to make the occupation of Mesopotamia permanent. Later, Gorringe gave evidence to the MC and in the Report he is quoted as saying:

> *I have no doubt that great improvements could and should have been effected during the first twelve months and so on in proportion afterwards. There was reluctance to spend money on improvements, which would partake of a permanent character.*[76]

That view is interesting because, as far as Hardinge, Duff and Nixon were concerned, the permanent annexation of Mesopotamia was the aim. This suggests that, although Meyer was at the centre of the IG, he was unaware of the political ambition of Hardinge.

The campaign was being conducted as cheaply as possible and in line with the limited budget available. On that basis, funding the building of railways was unlikely to win financial support. Meyer has been cast as the dead hand of inertia on the tiller of military success, but he did not set the Government of India budget – he administered it. Gorringe was damning when he said, in evidence, that there was:

> *No improvement in the unloading wharves for ships was made until December 1915, when the reinforcements for two divisions were coming out.* [77]

Notwithstanding Nixon's ambition and Townshend's undoubted flair, IEF'D'did not have, readily to hand, the means to fry those other 'different fish'.

**22. Major General G.F. Gorringe DSO, later,
Lieutenant General Sir George KCB KCMG DSO.**

Chapter notes

57 The Army List 1914, HM Stationery Office.
58 Napoleon, 9 December 1817, B.E. O'Meara, *Napoleon in Exile*, 1822.
59 MC Report, p.15.
60 Townshend, Sir C.V.F., *My Campaign in Mesopotamia,* p.41.
61 MC Report, p.17.
62 Later, Vice Admiral Wilfred Nunn CB CSI CMG DSO, author of *Tigris Gunboats*.
63 Sir Joseph Austen Chamberlain KG (1863–1937). He was Secretary of State for India 1915–17 and, as such, a key player in the military debacle in Mesopotamia.
64 Hardinge papers, 26 May 1915, 93/No. 10.
65 Nunn, W., *Tigris Gunboat*s, p.98.
66 Townshend, C.V.F., *My Campaign in Mesopotamia*, p.62.
67 Nunn, W., *Tigris Gunboats*, p.105.
68 Ibid, p.174.
69 Ibid*,* pp.107–108.
70 General Staff Officer Grade 1. In this case, his senior staff officer.
71 Sun Tzu (544–496 BC) was a philosopher, soldier and military strategist. He is credited with the authorship of the influential book *The Art of War*.
72 Maurice (539–602) was a Byzantine emperor and prominent general of his time. George Dennis translated *Maurice's Strategikon* in 1984.
73 MC Report, p.18.
74 Major General von Clausewitz, *Principles of War*, 1812.
75 Townshend, C.V.F., *My Campaign in Mesopotamia*, p.72.
76 MC Report, p.55.
77 Ibid.

Chapter 6

The Capture of Kut

'The most essential quality of a general
is firmness of character and the resolution
to conquer at any price.'

(Napoleon, Gourgaud, *Journal inédit de 1815 à 1818*, Vol. 11, 1816)

It will assist the reader at this stage to provide a simplistic summary of the geography of that part of Mesopotamia covered by this book. First, one should place the right hand flat on a table, palm downwards, all fingers extended. On this basis, 'the wrist is the Persian Gulf; the vein running up the back of the hand is the Shatt al-Arab – running past Abadan to Basra; the little finger is the Karun River – at its tip Ahwaz and oil; the thumb is the Euphrates – at its tip is Nasariyeh. The junction of the thumb and first finger is Kurnah; the first finger is the Tigris – at its first joint Amara and at its tip Kut–al-Amara. Running sluggishly down from the tip of that first finger, is the shallow Shatt-al-Hai.'[78]

By June 1915, Nixon controlled the wrist and the back of the hand (Abadan and Basra), the little finger (Ahwaz and its oil), the junction of the first finger and thumb (Kurnah) and the first finger as far as the first joint (Amara). The Turks held the tip of the first finger (Kut–al-Amara) and the tip of the thumb (Nasariyeh).

With Amara secured and now occupied by 17th Brigade, Nixon turned his sights to the west and, specifically, to the Shatt-al-Hai, which is an apology for a river. It is very wide but far too shallow to allow the passage of any significant vessel; indeed for seven months of the year it is unnavigable, but nevertheless it runs from Kut to near Nasariyeh.

Nixon obviously thought that the Turks, who were unable to sail down the Tigris to Kurnah and Basra, might just see the Shatt-al-Hai as presenting a passage to that town and, from there, threaten Basra. That all seemed to be unlikely but, nevertheless, in order to thwart that possibility he gave orders to the GOC 12th Indian Division to take Nasariyeh, located 68 miles west of Kurnah. The Indian Government approved this excursion, as did

53

Chamberlain, in London, who would have been hard-pressed to forbid it.

Townshend had his name in lights and there can be no doubt as to his bold, inventive and practical soldierly skills. The successes thus far were, predominantly, Townshend's. At this time he was the most successful general on the Allied side and far more newsworthy than his fellows who were bogged down in the trenches of Flanders and Gallipoli.[79] Nixon wallowed in the reflected glory of his subordinate and cast such common sense as he had to the winds.

He had done little to improve the berthing arrangements in Basra and nothing to bring the medical support to a level commensurate with likely casualties. Hardinge and Duff had given him his head and he was deaf to Townshend's plea to release those of his soldiers who were now carrying out line of communication defensive duties. Relations between the two generals cooled but remained strictly professional.

Sight must not be lost of the fact that this campaign was being fought 'on the cheap'. The IG had starved its army for a decade or more and Sir William Meyer,[80] the civil servant appointed as Finance Member of the IG, could not allocate funds that did not exist. The parsimony of the IG was coming home to haunt it.

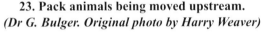

23. Pack animals being moved upstream.
(Dr G. Bulger. Original photo by Harry Weaver)

Townshend intended to establish a firm base at Amara on the right bank overlooking the town and, to this end, he asked for six months' reserve of food and ammunition. Nixon sheltered behind the Indian Army regulations and declined. This caused Townshend uncharacteristically to burst into print and he lucidly addressed his ire to Nixon's Chief of Staff (who was the same rank),[81] saying among other things, 'I do not think that regulations should come into the question.'[82] This illustrates the curious manner in which, although Nixon prosecuted the campaign aggressively, he was nevertheless unable or unwilling to provide Townshend with the means to do his bidding. He wholeheartedly supported his staff, who seemed to be incapable of recognising that the situation the force faced was quite unlike anything for which the 'regulations' had been written. Eventually the desired supplies were located at Amara, but only after a protracted bureaucratic battle.

Nixon had a number of shortcomings; perhaps one of the most significant was that he never solved the problem of river transport. From that flowed all manner of crises. It was a task given to him on appointment and although he had made requests for more ships, it was only on 10 July 1915, eight months after the invasion, that he got around to asking the IG to provide six paddle steamers, three stern wheelers, eight tugs and forty-three barges. This points to a significant gap in the transport inventory that Nixon and his staff had recognised, albeit belatedly. However, despite the serious impact the transport deficiency had upon his logistic capacity, he did not adapt his master plan to take Baghdad.

The river transport requested by Nixon did not exist and the Mesopotamia Commission Report (at page 19) observed:

> *The additional transport asked for was sanctioned after lengthy correspondence but the execution of the order under any circumstances would have taken from eight to ten months before completion, and the ships would then have had to be conveyed whether under their own steam or piecemeal to Basra. Under no circumstances would they have been available till towards the middle of 1916.*

Townshend's 18th Brigade lost its sappers, miners and supporting field artillery, all of which were now moved to the command of General Gorringe to support the attack on Nasariyeh, where there was a Turkish concentration, and so Nixon's fears were justified. Access to the objective was by way of the Euphrates River and the very shallow Lake Hammar. In fiercely oppressive heat, on 25 July, Major General Gorringe,[83] aided by a flotilla of small boats, attacked and took his objective – and 950 prisoners. British

24. Austen Chamberlain, Secretary of State for India, 1915–1917.

casualties were 553 all ranks, but there was much sickness in addition.[84] The Indian Army Medical Service was kept fully occupied.

Ignoring the practical problems that confronted it, and as success piled on success, the IG's ambition knew few bounds – it really was all just too easy. Hardinge sent a telegram to Austen Chamberlain on 27 July, which read: 'Now that Nasariyeh has been occupied the occupation of Kut-al-Amara is considered, by us, to be a strategic necessity.'[85] Chamberlain demurred initially but, when furnished with the details of Nixon's military arrangements, he gave his assent. This followed the usual pattern of London balking initially at a request but then, belatedly, conceding and giving permission.

Wilfred Nunn noted that it was 112 river miles from Basra to Amara and a further 152 river miles from Amara to Kut. Ctesiphon, on the outskirts of

Baghdad, is about 170 miles above Kut, 'on the river upon which we were depending for our supplies and ammunition, as we had no railway.'[86]

To 'fast forward' ninety-two years to 2007, when Major Chris Hunter RLC found himself fighting a different war but in the same place (modern spelling Al-Amara), he wrote:

> As I climb out of the warrior, I am blinded by the brilliant sun. The stench of rotting garbage and crap is all too familiar now, but it still makes me want to puke. It's just like being in the back streets of Basra. I'm beginning to wonder whether every city in this country smells of shit or they just saved the best ones for us. Among the two-storey flat-roofed buildings and palm-lined boulevards I can feel the blue touchpaper and the whole place is going to explode any second.
>
> This is supposed to be the location of the Garden of Eden and to those that live there I'm sure Al-Amara is the most wonderful place on earth. But as far as I am concerned, this collection of flyblown hovels in the middle of nowhere is one of the most violent shit-reeking slums I've ever visited. Burnt-out cars, festering rubbish and piles of brick and rubble litter every street. Centuries-old buildings have been destroyed by insurgent mortar and RPG fire. Al-Amara is a city in ruins and the people who live here don't give a damn.

It is difficult to imagine the extreme squalor that faced Townshend in this, his latest prize. The 6th Division now spent from 3 June until mid-September, about ten weeks, encamped outside Amara. Townshend did not want his troops to be billeted in this health-threatening place, and of necessity a tented barracks sprang up. For the soldiers this was not by any means a holiday; quite the reverse, it was an uncomfortable, miserable and very boring existence. It generated physical and mental illness.

The rate of physical sickness had risen to alarming proportions and was no respecter of rank. The soldiers who had not succumbed to 'fever' reacted to their surroundings in different ways. Their lifestyle gave rise to extreme boredom, anxiety, restlessness and frayed tempers, although it was reported in the Press, specifically *The Times*, that 'some efforts were made to alleviate their circumstances with the provision of mosquito nets, ice, mineral waters and fresh vegetables.'

That was quite untrue.

It was the work of an early twentieth-century, cynical, spin doctor – the reality was very much removed. At 0500 hrs in Mesopotamia it was already too hot to sleep. For those who ventured out, sunstroke and heatstroke were common occurrences. The mercury habitually exceeded 110°F and often reached 116°F. In one period from 7 to 28 July 1917, the temperature did not fall below 116°F in the shade. The climate was lethal, and 423 British and fifty-nine Indian troops died of heatstroke.[87] William Bird, a soldier in that most excellent battalion, the 2nd Dorsets, alleged in a letter that he had experienced '127°F in the shade'.

The Tigris water was unclean, but it was the only source and so dysentery and paratyphoid cases multiplied. Men lay all day on 'beds' with rushes used as mattresses. Any exertion was hazardous, as the following demonstrates:

> I remember very vividly a burial party. We started out for the cemetery, about a mile away, at about 6.00 am. Before we had gone half the distance a man went down with heatstroke and was carried back, limp and twitching to hospital.
>
> As the corpse was lowered into the grave, one of the men on the ropes stumbled forward and fell limply into the grave on top of the dead body. As we fell in to march back, another man went down. Luckily, we had brought a spare stretcher and with one man on this and the other on the stretcher on which the dead man had been carried to the grave, we returned.
>
> We had buried one man, and lost three others over the job.[88]

The impact of all of this on Force levels is evident. Townshend's division was evaporating. Townshend recorded that, within ten days of taking the town, about 1,200 of his men 'were on the sick list.' Townshend undertook a reconnaissance north of Amara and he soon, thereafter, contracted a fever; he was rushed downriver to Basra and thence to Bombay, where he had time to recover, free from the attention of the flies. In a curiously un-soldierly letter to his wife, he wrote:

> This is the first day my darling, I am up and dressed and I am now rapidly getting stronger. After the business at Amara, I was on a long reconnaissance all day along the road to Baghdad. No one looked after me to see that I had any food and I was too much taken up with my work to think of food, and so went empty all day under a blazing sun.[89]

Townshend was in command of that reconnaissance party; he decided where it went and where it would stop to eat, drink and water its horses. To suggest that he, an able bodied, fit soldier on active service should have had to be 'looked after' is complete nonsense. The tone of the letter is very revealing and this wimpish 'poor me' attitude would surface again in the future.

He was most fortunate in the priority treatment he received while he was ill. This was a service not available to his soldiers, who took their chances with the regimental medical officers, the enervating heat, poor diet, dirty water and those 'bloody flies'.

Townshend was evacuated and treated in India. As he remarked in his book, 'It was only my splendid constitution that pulled me through.'[90] Many of his soldiers were not so fortunate. Cemeteries were being filled and his soldiers' bones are there to this day. That letter to Townsend's wife ended with:

> I told you darling, that I only wanted my chance! You should have seen the British and Indian soldiers cheering me on as I stood on the *Comet.* I must have the gift of making men (I mean soldier men) love me and follow me. I have only known the 6th Division for six months and they'd storm the gates of hell if I told them to.

Townshend was heroically heterosexual. He was an averred and enthusiastic admirer of the female form – so it is curious that he needed to include the phrase in parentheses, and to his wife, of all people.

While in India, Townshend stayed with Hardinge as his guest and during that sojourn he wrote to his friend, General Sir James Wolfe-Murray.[91] At the time, Wolfe-Murray was the professional head of the British Army and the propriety of a relatively junior officer writing in the following terms may be doubtful. Townshend wrote:

> I believe I am to advance from Amarah to Kut-al-Amara[92] directly I get back to my division, my headquarters being at Amarah. The question is where are we going to stop in Mesopotamia? I stayed with the Viceroy, but could not get anything out of him as regards our policy in Mesopotamia. … We have certainly not good enough troops to make *certain* [Townshend's italics] of taking Baghdad, which I hear is being fortified, and guns of position are being mounted there.
>
> We can take no risks of a defeat in the East. Imagine a retreat from Baghdad and a consequent instant rising of the Arabs of the whole country behind us, to say nothing of the certain rise in the case of the Persians and probably the Afghans in consequence, as the Amir is only keeping his country out of the war with difficulty. You can afford to have reverses in France and retreats, witness that from Mons to the Marne; you cannot do that sort of thing in the East and retain prestige.
>
> Of our two divisions in Mesopotamia, mine, the 6th, is complete; the 12th Division (Gorringe) has no guns! Or divisional troops – and Nixon takes them from me and lends them to the latter when has to go anywhere.
>
> I consider we ought to hold what we have got and not advance anymore

– as long as we are held up, as we undoubtedly are, in the Dardanelles. All these offensive operations in secondary theatres are dreadful errors in strategy: the Dardanelles, Egypt, Mesopotamia and East Africa! I wonder and wonder at such expeditions being permitted in violation of the greatest of all the great fundamental principles of war, especially that of Economy of Force. Such violation is always punished in history.[93]

The letter goes on at greater length and becomes a gratuitous lesson in military strategy to a general vastly his superior, albeit not with the same grasp of military history. The letter concludes by mentioning the plaudits that he has received and the record he has established 'in the way of pursuits'. Russell Braddon was no fan of Townshend and his book, *The Siege*, has a persistent, angry undertone. He commented very strongly on this letter, saying:

The letter was completely in character. It revealed a gift for strategic appreciation amounting almost to prescience. It revealed Townshend's chronic tendency to criticise his superiors and his obsession with his own affairs to the exclusion of all others. It revealed his habitual lack of generosity to colleagues whom he praised only if they were of inferior rank to himself – his tendency to whine and his almost embarrassing immodesty.

Norman Dixon thought that the letter, and Braddon's observations upon it, were sufficient evidence to include Townshend in his work on Military Psychology.[94] This calls into question the depth of Dixon's research into other subjects upon whom he passed judgment in his book.

Setting letter writing to one side and to return to the chronology: Townshend met with the Commander-in-Chief on 10 August. And the senior man was given an up-to-date, if shaded, briefing on the situation of 6th Indian Division. At his meeting with General Sir Beauchamp Duff, Townshend made the valid point that to take and hold Baghdad would require a corps of two full divisions. According to the GOC 6th Division, Duff replied, saying, 'Not one inch, Townshend, shall you go beyond Kut unless I make you up to adequate strength.'[95]

Townshend was itching to put up the third star that would go with command of a corps. The 'K' that usually went with promotion to lieutenant general would be a very acceptable bonus. It had not occurred to Townshend that anyone else might be given the job – if indeed a job was created. As Townshend's biographer, the author (who studied his man in some depth) believes Charlie's overriding and dominant characteristic was his utterly unbridled and unattractive ambition. It shaped everything in his life and affected the way he related to all other people. He made it his business to cultivate his seniors and he used his association with them shamelessly. His soldiers were no more than a means to his ends and there is no recorded indication of his personal care for any of them.

Townshend started his journey back from India and at about the same time the MC noted:

> *On 15 August 1915 Surgeon General Hathaway made application to the Inspector General of Communications at Basra for a steamer to be set apart and fitted for the conveyance of sick and wounded or alternatively for a tug and two* mahailas. *The steamer and tug were refused on the ground that all were required for the movement of troops and supplies.*[96]
>
> *Surgeon General Hathaway did not impress the need on General Nixon and he showed little foresight ... his request on 15 August 1915 for an improvised steamer was not urged persistently or with sufficient emphasis.*

Townshend returned to his duty and Nixon had briefed him that Suleiman Askeri Bey, who had commanded at Kurnah and Shaiba and suffered defeats in both places, had committed suicide – such was his shame. His successor was Nureddin (Nur-Ur-Din), a very capable soldier, who had taken a position astride the Tigris at Es Sinn. He was thought to be particularly strong on the right bank. His strength was estimated at about 10,000 men and thirty-two guns. There is no record of whether or not Nixon and Townshend discussed river transport at this meeting. If they did not, then they should have done so. If they did, then the conversation was unproductive.

25. Nureddin Pasha.

Townshend concentrated his force at Ali Gharbi and took stock. In addition to his three-brigade division he had 6th Indian Cavalry Brigade, 10th Royal Field Artillery Brigade and two battalions of 30th Indian Brigade. All up he commanded 11,000 men and twenty-eight guns. The downside was that his riverine assets were, at best, barely adequate and he could not afford any losses. A wise man once said, 'Victory is the beautiful, bright coloured flower. Transport is the stem without which it could never have blossomed.'[97] In this case and, indeed, throughout the campaign, the 'stem' was weak, thin and vulnerable.

Numerically the two sides were evenly matched, but the attackers were always the most at risk and never more so than in the flat, almost featureless desert around Kut. The Turkish forces that lay in wait for Townshend were the remnants of the 35th and 38th divisions that had been soundly beaten at Shaiba, Nasariyeh, Kurnah and Amara. Morale was low and lowered further by the same logistic weaknesses that faced the British. Medical support was minimal and resupply was just as dependent upon the Tigris. Nureddin's riverine assets consisted only of those craft that had been upriver of Amara when it was taken. His soldiers were, in the main, conscripts with only minimal training.

Nureddin's grandiose brief from Enver Pasha[98] was to defeat Townshend and retake Basra. As we say today, 'this was a big ask'. Taking one hurdle at a time, the Turkish commander had sensibly concentrated his force at Es Sinn. This is one of the few significant points on the Tigris north of Amara and distinguished by the easily defended and commanding ridges on the right bank.

Nureddin anchored both his formations on the river and incorporated the Suwaikiya, Suwada and Ataba marshes into his defence on the left bank (looking downstream). These marshes were lined with mines and in any depression *punji*[99] stakes had been sown. Wire entanglements were extensive. Although Nureddin's men dug in and created a formidable series of redoubts and trench systems on the left bank nevertheless, he had left two gaps that were revealed by aerial reconnaissance (see map on page 63).

Nureddin installed a boat bridge about 6 miles behind his lines to enable him to move forces from one bank to another. It would take any redeployed soldier, using the bridge, too long to join the fray, and from all accounts he had a second boat bridge linking his two front lines either side of the river. This is not shown on the map, although a ferry is marked.

Townshend, ever the faithful disciple of Napoleon, was always going to look for something other than a frontal assault. To this end he put together a complicated plan that was dependent upon all the component parts working in concert and in time, each with the other. He was pleased to describe this as a 'turning attack' and in simplistic terms it meant attacking the Turks from deep on their left flank whilst holding their right flank in position and unable to move.

An idiosyncrasy of Townshend's was that he never referred to his formations as, say, '17th Brigade'; he much preferred to designate them as 'columns', 'forces' or 'bodies' (as in 'Main Body'). Facing Nureddin at Es Sinn he promulgated his plan, and in this he split his division into three columns, thoughtfully entitled 'A', 'B' and 'C'. In command style this was very Napoleonic.

Brigadier General W.S. Delamain CB DSO would command Column 'A' –

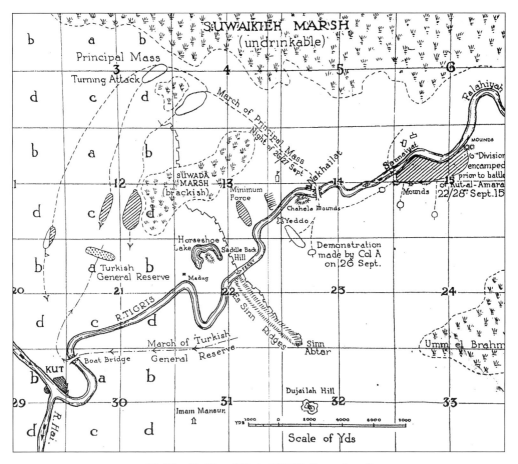

26. The Battle of Kut. *(C.V.F. Townshend)*

a mixed force composed of an enhanced battalion and three batteries of Maxim machine guns together with a company of sappers. It was his job to overrun and take the three redoubts between the Ataba and Suwada marshes. The Ataba Marsh is not named on the map above. It is that area below Suwaikieh and above Suwada.

Brigadier General C.I. Fry commanded Column 'B', or the 'minimum force', using Townshend's nomenclature. He had his own 18th Brigade and his function was to 'demonstrate' on the left bank between the river and the Suwada Marsh in an effort to convince the Turks that this would be the axis for the main attack.

Column 'C' was the command of Brigadier General F.A. Hoghton and he had his own 17th Brigade, supplemented by two battalions from Delamain's 16th Brigade and four machine guns. In addition he was furnished with two armoured cars and a cavalry component. His aim was to

27. Brigadier General Fry and staff officers of HQ 18 Brigade.

pass through the 300-yard gap between the Turkish north redoubt and the Ataba Marsh and, from there, spread mayhem in the Turkish rear.

On the face of it, the plan was attractive, but unless Column 'A' could engage the redoubts from the front there was going to be a reduced chance of Hoghton being able to approach them from the rear. Once the troops were committed Townshend had no part to play.

The 6th (Poona) Division assembled at Sheikh Sa'ad, about 8 miles short of the busily digging Turks. The advance to this point had been up the right-hand bank; some of the troops travelled on the river but the bulk of the troops had marched in the blistering sun. The right-hand bank (British left) was Hobson's choice because it was easier for ships to moor on that side of the river.

There was a pause for ten days to await the arrival of the divisional artillery. A river crossing was going to be the first phase of Townshend's plan. In the interim, further aerial surveys were made by the very few intrepid airmen in the theatre. It was clear that on this right-hand bank the Turks had developed a defensive 2½-mile system along the line of an old, raised and abandoned canal. In the desert a 10-foot bank counts as 'high ground' and gives greatly improved line of sight. On the map this position is shown as 'Es Sinn ridges'.

The British plans for the battle to come were inhibited by an extreme shortage of land transport. Townshend was 300 mules short of his requirement and the consequence was that all the available transport was, of necessity, allocated to the 'main force' on the left bank. Those 800 camels sent home by Barrett, in October 1914, were being sorely missed.

Townshend had no water carts and, furthermore, there were no arrangements in place to resupply drinking water.[100] This was an unbelievable and reprehensible oversight that would have dire consequences for the men committed to long approach marches and violent action in temperatures of over 100°F. The only form of ambulance was the awful, inadequate, bone-shaking, mule-hauled army transport cart (ATC).

The MC later endorsed the Vincent-Bingley view on the subject of water, which said:

Water supply arrangements at the actual front were also far from satisfactory. The recent outbreak of cholera is attributed by sanitary experts to the failure to supply the troops with a sufficient amount of purified drinking water.

On 25 September, a telegram was received from General Sir Beauchamp Duff, the Commander-in-Chief, India. The telegram said, 'No going beyond Kut–al-Amara.' Townshend mused in his diary, 'When was Sir Beauchamp Duff induced to change his mind; and who persuaded him to do so?' Then, a man who can change his position so radically is just as likely to change it back.

For the soldiers who had been waiting in fearful anticipation, 27 September came as a relief as operations against Kut commenced. Column 'C', under Hoghton, put the ball in play by starting a forced march on the night of 27/28 September to outflank the Turkish line. 'Darkness is the friend of the skilled infantryman,' or so said Liddell Hart,[101] but then he was not present on this particular night.

As dawn broke, the Turks saw a large body advancing on the right bank; it reached the Chahela Mounds and created a great cloud of dust. Tents were pitched to give the impression that this body was there to stay and this was the axis of the impending attack. Nureddin was now convinced that the British thrust would be up the right-hand bank and the dust cloud and tents served to reinforce his view. He thinned out his troops on the opposite bank

28. Brigadier General W.S. Delamain DSO. Photographed by Swain as Lieutenant General Sir Walter Delamain KCB KCMG DSO in about 1923.

and moved them across the river by means of a boat bridge (not shown on the map). On the left bank, Fry's force was 'demonstrating' as planned. It reached Nukhailat village and dug in with its left wing on the river.

The air component suffered and four aeroplanes were damaged, but the sole survivor provided invaluable, up-to-date intelligence throughout the battle.

The fog of war descended; Delamain was waiting to launch his attack but could not do so until Hoghton appeared over to his right, from the direction of the Ataba Marsh. Hoghton's night march had eluded the enemy but the compass readings that had been provided were found to be in error.

66

The effect was that Column 'C', instead of marching south of Ataba Marsh, marched around it. This added several miles to the journey for the heavily burdened soldiers, but more importantly, it took valuable time and exhausted the stock of telephone cable carried to ensure communication between the commanders.[102]

The sun was climbing into an azure sky before Delamain could see Hoghton in the far distance at about 0830 hrs. Delamain decided that delay was dangerous, so he initiated the attack. Hoghton, somewhat belatedly, joined in. Eventually, and after heavy casualties on both sides, the three positions were all taken. Kipling's verse applied:

> *When first under fire and you're wishful to duck*
> *Don't look or take heed of the man that is struck*
> *Be thankful you're living and trust to your luck*
> *and march to your front like a soldier.*[103]

The sun was now scorching. Hoghton's men were utterly exhausted and so weak from thirst that many collapsed on the enemy position. A number of mules stampeded into the nearby marsh, seeking water, and were inextricably bogged down. They had to be shot in situ, the transport situation was exacerbated and the 'stem' was even weaker.[104]

Fry's Column 'B' was facing stiff opposition and he needed help. He appealed to Delamain and, just before the sun set, his soldiers made an assault on the left flank of the Turkish position. The advance was over 1,000 yards of flat desert and it called for great courage and fitness to arrive at the enemy position and then take it at bayonet point. Napoleon once said, 'The bayonet has always been the weapon of the brave and the chief tool of victory.' It proved to be so on this day.

The cartoon overleaf, extolling the power of the bayonet and the aggression it generates, was published in *Mr Punch's History of the Great War* in 1919.

As night fell, and the temperature with it, the wounded lay out in the open. The Turks still blocked the way to the river and water. The unwounded strove to bring in the wounded as Marsh Arabs were about, robbing, killing and mutilating any soldier they found in the dark. They were indiscriminate and murdered Turks with similar lack of compassion. The medical service, always fragile, had all but broken down and could not cope with the scale of the casualties, some of whom died of exhaustion in the biting cold that night.

Later, the Vincent-Bingley Report (which was incorporated into the MC Report) would note:

THE RECRUIT WHO TOOK TO IT KINDLY

29. Cartoon from *Mr Punch's History of the Great War.*

No satisfactory reason has been assigned for the failure to provide the ordinary form of land ambulance transport for these operations ... but throughout the campaign the usual form of ambulance transport has been the army transport cart that is, a small springless cart made of wood and iron, drawn by mules or ponies, and ordinarily employed for the carriage of supplies. When the evidence of the suffering caused by this means of conveyance, particularly in cases of fracture and severe injury, is considered, it is difficult to avoid criticising the action of those responsible for this deficiency in severe language.[105]

The person responsible was Lieutenant General Sir John Nixon, the Corps Commander. He had decided that he would attend the battle, assuring Townshend that he was just a spectator but that he 'would be available to deal with matters of policy.' If there was any glory to be won at Kut, Nixon wanted to be on hand to reap his share. His reference to 'policy' is fatuous, because 'ambulance policy', which should have been at the top of his priority list, clearly was not. Townshend had no option but to accept Nixon's presence, which served no practical purpose, and he could well have done without it.

Nixon was close enough to see for himself the suffering of his soldiers in the aftermath of this battle and to observe the breakdown of the logistic chain, such as it was. In any army over the last 500 years, the four prime requisites have been water, bread, bullets and bandages. In this case, at least two of these requisites were not available. Water replenishment was such a basic need that Townshend must be held responsible for its dreadful omission from his great plan. There is no evidence that Nixon drew any conclusions from that either.

Townshend called up his river flotilla and told it to try to force a passage to Kut under cover of darkness. The leading ship was *Comet*, commanded by Lieutenant Commander Cookson. Under heavy small-arms fire, *Comet* steamed upriver until it was halted by an underwater obstruction that turned out to be a thick chain strung across the river. Cookson, axe in hand, leapt into a ship's dingy and, under fire, paddled to the *mahaila* that anchored one end of the chain. He boarded the *mahaila* but then he fell, riddled with bullets. He was later awarded a posthumous Victoria Cross. Most of his crew were dead or wounded and *Comet* drifted back downstream.

The Turks had started to withdraw from the right bank (looking downstream) the previous afternoon but mirages had obscured their movement from Townshend. Now using darkness as his cloak, Nureddin

30. Lieutenant Commander E.C. Cookson VC DSO RN. *(Photo Central Press)*

stole away and skilfully took away half of his guns with him.[106] It was a very professional operation.

As the sun rose on 29 September 1915, it revealed a bleak scene. The battlefield was silent save for the cries of the unrecovered wounded of both sides. The field belonged to Townshend; it was yet another victory. Access was now available to the river, and parched Indian and British soldiers were able to slake their raging thirst in the murky waters of the Tigris – the water tasted like champagne.

Townshend despatched his cavalry brigade in pursuit of the Turks but its performance was mediocre. When it caught up with the Turkish rearguard, the commander, Brigadier General Roberts, held back, ostensibly waiting for reinforcements. However, one of the reasons for the Brigade's dilatory performance was that the cavalry were Indian and they were not carrying with them their cooking pots. It was unconscionable that they would use Arab vessels in lieu. The Indian caste system in operation would show its face again a few weeks later.

Townshend took to the river, upon which the water level had fallen. The difficulties then encountered with shoal water and tight bends delayed his triumphal entry into Kut for two days. River traffic downstream was filled with the wounded. Townshend had estimated 6 per cent casualties; in fact, 6th Division suffered 12 per cent, or 1,229, of which only ninety-four were killed.[107] This is a very small proportion of about 1:13. The Turkish losses were reported to be 1,700 killed and wounded and 1,289 taken prisoner.

Surgeon General Hathaway's arrangements to care for these wounded men were wholly inadequate and some died of no more than neglect as they lay in their own excrement and blood during the interminable, agonising journey in open barges to Basra and what passed for a 'hospital' in this benighted land.

Chapter notes

78 Braddon, R., *The Siege*, p.49. Braddon's book is an important source document because when he wrote it, in 1967, many of the participants were still alive and available for interview.

79 The Gallipoli peninsula was invaded on 26 April 1915 and eventually abandoned on 9 January 1916 after very heavy losses. The small populations of Australia and New Zealand lost proportionately more than Britain and India.

80 Sir William Meyer GCIE KCSI ICS (1860–1922). Served as Finance member of the Indian Government from 1914–18. He was appointed High Commissioner of India in September 1920 but died suddenly, in London, in October 1922.

71

81 Major General George Kemball CB DSO (later, Sir George KCMG CB DSO 1859–1941).

82 Letter from Townshend to Chief of Staff IEF'D', 6 June 1915.

83 Later, Lieutenant General Sir George Gorringe KCB KCMG DSO (1868–1945). He was described by Braddon (p.51) as 'a big man, highly coloured, deeply tanned, officious and utterly without tact. He allowed nothing – not Turks, Nureddin (the Turkish Commander), counter-attacks, casualties, swamps, Marsh Arabs or deeply entrenched redoubts – to stop him.'

84 MC Report, p.18.

85 Ibid, p.18.

86 Nunn, W., *Tigris Gunboats*, p.195.

87 Major Harry Weaver diary.

88 *Oxfordshire and Buckinghamshire Light Infantry Chronicles*, Vol. XXIV 1914–1915 (published privately).

89 Sherson, E., *Townshend of Chitrál and Kut*, p.266.

90 Townshend C.V.F. *My Campaign in Mesopotamia*, p.77.

91 General Sir James Wolfe-Murray KCB (1853–1919). He had been a mentor of Townshend in India. He was appointed as Chief of the Imperial General Staff on 30 October 1914 but, in that post, he was described as 'ineffectual'. He contributed nothing to public affairs and was overshadowed by Kitchener in the War Council. He carried some of the responsibility of the rapidly failing Dardanelles campaign and was dismissed from his post on 26 September 1915.

92 Kut-al-Amara (Townshend's spelling); better known as Kut.

93 Townshend, C.V.F., *My Campaign in Mesopotamia*, p.84.

94 Dixon, N.E., *On the Psychology of Military Incompetence*, 1976.

95 Townshend, C.V.F. *My Campaign in Mesopotamia.* p86.

96 MC Report, p.57.

97 Churchill, W.S., *The River War*, 1899.

98 Enver Pasha (1881–1922) had two roles in the Turkish Government. He was War Minister and the Ottoman Commander-in-Chief. He was much influenced by the military training he had with the German Army although his performance as military commander was mixed. After the war, his credibility now severely damaged, he fled to Germany. Thereafter, he involved himself in Russian politics and was killed in 1922 fighting for the Basmachi Muslim movement against the Bolsheviks.

99 A Punji stick or stake is a booby trap. It is a simple, sharpened spike, usually made of wood and placed vertically in the ground. Punji sticks are usually deployed in substantial numbers. The Viet Cong in Vietnam used them effectively and frequently.

100 Barker, A.J., *The Neglected War*, p.82.

101 Liddell Hart, Sir Basil, *Thoughts on War*, Faber, London, 1944.

102 Moberly, F.J., *The Campaign in Mesopotamia 1914–1918*, Vol. 1, pp.323–4.

103 Kipling, R. (1865–1936), *The Feet of the Young Men.*

104 Barker, A.J., *The Neglected War*, p.85.

105 MC Report, p.65.

106 Townshend recorded that seventeen enemy guns were captured (p.120). However, Barker said, 'fourteen, including one of 1802 vintage' (p.88). The *Official History* settled for thirteen.

107 Nunn, W., *Tigris Gunboats*, p.163.

Chapter 7

What Next?

'Principles of strategy should never transcend common sense.'
(Motto of the German Army Staff College prior to 1914)

Townshend had started his campaigning in April 1915 with three battalions of British soldiers. These were the 1st Battalion, the Oxfordshire and Buckinghamshire Light Infantry; the 2nd Battalion, the Dorsetshire Regiment; and the 2nd Battalion, the Norfolk Regiment. The three British battalions, one in each brigade, were the rocks upon which Townshend's victories, thus far, were built.

In every engagement since April, these battalions had suffered attrition in their ranks and they were now significantly weaker. For example, on 9 October 1915, the Dorsets numbered only 297,[108] or about 50 per cent of their strength. Nixon had exacerbated matters by appropriating the services of many of these valuable infantry assets to staff his administrative tail, and that was a constant irritation to the GOC 6th Division, who recorded in his memoirs that he made 'repeated efforts to induce Headquarters at Basra to send back to my battalions the scores of British soldiers of the Norfolks, Dorsets and Oxfords who were employed in every imaginable kind of billet in Basra – as police, extra clerks, batmen for officers (including staff officers of the Indian Army, who were not entitled to British soldiers as servants), improvised chauffeurs for a regular fleet of motor launches, marines on gun boats, extra hands to strengthen reservist crews of blue jackets – all taken from the bayonets of my division!'[109]

Despite his entreaties to Nixon and his staff, those well-trained, regular infantrymen continued to be misemployed and Townshend's anger can be readily understood. However, a Norfolk man himself, Townshend asked the Norfolks to furnish him with another batman when Private Whitmore, his long-serving soldier servant, collapsed. Private John Boggis, who had volunteered for the job, drew the short straw. Boggis was a valuable source for Russell Braddon and, when interviewed, gave an interesting view of his commander's behaviour.

Townshend reflected on his victory at Kut and, when he wrote his memoir in 1920, he said:

> The Battle of Kut-al-Amara can be said to have been one of the most important in the history of the British Army in India. There had been nothing of its magnitude either in the Afghan war or the Indian mutiny. For it was fought against troops equally well armed and of equal numbers to ourselves. In addition we ejected them from a very strong and up-to-date position, commanding ground as flat as a billiard table with nothing to check their fire-sweep.[110]

Townshend's judgement may well be correct, but what he did not know was that this was the high water mark of his career and from this point it was downhill all the way, ultimately to failure and disgrace.

His wounded and their treatment were not mentioned. The battle had been concluded on 29 September but the journey back to Basra took over a week, and for the unfortunates packed into ill-equipped ships and barges that journey was a misery and a worrying prelude to things to come. The Indian Medical Service, under the leadership of Babtie and Hathaway, was failing.

31. Wounded Indian soldiers.

74

At Kut the medical personnel allocated to 6th Division were barely sufficient. Any further forward movement up the river with a commensurate level of casualties was almost certain to convert the existing deficiencies in medical personnel and materiel into total breakdown of the whole system. That is, *'unless continuous good luck should attend the new offensive movement.'*[111] The availability of 'good luck' is not the basis upon which war should ever be waged but Nixon was to set a precedent by depending upon it.

The Mesopotamia Commission Report was not expected to comment on undeniable success. It merely summarised the capture of Kut in one paragraph:

> *On September 14 the Headquarters of Sixth Division reached Sheikh Saad, and on 15th, Abu Rummanah, which had been very strongly fortified by the Turks was captured by us. On 29th, after severe fighting, the Turks were in full flight and our cavalry had entered Kut-al-Amara. During the fight we captured more than 1,700 prisoners and thirteen guns, and inflicted heavy losses in men and materiel. This part of the campaign was brilliantly executed by General Townshend and the Sixth Division of the Indian Army and the whole series of military operations during the past three months had been so extraordinarily successful that it is not surprising that a spirit of optimism and over-confidence as to what could be achieved overcame General Nixon and his Headquarters Staff.*

Mention has been made of the Marsh Arabs and their malign and cruel presence on the fringes of all of the engagements of this campaign. Proximity to loot was their incentive and, along the way, they added to the fatalities of both sides. Colonel A.J. Barker wrote of them in 1967 and his judgement was that, 'In theory, they made their living as herdsmen of water buffaloes or fishermen, or as odd job men, but their environment and natural traits produced a highly developed predilection for any form of thieving and dirty work – so much so, that even to people who regarded robbery with violence as a gentlemanly pastime, the Marsh Arabs had the reputation of being degraded villains.'[112]

Wounded soldiers, on both sides, fell victim to these people who were merciless and rapacious. On 1 October 1915, an ill-informed King George V telegraphed General Nixon and said, 'I warmly congratulate you and my troops under your command upon the marked success which they have achieved under difficult and trying conditions. I trust the sick and wounded are doing well.'

King George, 'the Sailor King', set an example that few of his generals could match, because his concern for the rank and file and the lower deck was genuine. Nixon replied with weasel words that did him no credit. He telegraphed back to his Sovereign, 'Sick and wounded well and it is hoped many will be back in the ranks shortly.' Hardinge telegraphed similar sentiments and he too received the same bland and misleading assurances from Nixon, who had now added 'economy with the truth' to his portfolio of misjudgements. His conduct was dishonourable.

On 3 October 1915, Townshend, who never wavered in his opinion, sent a telegram to Nixon's Chief of Staff, Major General Kemball. The MC Report described that communication as *'important'* (p.27). Given the content of the telegram and the subsequent course of events, it was shrewdly worded and timed. Townshend wrote:

> By the aviator's report attached you will see that the chance of breaking up the retreating Turkish forces, which by now have taken up a position at Salman [Suleiman] Pak [Ctesiphon], no longer exists. The position is astride the Baghdad road and the Tigris and is estimated to be 6 miles of entrenchments … my opinion, if I may be allowed to express it,[113] is that up to the Battle of Kut our object has been to occupy the strategical position of Kut and to consolidate ourselves in the Vilayet of Basra. Ctesiphon is now held by the defeated Turkish forces.
>
> Should it be considered politically advisable by the Government to occupy Baghdad? At present, on account of the doubtful situation at the Dardanelles and the possibility of our small force being driven out of Baghdad by strong forces from Anatolia which would compel us to retire down a long line of communications teeming with Arabs, at present more or less hostile, whose hostility would become active on hearing of our retreat, then I consider that on military grounds we should consolidate our position at Kut. The sudden fall of water, which made the advance of our ships most difficult and tiresome, upset our plans of entering Baghdad on the heels of the Turks while they were retreating in disorder.
>
> If on the other hand it is the desire of the Government to occupy Baghdad, then, *unless great risk is to be run* [author's italics], it is in my opinion, absolutely necessary that the advance from Kut should be carried out methodically by two divisions or one Army Corps or by one division supported closely by another complete division, *exclusive* [author's italics] of the garrisons of the important places of Nasariyeh, Ahwaz and Amara.

This was a perfectly reasonable, professional opinion and he was entirely correct in airing it. However, 'there's none so blind as them's can't see', and

Kemball replied the same day. He said that Townshend had not taken into account Sir John Nixon's 'appreciation of the situation'[114] in which the Army Commander calculated that Townshend faced a Turkish force of only 4,000 bayonets, 500 sabres and twenty guns, and that this force was inferior in strength and morale to that defeated at Kut. He believed it was Nixon's intention 'to open the way to Baghdad as he understands that another division will be sent here from France and he would like your plan for effecting this object.'

32. Major General George Vere Kemball DSO (later Sir George KCMG CB DSO). Kemball went on from being Nixon's Chief-of-Staff to command of 28th Brigade.

Townshend's telegram found its way into the public domain. The author, who was already a darling of British citizenry as a result of his sequence of victories, found himself the subject of discussion in both Houses of Parliament. Later events would endorse Townshend's stated caution and his averred need for a second division that, of course, he expected to come under his command.

Nixon denied any knowledge of the telegram. In his evidence to the MC he stated that, *'If he says he sent it in, I suppose that he did. ... Personally I have no recollection of that appreciation and I'm not sure that it arrived. I never saw it.'* Kemball said he was sure Nixon must have seen it. Hardinge and Duff were unaware of Townshend's advice. Later, Duff wrote and said that he had not seen the telegram and if he had he would have ignored it. Duff added that such a communication would carry no weight at all. 'I never take the opinion of a junior officer in a case of that sort who had no more responsibility than a lance corporal. I would as soon go to the officer commanding a battalion.'[115]

Townshend, who kept a diary, noted accurately on receiving Kemball's reply that, 'There is nothing definite known about this, and no earthly chance of it [the additional division] being in this country in time.' He could recognise 'pie in the sky' when he saw it but it is an indication of the level of his moral courage that, despite his plainly stated professional objections to a further advance and the absurd response to his objections, he nevertheless wired straight back to Kemball, saying, 'You did not mention the arrival of a division from France in this country and that makes all the difference to my appreciation.' It was a very weak volte-face.

The MC Report observed wryly, on page 27, that, '*These two statements are not easy to reconcile but General Townshend, like many other born fighters, was somewhat mercurial and changeable in his views.*'

That was an overly generous summation. Townshend did not challenge his orders when eventually they were given. He justified this by saying that, as a soldier, he was obligated to follow orders no matter how much he disagreed with them.

Townshend was quite right; an army, any army, will degenerate into a leaderless rabble unless there is strict discipline, at all levels, and a strict adherence to orders legally given. Napier[116] hit the spot when he said, many years before, that, 'Soldiers must obey in all things. They may and do laugh at foolish orders, but they nevertheless obey, not because they are blindly obedient, but because they know that to disobey is to break the backbone of their profession.'

That is the received wisdom. In this case Townshend stood on the threshold of history and one could speculate that if he had declined to advance further, unless supported, he may well have been sacked; but his sacking and the reason for it would have brought him public acclamation. It would have drawn notice to the nonsense about to be perpetrated by Nixon, and the likelihood is that Nixon too would have been sacked. Thousands of soldiers would not have been killed and the world would be a different place.[117] On the other hand, Townshend would not have won the promotion he craved and his career would probably have been over – he would not take that chance, and who can blame him?

Compliance with 'orders' is a two-edged sword and can be ill-used. It was to be the refuge of criminals in the wars to come. In this campaign and in this case, it was a sorry excuse for disaster.

A complication in all of this was that Townshend had a track record in crying 'wolf'. He had emphasised at Kurnah, Amara and Kut how difficult it would be to achieve his aim and this of course added to the lustre of his victories, particularly when he had succeeded so effortlessly. It would be understandable if Nixon thought that his subordinate was, once more, 'over-egging the pudding'.

Townshend may have been a self-obsessed personality but he was probably better educated in military strategy than most of his contemporaries and he was aware that lessons learned by one generation have to be relearned by generations that follow. Military history is cyclic and on that basis he reflected, in 1920, on the lines of communication situation he faced at Kut and compared it to that facing Napoleon in 1812 when he advanced on Moscow. He wrote, 'Moscow was 570 miles from the Nieman River.

213,000 men actually marched with the Emperor; the remainder of the 600,000 men garrisoned Germany and guarded the line of communication to France.'[118] He made the valid point that the proportion of Napoleon's force assigned to the defence of the lines of communication was vastly different to the parlous allocation made by Lieutenant General Sir John Nixon along the Tigris more than 100 years later.

Napoleon lost anyway!

Sir Percy Cox, the Indian civil servant sent to the theatre of operations with Nixon, was an important opinion former. He had no executive power but he had the ear of those who had that power. The Arabs named him 'Supposi Kokus'. Not all of Cox's advice was well judged and mention was made earlier of his ill-considered suggestion that the British occupation of Basra would be a permanent feature of the post-war world. Unabashed by that, he was a firm supporter of Nixon, his boss, and they shared an ambition to attack Baghdad – practicalities ignored.

In early October 1915, Kut was secured, the Shatt-al-Hai was sealed at both ends and the 6th Indian Division was receiving battle casualty

33. Enva Pasha with unknown German officer.

79

replacements. There was considerable telegraph traffic between India and London to which Townshend was not privy. On 4 October, the Cabinet met and decided:

> *The position was reported yesterday to the Cabinet, and they have decided to appoint a committee of the Foreign Office, General Staff, Admiralty and India Office, to consider in all its possibilities and policy for an advance on Baghdad.*
>
> *If forces are available to take and hold the place, political reasons were thought to make occupation desirable ... it is thought that we might be able to capture Baghdad but that forces weakened by further losses would be insufficient to hold it against counter-attacks and maintain communications. Kitchener can hold out no hope of reinforcements from Europe and Egypt.*[119]

Common sense was alive and well and living in London. Townshend's views were supported and Kitchener's categoric advice that troops could not be found in other theatres seemed to put the lid on the matter. On 6 October, the Viceroy sent a telegram to the Secretary of State, saying, '*Orders to stop further advance were telegraphed yesterday to General Nixon.*'[120]

Nixon, however, would not be thwarted and the following day he advised the Secretary of State that, 'navigation difficulties had been overcome' and, 'the enemy is shaken, short of ammunition and has lost 13 guns.' His final remark was, 'Should we let such an opportunity slip by us, I can see no arguments by which we could justify ourselves.'

The phrase that is underlined above was subject to very detailed scrutiny and the MC claimed that '*misunderstanding arose from the first sentence of the telegram*'. Nixon later said that he was referring to the passage of ships to Kut through the now shallow water. He did not mean that he had resolved the broader transport issue. He was misunderstood and that misunderstanding had serious implications.

The air component at Azizieh at the beginning of October consisted of three aeroplanes under the command of Major H.L. Reilly, and the first reconnaissance flight over Baghdad took place on 6 October.

By 5 November, reinforcements of the Royal Flying Corps, with four B.E.2.C aeroplanes, reached Basra and reorganised as No. 30 Squadron RFC. Reconnaissance flights over Baghdad continued until 13 November, when an aeroplane, sent to cut the telegraph lines north and west of Baghdad, was damaged in landing and was captured by the Turks. The pilot, Major Reilly, was taken prisoner and paraded through the streets of Baghdad.

General Nixon, with his headquarters, arrived that same day at Azizieh. When he was told of the loss of Reilly and his machine, he feared further attrition among his few aeroplanes and so gave orders that no more long-distance reconnaissance was to be undertaken.

Soldiers, the world over, believe that 'time spent in reconnaissance is never wasted' and the same applies to 'effort spent'. To abandon reconnaissance was shortsighted, overly defensive and entirely illogical. Nixon's first need was for an accurate estimate of enemy forces. From this he could make a balanced 'appreciation of the situation', and from this in turn would flow a cohesive plan.

Hardinge was encouraged by Nixon's assurances on 'navigation difficulties' and was still sufficiently enthused by the golden prize that, on 9 October 1915, he sent a telegram to Chamberlain saying, 'I still hope to be the Pasha of Baghdad before I leave India.'[121] There can be no doubt whatsoever of the Viceroy's position. For him it was Baghdad or bust – and let's not worry about the details.

At this early stage Townshend's position enjoyed the support of Hardinge and Duff. The issue of river transport, in particular, exercised Duff. However, that topic was inconvenient and so Hardinge simply skated over the issue.

London signalled Nixon direct on 8 October and asked him most urgently to reply to the question, 'to both occupy and hold Baghdad what addition to your present force are you confident will be necessary?' Nixon responded immediately, saying, 'No additions are necessary to my present force to beat Nureddin and occupy Baghdad; of this I am confident.' He added that he would need an additional division and a cavalry regiment to hold the city.

Over the next fifteen days telegrams flowed to and fro, most of them marked 'Private' and thus not archived like all other routine correspondence. The MC did, however, obtain some and in its Report the escalation of the 6th Division's task was laid bare.

In the meantime, events in the Dardanelles were flowing Turkey's way. Its very stout defence of its territory was causing vast casualty lists and the tactically inept General Sir Ian Hamilton had no ideas, aims or ambition. Defeat was on the cards and if that were to take place, the Turks would then be able to move large bodies of battle-hardened troops to Mesopotamia.

On 21 October, the Secretary of State advised the Viceroy that Turkish forces confronting 6th Division consisted of:

> only 9,000 troops and some irregulars to deal with for the next two months. The Turkish forces may be somewhat increased by the end of the year and they could conceivably reach a total of 60,000 by the end of January 1916

and an even larger figure during 1916. On this basis, it is thought to be unwise to occupy Baghdad … Arabs are wavering and will probably join the Turks unless we can offer them great inducements. … we should occupy Baghdad, giving assurances to Arab leaders that we favour creation of Arab states independent of Turks … unless you consider possibility of eventual withdrawal is decisive against the advance, all other considerations seem to us to render it desirable and we are prepared to order it.

This was a curious message and the last sentence is at odds with the earlier argument. However, this was just the encouragement that Hardinge wanted and he replied blandly, assuring his reader that, 'We believe General Nixon has a fair prospect of being able to hold his own against 60–70,000 Turks provided that he has occupied Baghdad as soon as he is ready.'[122]

Hardinge probably did not draft this assertion and General Sir Beauchamp Duff and his staff must have been involved. Nevertheless, Lord Hardinge signed it and so ownership of this arrant nonsense is his.

The statement is so utterly absurd as to be off the scale of stupidity.

Even more worrying is that it was not challenged. Any soldier, of any rank, of any generation, of any nationality would know that to 'hold one's own' against odds of, say, 7:1 (or worse), with hopelessly inadequate medical cover, at the end of a very vulnerable 500-mile single line of communication, dependent entirely upon the vagaries of the Tigris and inadequate resupply transport, was quite impossible. Hardinge did acknowledge the possibility of a withdrawal but the human and materiel implications of a contested withdrawal were brushed aside.

General Barrow, the Military Secretary to the India Office, wrote a memorandum in which he expressed the opinion that to attempt to go to Baghdad with the forces currently available was to incur unjustifiable risk. He was *the* military adviser to the India Office. Then Barrow moved his position, having been assured of the availability of the two new divisions at some unspecified date in the future. Barrow was an experienced soldier, operating at the highest level, but at no point did he give any indication that he had considered time and geography.

The MC turned its attention to the committee that had been set up to consider the future policy of British Forces in Mesopotamia. Sir Thomas Holderness, the Permanent Under Secretary of State in the India Office,[123] chaired this body. His colleagues were General Sir Edmund Barrow, Vice Admiral Sir Douglas Gamble, from the Admiralty, Sir Louis Mallet and Mr Lancelot Oliphant, both Foreign Office officials, Colonel Talbot and a Captain Paddon, from the War Office. The latter was probably the secretary.

34. General Sir George de Symons Barrow GCB KCMG.

The MC expressed disquiet over the composition of the committee and was singularly underwhelmed by its performance. Holderness admitted that the assurances received from Nixon were taken at face value. The kindest judgment on Holderness was that he was ingenuous. It is not necessary to labour the point but the MC Report said, acidly:

> *It was the promise of reinforcements that alone induced this Committee to advocate an advance on Baghdad but, as in the case of other authorities*

consulted, they apparently passed over the all important problem of how these reinforcements, after arrival at Basra, were to be conveyed as fighting units to the front, a distance of some 500 miles. We lay stress upon this serious omission ... the despatch of troops from France or Egypt could not affect any fighting around Baghdad after its capture, unless they were conveyed as an organised force to the scene of the action. The arrival of troops in Basra, without transport or their proper medical complement with their headquarters staff scattered and disorganised, was not a reinforcement in the sense defined by the Viceroy in his private telegram of 9 October in which he expressed himself thus, 'We may add that the reinforcing troops should reach Baghdad not later than a month after the capture of the city, and this is the period which we calculate must elapse before the Turks could concentrate in strength to attempt its re-capture.'[124]

Chamberlain looked to this committee for guidance and he was badly served, especially by General Barrow, the senior military figure who, by dint of his calling, would have had great influence on this strategic military issue. To Barrow must be accorded a significant degree of blame for the events that followed. In the face of all the rational and practical reasons not to advance on Baghdad, on 23 October 1915 the die was cast. The fate of thousands of men was decided when Austen Chamberlain, Secretary of State for India, sent the following telegram:

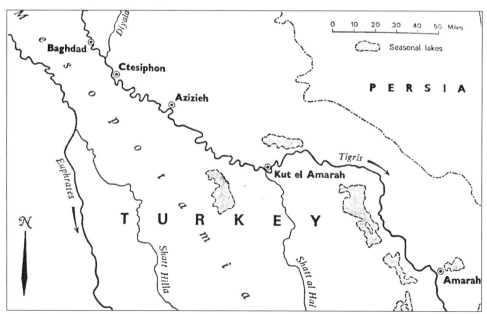

35. The line of advance of the 6th Division. *(The War at Sea)*

If Nixon is satisfied that the force available is sufficient for the operation he may march on Baghdad. Two divisions will be sent to him as soon as possible, but owing to relief and transport arrangements, reinforcements will take time to despatch. Probable date will be wired later.[125]

Had the two promised divisions suddenly arrived upriver in Kut, fully armed and equipped, with ample river transport, then Townshend could have taken Baghdad and probably Constantinople as well. However, this was another case of 'jam tomorrow' and the stark fact was that Townshend was not strong enough for the task he was to be set.

Chapter notes

108 Townshend, C.V.F., *My Campaign in Mesopotamia*, p.121.

109 Ibid, p.144.

110 Ibid, p.121.

111 MC Report, p.19.

112 Barker, A.J., *The Neglected War*, p.42.

113 It was Townshend's unquestionable duty to express a view. His shallow servility was unnecessary and not to the credit of a general in command of a major formation.

114 An 'appreciation of the situation' is the time-honoured manner in which a commander weighs up all the factors affecting him and his command. From this examination of the factors he draws conclusions and from those he develops his plan. If his information is inaccurate, then the appreciation will be flawed and so will any plan based upon it.

115 Davis, P.K., *Ends and Means*, p.115.

116 General Sir William Napier KCB (1782–1860), soldier and historian.

117 Twenty-seven years later, in 1942, Lieutenant General A.R. Godwin-Austen resigned command of XIII Corps, while on active service in North Africa and in the face of the enemy, as he disagreed with his Army Commander (Ritchie). Curiously, he suffered no penalty. He was later General Sir Alfred Godwin-Austen KCSI CB OBE MC (1889–1963). He went on to be Quarter Master General of the Indian Army (see Nash, N.S., *Strafer – Desert General*, Pen & Sword, Barnsley, 2013, p.164).

118 Townshend, C.V.F., *My Campaign in Mesopotamia*, p.128.

119 MC Report, p.22.

120 Ibid.

121 Viceroy Telegram No. 1148 to Seccretary of State, 9 October 1915, Hardinge papers, 99/No. 655.

122 MC Report, p.24.

123 Sir Thomas William Holderness, 1st Baronet GCB KCSI (1849–1924), was the first former member of the Indian Civil Service to be appointed to the post of Permanent Under-Secretary of State for India. He was vastly skilled in Indian domestic affairs but had no military experience – and it showed.

124 MC Report, p.25.

125 Ibid, p.24.

Chapter 8

Advance to Ctesiphon

'A good general not only sees the way to victory:
he also knows when victory is not possible.'
(Polybius, *Histories*, 125 BC)

While all the political manoeuvres were being conducted by telegram and in various committees, for six weeks after the taking of Kut, the 6th Indian Division rested in a concentration at Azizieh, some 90 miles further upriver. Here it erected suitable defences and Townshend requisitioned from Basra the myriad items of stores he required. Incredibly, the Staff in Basra, with the concurrence of Nixon, refused to supply among many items, for example, wire cutters and Very lights. The Staff deemed them to be unnecessary.

**36. Khalil Pasha, the aggressive leader of Turkish
forces in Mesopotamia in the autumn of 1915.**

The Division made do without the kit and applied itself to the absorption of its piecemeal reinforcements. The pre-war British battalions composed of regular soldiers had suffered serious loss and the corporate skill level of these battalions had been diluted by the absorption of less experienced replacements. The losses incurred by the Indian infantry had been no less severe but the quality of reinforcements caused Townshend concern. He recorded that, 'I have never seen such a wretched class of recruits in the whole of my Indian experience and the battalion commanders did not mince their words on the matter.' The quality was such that Townshend sent back to Basra an entire battalion's worth of unsatisfactory trans-border soldiers from the north-west of India.[126] This decision was on the basis of 'numerous desertions to the enemy'.

> On the night 23/24 October an incident occurred which led to the withdrawal from the 16th Infantry Brigade of the 20th Punjabis and to their replacement by the 66th Punjabis from the 12th Division at Amara. The Turks were making great efforts by propaganda to seduce Indian Mahomedan troops from their loyalty and at this particular period were making much capital out of the fact that the British were approaching the tomb of Suliman Pak, a servant of the Prophet, which was one of the Islamic Holy Places. The Turkish propaganda had, however, no great effect. Whatever their religious scruples may have been, the Indian Mahomedans as a whole proved thoroughly loyal, the few exceptions being generally Pathans of trans-frontier tribes; and they were not always swayed by purely religious factors. The 20th Punjabis had one and a half companies of trans-frontier Pathans; and, on the night in question, one of their Afridi sentries shot the other sentry and the non-commissioned officer of his piquet — both Sikhs — and, pursued by the fire of the remainder of the piquet, deserted to the enemy with another Afridi.[127]

It was customary, in Indian regiments, to enlist different races and to mix these races in all guards, piquets, etc., in order to minimise the dangers arising from racial or religious scruples such as that described above. In practical terms each race policed the others.

Charlie was an officer of the Indian Army but, unlike the overwhelming majority of British officers of that army, he did not admire his Indian soldiers and whenever possible depended upon their British counterparts. It was a curious attitude but then Townshend was a curious man. To be fair it must be noted that Delamain had told Townshend at the conclusion of the battle for Kut that he did not think his 'soldiers would storm trenches again if they were put to it'. This had the effect of endorsing Townshend's negativity.

As the Division waited for its orders, the GOC, comfortable aboard ship, got down to his letter writing. He was an assiduous correspondent and shared his views with a wide circle of civilian and military associates. The civilians tended to be theatricals and the military were senior and career enhancers.

It was on 22 October that, for the second time, Nixon was warned in a direct telegram from London that 30,000 Turkish troops, under the command of Khalil Pasha, were on their way to the theatre. Further intelligence revealed that the German Field Marshal von der Goltz[128] was also in transit and that he would assume command on his arrival. This German had a track record as a brutal and ruthless individual. He was going to be a formidable adversary.

37. Field Marshal von der Goltz.

Nixon, in a display of extraordinary insouciance, decided to ignore the intelligence reports and did not deviate from his crusade to Baghdad.

This was folly of the very highest order.

Nixon issued his orders on 26 October and Nunn observed that 'they had an excellent effect on our men who though suffering a good deal from sickness and worn with the long summer campaign, were confident of beating the Turks and of capturing Bagdad.'[129] The Mesopotamia Commission some months later, and with the advantage of hindsight, observed:

> *A spirit of intense optimism animated the headquarters and administrative staff. This is shown by their estimate of impending casualties, preparations being made for only 500 severely wounded. Two river steamers, the* Mosel *and the* Julnar*, were put on one side to be temporarily fitted up by Surgeon General Hathaway for the reception of wounded, the arrangements being that the more seriously wounded would be moved down to Kut in these vessels and the more lightly wounded located in Baghdad.*
>
> *No apprehension of an effective repulse or our inability to reach Baghdad seems to have been entertained by those directing the advance.*[130]

Townshend was 30 miles short of the Turkish defence line at Ctesiphon. A valuable asset peculiar to the British was its few last surviving aeroplanes, one flown by a courageous officer called Yeates Brown. Hitherto, he had carried out invaluable reconnaissance and his reports to Townshend were as gold dust. It was he who had alerted Townshend to the disposition and strength of the Turks at Kut and most recently at Ctesiphon. He volunteered to overfly the enemy position and cut their telephone lines to Baghdad. This he accomplished but he was shot down and captured. The loss of this one officer was as serious as the loss of a battalion.

Townshend penned one important letter, privately, to the Viceroy on 2 November. Townshend had a track record of bypassing the chain of command and this was just another example. He told Hardinge that the morale of his division was 'very low, and the men had their tails down. The Mohomedans are not pleased at approaching the sacred precincts of Suleiman Pak at Ctesiphon – the troops are not confident and have had enough. Now the British soldier and the sepoy look over their shoulders and are fearful of the distance to the sea. In consequence they go down with every imaginable disease.' He added that the British battalions 'could be relied upon but the Indians are now shaken and unreliable.' On the day he wrote those words, only fifty-four Indian but seventy-five British soldiers had reported sick.

This was all very negative and in writing in these terms to the Viceroy, one wonders if he was hoping that Hardinge would abort the plans to advance. Townshend's opinion of his troops was disputed. Others said that the Division had won a famous battle and the morale of the survivors was predictably high. The MC, in observing on his letter to Hardinge, remarked that, *'These are not the words of a general commanding a force in the field who has confidence in the capacity of his troops to achieve the task assigned to them.'*[131]

Townshend, not for the first time, had misled Hardinge when he spoke of his Indian soldiers' reluctance to go to Suleiman Pak. This was not the case; the sepoys were in ignorance of their objective, which was always referred to as Ctesiphon (known to the British soldiers as 'Pissedupon'). Religious matters were never an issue and Townshend's motives are unclear. What is clear is that he was disloyal to his Indian soldiers who, in earlier days, had been paid in salt. This was the origin of the expression to be 'worth one's salt' or *Nimak hilal.* It was the Indian soldier's creed and he would follow his British officer anywhere.[132]

It was on also on 2 November that the Prime Minister, Asquith, told the House of Commons, 'General Nixon's force is now within measurable distance of Baghdad. I do not think that in the whole war there has been a series of operations more carefully contrived, more brilliantly executed, and with a better chance of final success.'[133]

These remarks by the Prime Minister, delivered with the authority of his post, were well received but, time would show, ill-judged.

At El Kutunie, 7 miles above Azizieh, the Turks had established a defensive position, but on the approach of the leading British brigade, the Turks encamped there promptly fled. This augured well for the battle ahead. Townshend burnt the Turkish installations and destroyed all the equipment that was found. He was obliged to send a gunboat downstream to protect the journey upstream of *mahailas*, under sail, bearing his supplies, of which he needed 208 tons per day but received only 150 tons. The danger from the Arabs had increased as the line of communication lengthened, and any river journey was now dangerous – despite the arrival of several of the new 'Fly' class of river gunboat, of which HMS *Firefly* was the first. Townshend continued to bombard Nixon's supine headquarters with requests for his misemployed infantrymen – to no avail.

It was at this point that Townshend first started to display some irrational behaviour. With his immediate staff he was taking passage in the steamer *Mejidieh*. In this position there were creature comforts to enjoy and among these was a warm bed. Not so for Private John Boggis who, at night, curled up in his blanket outside Townshend's cabin door. Townshend bestowed much of his affection on his small dog called Spot, in recognition of his one engaging black eye. Spot was a Jack Russell, or closely related to that breed. One very cold night Spot curled up against Boggis, and man and dog shared such body heat as they could conjure up. In the morning, a furious Townshend thrashed the dog unmercifully.

'Why are you doing that, Sir?' enquired a bemused Boggis.

'He was sleeping with you,' growled Townshend as he continued to belabour the small creature. 'He's my dog and he's got to learn.'[134]

Townshend ordered his entire division to abandon and stack all its surplus equipment, mess silver, clothing and personal possessions not needed in battle. He intended to travel light, defeat the Turks and return for the mountain of kit later.

Meanwhile, Nixon was determined not to miss the triumphal entry into Baghdad, so he and his entire staff had embarked in a steamer and sailed upriver as if to a picnic. For Townshend, slow progress of the river transport was a constant frustration, as was the shortage of equipment. At one point he decided he wanted a boat bridge so that he could send out a foray on the far bank. He was engaged in conversation with the major who was dealing with the problem when Nixon strolled by. Nixon enquired of the major if the boats he had were satisfactory.

'No, Sir,' replied the officer.

'Why don't you use pontoons?' asked Nixon.

'Only eighteen are authorised, Sir.'

'Wire India for more,' Nixon ordered, turning to one of his staff officers. Then, addressing the major, he continued, 'How many do you want?'

A pontoon cost over £100 and the major wondered if he could ask for twenty. He was well aware of the parsimony of the Indian Government.

Nixon, exuding authority, said, '100?'

The major was amazed and did not answer at once.

'200?' interrogated Nixon.

'Fifty, Sir,' responded the major eventually.

Nixon instructed the staff officer to wire for the pontoons at once.[135]

It was an absurd moment of military theatre. As Braddon wrote, 'He might as well have wired for a million because there were none available in India.'

On 12 November, Hardinge penned a petulant letter to Chamberlain objecting to the Secretary of State's suggestion that Nixon should reconsider his next move. There were more than sufficient dark clouds on the military horizon, but Hardinge wrote defensively as follows:

Nixon will act as he thinks best. He is in command, and we have full confidence in him to perform his duties properly, and if he needed our interference in such matters, we would not think him fit to hold his post and would remove him … Nixon is a very fiery little man and nobody would resent it more than he.[136]

The tone of this indicates that Nixon's strong personality was a factor in the decision-making and that, despite Hardinge's use of the royal 'we', Nixon was on a very loose rein and probably difficult to control.

Townshend was as ready as he was likely to be when finally his long-awaited supply ships arrived on 18 November. With their welcome arrival, but from an identified source, came the unwelcome news that, 'a Turkish advance, five or six thousand strong, was closing on Zeur.' Zeur, a mere dot on the map and of no particular significance, was some 14 miles distant and Townshend responded vigorously. He formed his force into two columns and marched them, about 3 miles apart, towards the enemy, who promptly withdrew.

A bloodless victory? Well, perhaps.

But Townshend was now about 104 miles from the security of Kut and in close proximity to a well-prepared enemy. He bivouacked for the night and the following morning moved further upriver to Lajj, with its groves of tamarind and casuarina.[137] The Turks had ample time to prepare their positions and, as the British force looked to its front, on its right-hand side (the left bank, looking downstream) were two very strongly fortified lines, each anchored on the Tigris and over 5 miles long. There was a gap of about 3½ miles between the lines. On the other bank were similar, shorter fortifications but in front of those the ground was broken by old watercourses and abandoned canals. It was impossible going for either cavalry or horse gunners.

Behind the Turks and parallel to their position, the Diyala River flowed into the Tigris. It was a bar to a withdrawal, and Townshend took note of that. He hoped to trap retreating Turks on the banks of the Diyala when he drew up his plan. Nixon, who was a mere spectator to the preparations, realised fully to what extent his career and reputation rested on Townshend's shoulders. He asked him if he was confident of winning. Townshend provided the right measure of reassurance to his commander and said that he expected success.

In simple terms, Townshend's plan was a rerun of his tactics at Kut in that he would initiate a turning attack on the right bank (looking upstream) to outflank the Turkish left, at the same time holding in position Turkish troops on their right in order to prevent them moving once contact had been made.

There were several features on the battlefield that had to be accommodated. The first of these was the Great Arch of Ctesiphon,[138] which was between the Turkish front and second lines. This venerated structure had to be safeguarded and the hope was that the enemy would not fortify it. Another feature was 'High Wall', the remnants of an old structure. In desert conditions a 12-foot wall counts as high ground; a 50-foot wall, as in this case, affords commanding views and provides an invaluable firing point. The third feature was what Townshend called Vital Point, or VP. This consisted of two redoubts at the northernmost point of the first line. Taking the VP was the key to victory.

Chapter notes

126 Townshend, C.V.F., *My Campaign in Mesopotamia*, p.143.
127 Moberly, F.J., *The Campaign in Mesopotamia. 1914–1918*, Vol. 1, p.47.
128 Wilhelm Leopold Colmar Freiherr von der Goltz (1843–1916) was a Prussian field marshal and military writer. His extreme brutality in Belgium in 1914–15 was much admired by Adolf Hitler, for whom he was a role model.
129 Nunn, W., *Tigris Gunboats*, p.166.
130 MC Report, p.29.
131 Ibid.
132 Raynor, C.A., Lieutenant Colonel, in an interview with Braddon, 1968.
133 *Hansard*, 3 November 1915.
134 Boggis, Mr J., in an interview with Braddon, c. 1968.
135 Sandes, E.W.C., *In Kut and Captivity*, 1919.
136 Hardinge to Chamberlain, 12 November 1915, Chamberlain papers 62/1.
137 Spackman, Colonel W.S., *Never come back no more*, private papers.
138 Ctesiphon is located approximately at Al-Mada'in, 20 miles south-east of the modern city of Baghdad. Ctesiphon was once a great city; it dates back to AD 540 and covered an area of 18 square miles. The only visible remains today are the great arch (Taq-i Kisra) located in what is now the Iraqi town of Suleiman Pak.

Chapter 9

The Pyrrhic Victory at Ctesiphon

'The object is not the occupation of a geographical
position, but the destruction of the enemy force.'
(General Pyotr A. Rumyantsev, 1725–96)

The force opposing 6th Division was composed of 18,000 infantry, 400
cavalry, two regiments of camelry, an uncounted mob of Arabs, certainly
numbering several thousand, all supported by fifty-two guns and nineteen
machine guns. So much for Nixon's 'appreciation' that had identified an
enemy force of only 4,000 Turks with low morale. There was also the
prospect of further large Turkish reinforcements joining the battle in the near
future.

Townshend had an enhanced division; numerically he had 13,700
infantry, five batteries of guns (thirty-five) and eleven squadrons of cavalry.
In addition, the Royal Navy was present and its guns might come into play.
The naval force consisted of HMS *Firefly*, *Butterfly*, *Comet*, *Shaitan*,
Sumana, *Shushan* and *Massoudieh*. Captain Nunn was in command and for
a 'blue water' sailor, he was a long way from home.

* * *

As 6th Division prepared for action, in London an
MP, Sir Mark Sykes, was drafting a letter to *The
Daily Telegraph*.

Sykes had seen active service in South Africa
and commanded a militia regiment. He was affected
by what he saw when he visited the theatre of
operations and wrote:

**38. Colonel Sir Mark Sykes
Bt MP (1879–1919).**

There are paddle steamers which once plied with passengers, and now waddle along with a barge on either side, one perhaps containing a portable wireless station and the other bullocks [to draw] heavy guns; there are once-respectable tugs which stagger along under a weight of boiler plating, and are armed with guns of varying calibre; there is a launch which pants indignantly between batteries of 4.7in looking like a sardine between two cigarette boxes. There is a steamer with a Christmas tree growing amidships, in the branches of which its officers fondly imagine they are invisible to friend or foe … *and this fleet is the cavalry screen, advance guard, rear guard, flank guard, railway, General Headquarters, heavy artillery, line of communication, supply depot, police force, field ambulance, aerial hanger and base of supply of the Mesopotamia Expedition.* [Author's italics][139]

In his short letter, Sykes had encapsulated everything that had made Townshend and his soldiers so vulnerable as they prepared for battle. The letter prepared *Daily Telegraph* readers for stormy water ahead but it was far too late to effect any change.

* * *

The Mesopotamia Commission observed that, after the capture of Kut, *'there was a spirit of intense optimism, and over confidence as to what could be achieved overcame General Nixon and his Headquarters Staff.'*[140] Townshend, in his memoir, written five years later and with the benefit of hindsight, said:

I knew nothing about this 'intense optimism'. All I do know is that I was determined to carry through the operation if it could possibly be done, and it was my plain and simple duty to carry out the orders of my superior to the best of my ability, although his orders were against my better judgment. Personally, I had no doubts in my mind as to the extreme gravity of the results of this advance, an offensive undertaken with insufficient forces, and not only that, but an offensive undertaken in a secondary theatre of war, where our strategy should have been to have remained on the defensive with minimum forces sufficient for that purpose. All my study indicated disaster to me. However, the die was cast. And so when Sir John Nixon asked me on the eve of battle, 'Are you confident of winning, Townshend?' I replied, 'Yes, I shall win all right.' And I did.[141]

In military circles, the rule of thumb is that the attacker needs a numerical advantage of 3:1 or better if he is to succeed. Here the forces were about numerically equal; moreover, in this case the attack would be across a flat desert, in good light, into well-constructed redoubts, fifteen in total. The flank attack had to carry the day or 6th Division would be slaughtered.

Operations started on the night of 21/22 November with a night march from Lajj. Townshend had again divided his command into four columns and the first into action was Column 'C' (Brigadier General Hoghton), with the task of engaging the enemy in the area of the so-called 'Water Redoubt' and 'High Wall' in the middle of the Turkish first line. The object of the exercise was to pose sufficient threat to cause Nureddin to move troops to that redoubt.

The remainder of the force, Columns 'A' and 'B', marched through the night to develop Townshend's signature 'turning attack'. They were under the command of Brigadier Generals W.S. Delamain and W.G. Hamilton; the latter was newly appointed, having relieved Major General Fry in 18th Brigade.

The cavalry 'Flying Column', or Column 'D', was commanded by Major General Mellis. Townshend did not trust Brigadier General Roberts after the abject performance of the cavalry at the Battle of Kut and so had summarily reduced his responsibilities. Roberts was superseded and was required to serve under Mellis, which must have been difficult for both men. In Mellis, Townshend had a profane, robust, hard-charging, unsophisticated warrior and a man to be relied upon. An infantry battalion was added to the Flying Column, but quite how Mellis was to employ and deploy foot soldiers when the bulk of his force was mounted was not immediately obvious but became clear later on.

Hoghton's approach across the almost featureless desert did not draw the expected fire, much to the surprise of the participants. The enemy were clearly prepared to wait and engage at a shorter and more lethal range. The lack of response from the Turks was discommoding Hamilton, who was to launch his attack on the Turkish second line behind the Vital Point, but only when he heard that Hoghton was in contact with the enemy.

It was when Hoghton and Hamilton were fully engaged that Delamain was to sweep forward and take the VP. There was no contact and so Hamilton marked time, and eventually had to ask for permission to crack on with his part of the plan.

The Battle of Ctesiphon then unfolded, initially, much as Townshend planned. As the attacker, the initiative was his to exploit, and this he did. What neither he nor Nixon had anticipated was the stout and heroic defence put up by Nureddin's troops. The battle was noted for the ferocity of the hand-to-hand fighting and the brutal losses on both sides. These Turks were every bit as obdurate as their fellows who were winning at Gallipoli.

It will aid the reader if they consider two sketch maps of the battle from different sources. The first of these is taken from Townshend's book at page 156, produced in 1920. It shows the Diyala River, against which he expected to trap the remnants of Nureddin's force. It should be compared with the second map of much the same ground on page 102.

The VP was carried by troops of 30th Brigade under the command of 'the gallant Climo',[142] as the defenders streamed back to their second line. Delamain, seeing his objective already taken, presumed that the whole Turkish front line had collapsed and so he swept on to the second line. Unfortunately he left a substantial body of enemy behind him. These unforeseen changes left Hoghton to face a well-entrenched enemy. A frontal attack was so clearly suicidal that Hoghton opted to move his formation across the battlefield at 90°. This was an extreme manoeuvre, very hazardous, and Hoghton's column was punished as it moved across the Turkish front. Townshend watched horrified as his master plan started to unravel. A counter-attack swiftly followed the taking of any position and the dead started to pile up around the breast works. Gurkha and Punjabi dead were unhappily abundant.

Townshend rode across the shell-swept battlefield to discuss the situation with Delamain, now back at the VP. Townshend commented in his book (p.173) that,

> A mass of tangled wire and deep trenches compelled us to dismount … and in getting to Delamain with whom I wanted to speak … I had to traverse a length of trench. The dead lay so thick that we literally walked on the bodies. I found him behind a small sand hillock, for the spot was under fire from some Turks cut off from retreat and installed in a redoubt some 700 yards south of the VP.

Delamain briefed Townshend, who was really on top of his game as he responded quickly and calmly. His demeanour under fire was noted by many of his officers and soldiers and there is no doubting the physical courage of 'Charlie'. He seemed inured to the eleven dead Gurkhas at his feet and to the products of their kukris – each with his head split open or severed. He sent a message to Hoghton to bring up his left shoulder and move at once on the VP because he saw 'that the battle was by no means finished'. Battered Hoghton strove to comply.

Unfortunately, the guns of the Royal Navy could not be brought to bear;

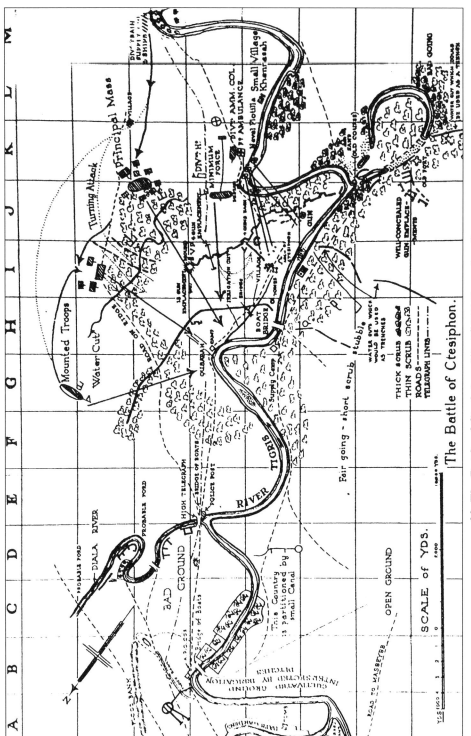

39. The Battle of Ctesiphon (1). (*C.V.F. Townshend*)

they were held up at Bustan by the menace of heavy Turkish artillery at the bottom of the river loop on the right-hand bank.

Townshend moved his headquarter to the VP and it was not a bonus when Nixon and his acolytes came to join him, just in time to hear that strenuous opposition had bogged down Hamilton's column. He had taken the second line but was facing tenacious counter-attacks. Mellis was unable to come to the rescue as his cavalry formation was also having difficulties. The cavalry were now in a dismounted role and being held up by a strongly held trench line. At this point, 'Mellis sent in 76th Punjabis [who were in support of his cavalry] with the bayonet and they carried the position in fine style.'[143]

Townshend called out, 'Boggis.'

'Sir,' responded his batman, who was never far away.

'A change of clothing.'

'*Now*, Sir?'

'I always change at this time.'

John Boggis was committed to making a hazardous journey of about a mile, on foot, across a very active battlefield to the river to collect clean clothes for his general. He had then to retrace his steps. Boggis stepped out of the trench and he was lost to view. There was a lengthy pause, but Boggis returned safely bearing the fresh linen.

'Your clothes, Sir.'

'Thank you, Boggis.'

Townshend stripped and stood naked, surrounded by the dead and the dying and in the sight of his staff officers. Deliberately, he donned a silk vest, silk underpants, a khaki shirt, his riding breeches, boots and his solar topee. A junior officer passed to him a piece of plum cake, of which he was very fond. The death and destruction all about him continued unabated.[144]

Lieutenant Colonel C.A. Rayner, who had witnessed this performance, endorsed John Boggis's account of this extraordinary event when both were, later, interviewed by Braddon. Quite what was in Townshend's mind is unknown. It was either a demonstration of incredible *sang-froid* or exhibitionism. What it certainly showed was his complete disregard for the life of the young soldier who ministered to his needs, and that perhaps overshadows the theatre of the change of clothes.

The day wore on and the sun blazed down on men lying in pools of their own and their comrades' blood. The tenor of the hand-to-hand fighting was ghastly, and in the confusion units became mixed and command and control weakened. There was fighting all along the front and a series of small, almost self-contained actions. The officer casualties in the Indian battalions were particularly heavy and particularly critical. Cohesion started to evaporate and at this point the Turkish reinforcements, which had been so airily dismissed by Nixon, made their appearance on the field.

At 1100 hrs, Hamilton's Norfolks, 110th Light Infantry, 7th Rajputs and 120th Infantry effected a secure lodgement in the second line. He could go no further but had to face an enemy refreshed and revitalised by the injection of fresh troops.

These reinforcements saved the day for Nureddin.

Officerless Indian troops started to stream back from the second Turkish line to the VP and a withdrawal was in process, although no orders to that effect had been issued. Townshend could see that 'panic' was knocking on the door and wanted to join his friend 'despair'. Townshend rounded up every officer he could get hold of, and that included Nixon's Chief of Staff, Kemble. This ad hoc group,

40. Lance Corporal John Boggis, R. Norfolk Regt, Townshend's batman.

of mainly staff officers, revolvers drawn, stemmed the rearward movement with a mixture of good humour, cajolery and, in some cases, the threat of death. The informal retreat was stopped. Common sense was restored and

41. The Great Arch at Ctesiphon. *(E.O. Mousley)*

soldiers who had seen what Arabs did to isolated individuals realised that it was probably safer to be on the battlefield in the company of one's comrades than to be alone, out in the desert. Death at the hands of Arab women was not to be contemplated.

The next crisis was shortage of ammunition; the normal process of resupply by companies had broken down as Norfolks, Gurkhas, West Kents and Punjabis fought alongside each other. The colour sergeants were willing, but unable, to get ammunition forward to anything they could identify as their company. Volunteers ran back over the ground, so expensively bought in blood and pain earlier in the day, to the mule lines where terrified animals carried on their backs panniers of SMLE .303in ammunition. The ammunition boxes were firmly sealed, watertight, and opening them with a bayonet slowed down the distribution of the copper-jacketed rounds, all neatly packed in clips of five and cotton bandoliers of a hundred. 'Who'll say no to a bunch of fives?' was one of the cries reported by Colonel W.S. Spackman, emerging from the melee.

The rate of fire being brought down on Turkish trenches increased as the ammunition was put to its designed purpose as units were formed from scratch; sound training paid off and order was restored. The conflict ebbed and flowed and these Turkish troops were a different proposition to the enemy encountered at Amara, Kurnah and Kut. They were tenacious, courageous and well led. It must have occurred to Townshend that he may have bitten off rather more than he could chew. Nevertheless, he maintained control as he moved bodies of his troops to best advantage and set artillery tasks. On several occasions as the fighting rolled around him, he drew his revolver.

Operations did not cease as night fell on 22/23 November and the Turks made a series of forays that jangled the nerves, prevented sleep but did not achieve any gains. The following day, the fighting resumed, with troops of both sides exhausted. It was a long, savage day with neither side yielding ground but taking casualties – Townshend was confident that he had had the better of the exchanges and fully expected Nureddin to withdraw. It was a forlorn hope and the killing continued.

The medical teams were faced with a massive task. There were British/Indian wounded spread out over a wide area and all of them had yet to be carried, by one means or another, to the river as the first stage in their journey.

> According to the Turkish account the general situation and the condition of
> their force at nightfall — exhausted and reduced by casualties heavier than

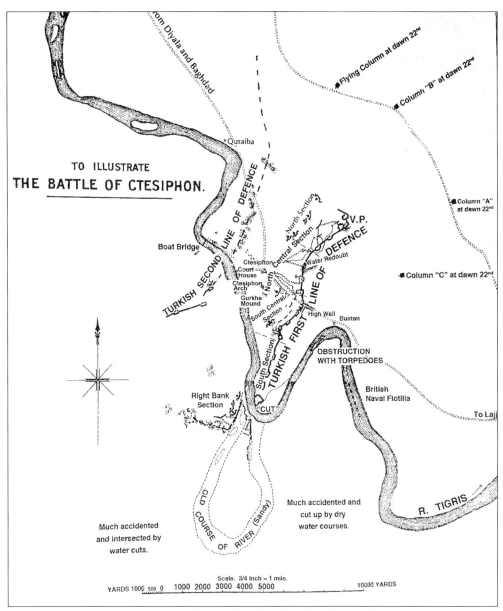

42. The Battle of Ctesiphon (2). *(Map by The Historical section of the Committee for Imperial Defence. Ordnance Survey 1924)*

those of the British — occasioned Turkish headquarters grave anxiety. The whole of their first line of defence, laboriously constructed during the previous months, had been lost; and the only fresh troops available were the remaining two battalions of the 51st Division, which were then being hurried forward from the Diyala River.[145]

102

The sun set on the evening of 23 November. Men slept fitfully and dreamt of home. At about 0200 hrs on 24 November, the Turkish firing died away. The battlefield was silent, save the cries of the wounded British, Indian and Turk. When dawn broke on 24 November and the British 'stood to', it was clear that the Turks had stolen away in the night in a very professional manner and quite undetected. The Turks had gone and the field was Townshend's.

He had won a victory, albeit a pyrrhic victory, because his division had been destroyed. He had incurred losses of 4,511 and his brigades were down to battalion strength. Briefly, Hoghton's brigade was only 700 strong, Delamain's about 1,000, and Hamilton's 900, at best. Wilfred Nunn was specific on the matter of officer casualties. He recorded them as being '130 British officers (out of 317), 111 Indian officers (out of 255). He estimated rank and file casualties at 4,200. Turkish losses were 9,500 including deserters.'[146]

On the 24th, the first ship to leave was HMS *Butterfly,* which carried away General Sir John Nixon and his staff! But not until Nixon, quite correctly shocked by what he had seen, had sent a telegram to General Hathaway saying, 'I see no possible excuse for what I am forced to look on as the most indifferent work done in the collection of the wounded.'[147]

Trenches that on the previous day were fought over with great ferocity were now 'full and spewing over with dead. Piles of Turkish corpses, dyed yellow with lyddite, lay everywhere.'[148] In the irrigation ditches the water ran red. Wounded men drowned in this ghastly desert. The sand was littered with wounded who had frozen overnight, but now groaned with thirst as the sun climbed high in the sky.

Lines of the hated unsprung carts jolted load after load of bleeding men to the riverbank at Lajj, where the steamers were moored. The 10- to 14-mile journey to Lajj would take three or four hours of aggravated pain even before the misery of a ten to fourteen-day voyage in a river steamer or an attached, facility-free barge could commence. This was all much the same as the evacuation of the wounded from Kut – the same problems but of a much greater magnitude.

Briefly, Townshend weighed up the options open to him and then he sent a message to his formations, saying that he would resume operations on the morrow, which must have been read with utter incredulity. His brigadiers were aghast – there was only one realistic option open to the 6th Division, and at this point Townshend had not grasped it. The Turks were consolidating beyond the Diyala and being massively reinforced. The brigade commanders made their views known and Townshend was obliged to think again.

43. The men in this photograph are smiling, but at other times and places, wounded men suffered badly as they were carried from the battlefield in the unloved army transport cart, pictured above. *(Dr G. Bulger; original photo by Harry Weaver)*

He decided that the remnants of his division would withdraw during the night of 24/25 November and reform at Azizieh. This was an interesting decision because, on the way upriver, Townshend had fortified Azizieh to a degree that had brought a rebuke from Nixon for his profligate use of defence stores, and especially barbed wire. Later, and before the 6th Division moved further upriver to its engagement at Ctesiphon, Azizieh was de-fortified and its use as a defensive position was greatly reduced. This was now Townshend's preferred site at which to give battle to his pursuers.

* * *

Albert Maynard was a soldier on HMS *Butterfly,* and many years later, he alleged that their ship was attacked during its passage to Basra and taken by a band of Arabs. Nixon, the GOC-in-C, was in the ignominious position of being obliged to bargain with his assailants. He bought the freedom of the ship, crew and passengers and all were sworn to secrecy, on pain of death.

This story appeared on the Internet and it was mentioned in *Chitrál Charlie*, published in 2010. The story has not been corroborated and reference to it cannot now be found. Maynard is long since dead but his story is just credible as a single ship was very vulnerable to attack. However, see page 114.

* * *

That was an intriguing historical cul-de-sac; and so to return to Ctesiphon. Townshend demonstrated what a skilled soldier he was as he managed the silent and unopposed withdrawal from Ctesiphon. The reality is that this was not a tactical withdrawal but a full-blown retreat.

The wounded had somehow been squeezed on to river craft of some sort or another and were now making their ponderous and very slow passage back downriver. Colonel Hehir was now filling the appointment of Principal Medical Officer of the 6th Division. However, it was beyond even his powers of invention and innovation to provide efficient and caring treatment for his wounded. Later, those who had not faced his medical dilemmas did not appreciate the Colonel's 'make and mend' solutions forced on him on the battlefield. Major R. Markham Carter FRCS IMS, the doctor in charge of the hospital ship *Varela*, was at Basra waiting to receive those wounded, and in a graphic description of the day, he recorded:

> *I was standing on the bridge in the evening when* Mejidieh *arrived ... as the ship with two barges came up to us I saw that she was absolutely packed and the barges were too, with men ... there was no protection from the rain. The barges were slipped and the* Mejidieh *was brought alongside ... When she was about three or four hundred yards off it looked as if she was festooned with ropes. The stench when she was close was quite definite, and I found that what I mistook for ropes were dried stalactites of human faeces. The patients were so crowded and huddled together on this ship that they could not perform the offices of nature clear of the ship's edge and the whole of the ship's side was covered. This is then what I saw. A certain number of men were standing and kneeling on the immediate perimeter of the ship. Then we found a mass of men huddled up anyhow, some with blankets and some without. With regards to the first man I examined ... he was covered in dysentery, his thigh was fractured, perforated in five or six places. He had been apparently writhing about the deck of the ship. Many cases were almost as bad. There were cases of terribly bad bedsores. In my report I described mercilessly to the Government of India how I found men with their limbs splinted with wood strips from Johnny Walker whisky boxes, bhoosa (compressed hay) wire and that sort of thing.*[149]

105

44. The river steamer *Medjidieh*. (Photo by Major General H.H. Rich *CB)*

Markham Carter complained about the facilities available to him and he was told that he had been given all there was 'as laid down in regulations'. More significantly, two of the most senior officers in the theatre, Major Generals Cowper[150] and Hathaway, sent for him. He was advised in the strongest terms that if he did not 'shut up' and keep quiet he would lose his command because he was 'an interfering faddist'.[151] The MC would revisit this event some months later.

Chapter notes

139 The *Daily Telegraph*, 24 November 1915.
140 MC Report, p.18.
141 Townshend, C.V.F., *My Campaign in Mesopotamia*, p.161.
142 Acting Brigadier General S.H. Climo had assumed command of 17th Brigade when Dobbie was evacuated, injured, just before the Battle of Kurnah. He was an officer of 24th Punjabis and promoted acting Brigadier General. Now he commanded 30th Brigade. See Townshend, C.V.F., p.173.
143 Ibid, p.175.
144 Braddon, R., *The Siege*, p.95.
145 Moberly, F.J., *The Campaign in Mesopotamia 1914–1918*, Vols. 1–4, p.90.
146 Nunn, W., *Tigris Gunboats*, p.175.
147 MC Report, p.76.
148 Thompson, Colonel H.G. DSO, interviewed by Braddon, 1968.
149 MC Report, p.76.
150 Major General Maitland Cowper CB CIE (1860–1932).
151 Barker, A.J., *The Neglected War*, p.107.

Chapter 10

The Retreat to Kut

'To know when to retreat and to dare to do it.'

(The Duke of Wellington, when asked for his opinion on the best test
of greatness in a general, William Fraser, *Words on Wellington*, 1889)

The Iron Duke would, no doubt, have endorsed Townshend's decision to
leave the field at Ctesiphon to the Turks. It was never about winning control
of a worthless expanse of desert but about destroying Nureddin's force in
order to open the way to the ultimate goal – Baghdad. Townshend had taken
that patch of worthless desert but had failed in his aim or, to be more
accurate, the aim of his superior, the ever ambitious Nixon. In addition, the
aspiration of Hardinge to be 'Pasha of Baghdad' was going to have to be
put firmly on 'hold'.

In textbook fashion, the 6th Division withdrew from its captured
positions, at 2030 hrs on the night of 24/25 November 1915, and it turned
its face southward. There was no noise, no lights. The withdrawal was
accomplished with a clean break and, in the cold night air, some of the men
strode, while others limped or shuffled across the unforgiving desert. The
column of marching men could not stray too far from the river, which was,
as ever, its water source. Nunn's remaining ships kept pace with the column
as many anxious glances over the shoulder were made. The realisation had
dawned that the initiative had slipped from British hands and that, now, the
6th Division was no longer the aggressor.

It was the quarry, the fox – and the hounds were in full cry.

Townshend, having changed his mind, wired to Nixon that he intended
to stay at Lajj, 'until I have eaten up my supplies.' He added that he would
then move onto Azizieh and wait for the arrival of his second division, which
he assumed would be sent on to him. From here he would launch another
strike on Baghdad. His wire also included some patronising remarks that
probably irked Nixon – but that was no doubt the aim. He did not explain
what he thought Nureddin's masses would do while his division masticated.
Nor did he explain how he intended to confront an estimated enemy at four-

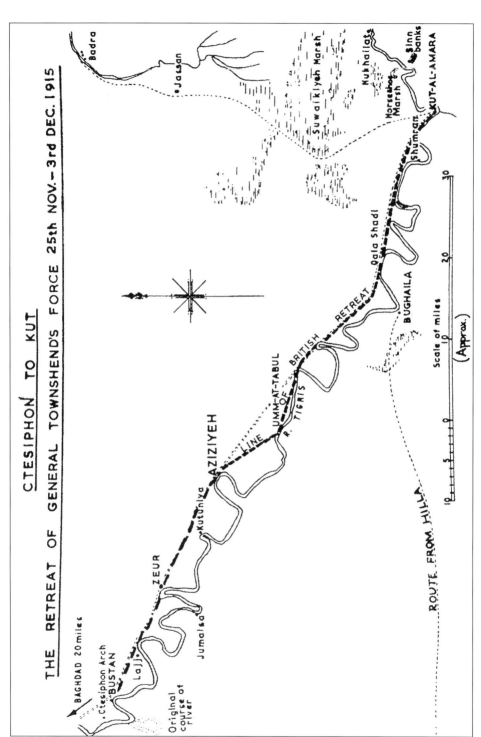

45. The route of Townshend's retreat to Kut. *(A.J. Barker)*

division strength of, say, 48,000 men in an unsuitable place like Lajj, or for that matter, Azizieh, with the badly battered remnant of 6th Division. All of that made this business of 'eating up supplies' seem surreal.

Nixon did not support Townshend's decision to retire and said so in a wire that read:

> I do not like your proposed retirement on Lajj for military reasons. ... You should, of course, prepare a fortified position at Lajj on which to retire in case of necessity and to cover your advanced base but for military reasons I do not consider retirement desirable at present.[152]

Nixon did not specify the 'military reasons' but Townshend rode the rebuke and, anyway, it was too late because 6th Division was already en route for Lajj.

The map on page 108 illustrates the sinuous nature of the Upper Tigris and explains, in part, why it took so long for the wounded to reach relative civilisation in Basra. The 6th Division's contested journey was to be an epic in itself. Townshend rode with the rearguard; his head on his chest. Colonel Thompson observed that, 'those who watched him were reminded irresistibly of Napoleon on his retreat from Moscow.'[153]

That first staging post at Lajj was about 10 miles south of the blood-soaked field at Ctesiphon. Lajj was neither 'fish nor fowl'. It was a village of no strategic importance, just a dot on the map. It was not far enough from Ctesiphon to provide significant distance between the two adversaries, it provided no obviously defendable position, nor did it reduce the line of communication by any significant amount.

It was an odd decision.

* * *

Braddon argued that, 'From the age of twenty-three to fifty-four, Townshend's diaries, cables and letters had revealed a man of ruthless consistency. But, from the moment his convalescence had begun in India, consistency had vanished.'[154]

This latest decision to 'eat up supplies' was irrational, as had been the beating of the dog and the need for fresh clothes. Another indicator was his position on an advance to Ctesiphon. This had varied from outright opposition to complete acquiescence, and his initial decision to resume operations on 25 November then rescinded. In total, all these incidents point to Townshend's behaviour being less than entirely normal. But, in late

November 1915, thousands of troops had complete faith in their 'Charlie'.

Townshend retained the affection of his men until the end of his life; he worked at being a 'soldier's officer'. This is a status all officers aspire to, and the usual device to achieve the aim is approachability. The general who chats to his soldiers, makes them laugh and is seen to care for them, even superficially, will achieve the accolade of 'soldier's officer'. It is fallacious to say that soldiers 'love' their general. It is more accurate to say that they 'admire and respect' him. This was the case with Townshend, but his officers were less convinced. They were in much closer proximity and could see the man, warts and all.

Braddon canvassed the views of Townshend's officers, and their opinions varied. 'A bit frenchified,' said one. 'A bit of a ladies' man,' opined another. 'A thruster, you know, the sort of chap that will ride too far ahead and destroy the scent for the hounds and drive the Master mad.' These are less than complimentary: 'A man who would rather go to the theatre than a shooting party' is almost damning, given the social mores of his contemporaries. Finally, 'The only real general in the Indian Army; but not exactly a gentleman.'

That last judgment would have cut Townshend to the very quick as he entertained strong aspirations not only to gentility but also of nobility. His ambition to be Lord Townshend was unabated, although the marriage of the 6th Marquess in 1905 had been a blow. But the union was childless and Charlie was still the heir and busting to don ermine – as 7th Marquess.

* * *

Townshend's stay at Lajj was very short-lived because aerial reconnaissance revealed that Nureddin's advance guard of 12,000 infantry and 400 cavalry were on their way from Ctesiphon and within 3½ miles. Further massive reinforcement was on its way. Chitrál Charlie urged his division to its feet and the retreat south was continued.

Townshend's force was accompanied by a miscellaneous but mostly unwieldy collection of barges, lighters and other river craft. The water was shallow and there were sand banks aplenty. The continuous need to refloat components of this flotilla took time and if one ship blocked the main stream then all behind had to heave to. It was a frustrating and tiring business. It was particularly fraught for the mariners, with Nureddin at their heels and aggressive, armed Arabs lining the riverbank. These Arabs had now thrown in their lot with the Turks and, like wolves, they stalked Nunn and his ships.

The passage downriver was difficult and just above Azizieh, *Comet* and

Shaitan had run aground. Grounding was part and parcel of navigation on this river and usually it was possible to back off a sand bank. In this case *Comet* did just that, but *Shaitan* was stuck fast and under speculative sniper fire from Arabs on the banks. *Comet*, *Firefly* and *Shushan* all put lines aboard *Shaitan*. However, she would not budge and eventually sprang a leak. The hull had been subjected to strains for which the ship was not built and a seam had opened. *Shaitan* sank in shallow water. She was unloaded, her guns and ammunition being a priority in the limited time available. *Comet*, *Shushan* and *Firefly* engaged the Arabs to cover this operation but the imminent arrival of the Turkish advance guard caused Nunn to abandon the ship.

46. HMS *Firefly*. (W. Nunn)

It was not possible to 'live off the land' as armies had done countless times in the past because in Mesopotamia there was nothing, but nothing, to live off. Nunn's ships did not just carry ammunition and food; they also transported fodder for horses and mules, firewood and a host of other prosaic items, all of which took up valuable cargo space, but without which life was bordering impossible.

The marching troops were often out of touch with the ships and it was only when their shorter route touched the apex of one of the innumerable bends that contact was re-established. The map on page 108 illustrates that point. The course of the river gave the Arabs ample opportunity to snipe the flotilla, and Nunn asked for cavalry support. The recently arrived 14th Hussars did what they did best and swept along the riverbank 'accounting for about 150'[155] of their adversaries.

Nixon wired to say that Townshend's plans to stand at Azizieh were approved and said comfortingly that about a third of the new reinforcement division would arrive there by 15 December. This was yet another hollow promise of 'jam tomorrow', and it did not impress Townshend. He now, belatedly, appreciated that the 6th Division was hopelessly outnumbered and that survival was his new aim.

A safe haven was needed, but where? Kut was 90 miles south, but Amara would be preferred. The latter was 130 miles away, as a mosquito flies, but 250 miles by way of the dawdling Tigris. The option to march in a straight line to Amara was impractical as the Tigris was the Division's lifeline – tenuous as it was. It was Hobson's choice, but the General resolved to press on and consolidate at Kut.

Previously, Azizieh (22 miles from Ctesiphon) had been strongly fortified but all the weapon pits had been filled in, the wire cut and dispersed, and the redoubts destroyed. The discarded heavy baggage of 6th Division was stacked ready for collection by a victorious army. When Azizieh was reached, on 27 November, the Division rested and hunted through the mountains of kitbags for prized possessions in a haphazard and ill-disciplined manner. The soldiers could only take what they could carry and all manner of treasures were left to the Arabs, who had been in constant attendance as they trailed the rearguard. There was going to be no use for ceremonial uniforms or mess silver from here on, and so these were regretfully abandoned.

Nunn asked Townshend if he could send on ahead, to Kut, any craft that could be spared. It was agreed that the naval 4.7-inch guns and the army 5-inch guns in barges, together with *Massoudieh* and *Shushan*, should leave for Kut in the south at once.

It had been a modest bonus when half a battalion of the Royal West Kents arrived with the 14th Hussars. These new members of the 6th Division were more than somewhat discommoded to be greeted with derision and then to discover that, having reached Azizieh, they would now have to retrace their steps. Mr Sherlock told Braddon that, when asked who they were, one of the newly joined soldiers replied, 'Half of the West Kents.' This drew the response, 'That's no bloody good; we need half the British Army.'

Other reinforcements were making their way north; among them were

47. The stern-wheeler HMS *Shushan*, photographed in the earlier Nasiriya operations and during which Nunn flew his pennant. *(Nunn)*

the Anglo Indian gunners from Amara. Their journey had halted at Kut because of the unavailability of river craft, most of which were making their slow, putrid passage south.

It was on 30 November that Azizieh was abandoned by 6th Division. Burdened with all that it could carry, its men had packed into their equipment food, souvenirs, personal possessions and also those of men long since dead. As the column struck out into the featureless desert, it left behind rising black smoke that besmirched a faultless blue sky. Everything flammable that could not be carried had been put to the torch. The smoke sent a clear message to Nureddin, about 6 miles behind, that the British were not preparing to give battle and the initiative was his to exploit.

It was winter in Mesopotamia, but as the sun climbed in the sky so the soldiers started to wilt and progressively they jettisoned their booty so rapaciously gathered only the day before. Four miles into their long day, Townshend called a halt to allow stragglers to catch up. To fall out and be left behind was to suffer a merciless and excruciating death at Arab hands.

Some did not catch up, gave up the struggle and became forever 'missing'.

Every soldier is dependent upon his comrades and Arthur Kingsmill wrote of one incident:

> He was lying on the ground, and when I told him to get up he said he was finished. I took his rifle, grabbed him by the collar, pulled him to his feet and kicked him. 'Now come on,' I said. He hung on to me and, as luck would have it, we caught up. 'Any more tricks and you get your throat cut,' I said, giving him half a biscuit and a piece of bully.

That unnamed soldier's life was saved by Kingsmill's unsympathetic treatment and he lived to fight another day. This was not an isolated incident and the bleak terrain, heat and thirst took their toll of men who had given their all at Ctesiphon and who had little left in reserve.

At about noon, the column, having advanced only about 8 miles, reached Umm-al-Tubal and was now much closer to the river, where the shadowing ships could be seen gliding slowly through the muddy water and providing, albeit briefly, an element of big gun protection. It was at this point that Nunn and Townshend had a misunderstanding that could have been very serious.

Townshend apparently thought that 10 'desert' miles as the insect flies was the limit of the ships' daily progress as they ploughed their way down the sinuous Tigris. Nunn, on the other hand, thought that he should halt because the troops were exhausted. Both men would have pressed on, but they did not discuss the matter and each deferred to what he thought to be the other's wishes. An unnecessary halt was called.

It was at this point that a message from Nixon arrived, telling that *Butterfly* was under a determined attack near Sheikh Saad. Although there was no mention of the ship being surrendered to Arabs, is this evidence in support of Albert Maynard's story? (See page 104.) However, after this incident Nixon demonstrated interesting and uncharacteristic concern about the security of his sole line of communication. This was concern that had come a little late in the piece as it had been needed some months earlier. Nixon asked the GOC 6th Division to help secure the river, and in turn Townshend detailed Mellis (30th Brigade) to move ahead of the column and eradicate any threat. It was agreed to lengthen the next day's march as Nunn wanted to make best use of daylight and his flotilla had a much longer journey than his khaki-clad comrades.

At Umm-al-Tubal, the British camp was roughly square, with the Tigris forming the southern boundary. Nunn positioned *Firefly* at the south-west corner. *Comet* was moored in the centre of that same boundary. It was a long night; the Turks fired star shells but made no assaults on the British line. Later analysis of events showed that the Turks had decided that the precipitate exit of 30th Brigade, to aid Nixon, with accompanying clouds of dust, was the 6th Division decamping. Drawing this fallacious conclusion, Nureddin halted for the night and gave orders to his 44th Regiment to occupy the abandoned British camp.

The 44th Regiment got lost in the dark and did not stumble over the encamped 6th Division.

The events that followed were extraordinary. Townshend decided that he needed Mellis to return and called for volunteers to ride to find 30th Brigade with the message. Captain C. Trench and Lieutenant W.J. Coventry volunteered, and they were to be accompanied by six cavalrymen. They knew that the desert was alive with hostile Arabs but were prepared to take their chances. Typically, Charlie gave an assurance that he would recommend them both for the VC;[156] he made no such offer to the six soldiers.

Nunn was told to send a similar message downriver in one of the launches. Lieutenant Wood RNR stepped forward and set off, but inevitably, his vessel was attacked and two of his crew were wounded. Wood extricated his launch from the engagement and returned to Umm-al-Tubal, his message undelivered. Nevertheless, he was decorated with the Distinguished Service Cross (DSC) for his trouble.

The Division posted sentries and the great majority climbed gratefully under their blankets. Townshend did too, but could not sleep and, when he was awake, so was everyone else.

He called out: 'Boggis.'

'Sir.'

'Can you hear wheels?'

'No, Sir.'

'Well, I can. Go and get Colonel Evans and we'll see if he can hear anything.'

Boggis crawled from beneath his blanket and set off to find the irascible, profane Colonel U.W. Evans, the formidable General Staff Officer Grade 1 (GSO1). Evans was the senior of Townshend's staff. He was a red-faced man with a bristling moustache and he did not suffer fools in any circumstances. He was not best pleased to be woken. Nevertheless, he hastened to his general's side.

'Evans,' enquired the GOC, 'can you hear wheels?'

'No, Sir.'

'I can. There are Turks on the move. Why have the sentries not reported it? See to it.'

Evans returned to his own tent, and an officer called E.J. Mant, one of those who shared the tent, recalled being woken by an irritable Evans who ordered Mant to 'listen and tell me what you hear'. By now any number of sleepers had woken and all were turned to listening. There were sounds, certainly the wind in the guy ropes, and the musical jingle of harnesses in the horse lines.

One officer ventured bravely, 'I think it's only the mules, Sir.'

'I know that's only the mules you pissbegotten bugger; but what else can you hear?'

'Nothing, Sir.'

'Well the General can!'[157]

The entire division 'stood to', donned its equipment and manned the shallow trenches that had been dug the previous afternoon. Tired men peered into the stygian darkness of the desert night. Just before dawn, the Division started to make preparation to move further in its odyssey to Kut. The move from Umm-at-Tabul started at 0800 hrs and thirty minutes later, the column was underway. It was a foggy morning and visibility was very restricted.

Lieutenant Edward Mousley, a gunner officer, remembered that at about 0900 hrs the fog cleared and 'before us some 1,800 to 2,000 yards off on the higher ground we saw a host of tents.'[158] There were lights among the tents and the immediate opinion was that it was the following Arabs. As the light strengthened, it became clear that it was not Arabs in those distant tents.

It was the Turkish Army.

Mousley observed that, 'The guns of the [10th] Field Brigade were limbering up ready to move but within two minutes they were down again, in action, and the first shell sang out the delight of the gunner at the prospect of so gorgeous a target.'[159]

The British, although surprised, were the first to react and within minutes the gunners were bringing down effective fire on the large number of advancing Turks and their encampment to their rear. The effect on the Turks was cataclysmic and very heavy casualties were sustained under the first few salvos fired by the artillery. Townshend commented later that, 'I have never seen artillery shoot with the precision with which 10th Brigade, Royal Field Artillery opened a rapid fire. This was most deadly. One saw Turkish lines of men dissolve in a regular cloud of our shells. What a splendid gun is our 18-pounder field gun.'[160] It was estimated, by Townshend, that the Turks were 12,000 strong, but by what means he made this estimate is unclear. Nevertheless, it was evident that there were hundreds of Turkish soldiers milling about among the multiple tents pitched on the crest of the distant dunes.

The Turkish response was brave but ill-judged. Thousands advanced across the flat desert into the fire of very professional gunnery and carnage was the only possible result. Gun teams limbered up and moved forward to shorten the range and give line of sight to fresh targets.

Comet and *Firefly* brought their guns to bear and added to the weight of shell falling on the Turkish XIIIth Corps. However, both ships were targets of Turkish artillery and *Firefly* was crippled when a shell hit her boiler. *Firefly* was towed away with great difficulty by *Comet*, a ship singularly ill-equipped for the purpose. *Comet* soon ran aground as her burden made her unwieldy, and she could not be freed. Nunn signalled to the little armed tug *Sumana* to drop the two barges she was towing and move upstream to assist with the recovery of *Comet*. *Firefly* meanwhile was drifting downstream 'not under command'. *Sumana* got a line onto *Comet* but could not free her. Turkish artillery was now operating at quite short range and becoming more and more effective. *Comet* was hit and set on fire. Captain Nunn decided that both *Comet* and *Firefly* should be abandoned. He ordered *Sumana* alongside and *Comet's* crew threw overboard the breechblocks of the guns and disabled the engines. Two men, Lieutenant Harden[161] and Seaman Ernest Gray RNR, pulled over to *Firefly* in a small boat and brought her officers and men to safety.[162]

On the river, the Turks had won the battle.

Two ships and several barges had been lost, together with invaluable stores. More worryingly, one of the barges dropped by *Sumana* was carrying wounded and those men had to be left to their fate. The only hope was that the Turks got to them before the Arabs.

The Turkish 44th Regiment that had been 'lost' now reappeared and joined the fight. Townshend ordered Delamain (16th Brigade) and Hamilton (18th Brigade), without formal orders, to attack, head on. The cavalry, with 'S' Battery in support, took up a position on the enemy flank and the Turks were receiving fire from two directions. This was an 'encounter' battle and quite unlike the more deliberate, formalised contests of the previous twelve months. There was no time to plan 'turning manoeuvres' and no room for subterfuge. This was a conflict that was 'played off the cuff'.

In the spontaneity stakes, the British were winning. Excellent gunnery and disciplined musketry did the trick. A little later in the morning, General Mellis's brigade, which had been sent for during the night, arrived on the scene of action, appearing from the south-eastern quarter. The Brigade's arrival was critical and effectively threw back the Turkish attack.

There had been countless acts of bravery and, as one example, Lieutenant Colonel J. McConville reported, 'a Norfolk with both legs broken, ignored his injuries. Spreading his ammunition carefully around him, he continued his deliberate fire, round after round.'[163]

Kipling might have had a battle like this in mind when he penned those famous words:[164]

> If your officer's dead and the sergeants look white
> Remember it's ruin to run from a fight
> So take open order, lie down and sit tight
> An' wait for supports like a soldier

Edward Mousley was able to observe Chitrál Charlie during this engagement and his view runs counter to those culled by Braddon and which appeared earlier. Mousley wrote:

> One could not but feel the keenest admiration for General Townshend, so steady, collected and determined in action, so kind, quick and confident. There, totally indifferent to the shellfire, he stood watching the issue receiving reports from various orderly officers and giving every attention to the progress of the transport. Some shells pitched just over us, one not 15 yards away, killing a horse and wounding some drivers. More than once I caught a humorous smile on the General's face as some shell missed us. … It was a most wonderful engagement and an exclamation of delight broke from him as he directed our attention to a charge of the 14th Hussars. Over the brown of the desert a mass of glittering and swiftly moving steel bore down upon the line of Turks, which broke and bolted.[165]

Townshend had the option of pursuing a broken but still numerous enemy. However, to his credit, and like the good soldier he was, he stuck to his declared aim, and that was 'to withdraw to Kut'. Accordingly, he issued orders to Delamain and Hamilton to 'retire in alternate echelons of brigades' – an order more likely to have been understood by the recipients than this author and perhaps his reader!

It had been a short, brisk battle, now out of living memory and forgotten. After the war, the Turks said that the British gunnery had paralysed them; they admitted to 2,000 casualties.[166] 6th Division had thirty-seven killed, 281 wounded and there were 218 missing. All the 1,500 Turkish prisoners were secure.

The engagement was broken off and 6th Division turned its face southward again. It faced a march of 36 miles. The naval component being now much reduced, the carriage of a fresh batch of wounded slowed progress. The 'road' alongside the river was regularly broken by old canals and irrigation ditches. Each of these had to be bridged for the wheeled vehicles and after the last wheels had passed, the bridging material, such as it was, had to be recovered and delivered to the head of the column for re-use.

The retreat was by no means the 'walk in the park' of legend. Mousley recorded:

> I was ordered to ride on and find a watering place, which I did; but the Turks still pressed in our rear, and we had to shove on without watering. I managed to water Don Juan (his much loved horse) however and gave him three of my six biscuits; we pushed on, the horses showing signs of fatigue. At 1800 hrs it was dreadfully cold and dark. The BGRA, the staff captain and I rode at the head of the Division. The orders were seventy paces to the minute with compass directing. We took it in turns of half hours. The strain was very severe. We'd had no food, except a sandwich for breakfast, for twenty-four hours, violent exercise under exhausting conditions.

There was no marked road, merely the occasional hoof mark to indicate that at some time, someone, or at least an animal, had passed that way before. The darkness, the cumulative effect of loss of sleep over several nights, the responsibility for guiding the entire force and now the extreme cold all added to the mix.

Mousley wrote that, 'I shall never forget that night. A halt was suggested but our Napoleonic general drove us on. Again, as we learned subsequently, he saved us. That night the Turkish Army, reinforced, was trying to out-march us.'

The 6th Division objective that night was a featureless place called Shadi. The ground locally was scarred with *nullahs* (watercourses or ravines) and there was but only one single track to bypass them. In one place a narrow stone bridge crossed a very deep *nullah* and here there was a scene of wildest confusion. Camels were being thrashed across, kicking mules hauled army carts and this caused a block as wheeled vehicles found difficulty – a bottleneck was created. Several vehicles overturned. Eventually the Division, a column 5 miles long, found its way over the bridge and the sappers blew it when the last man was safely across. The force bivouacked for what was left of the night and tried to sleep.

Mousley recalled the intensity of the cold but he did not sleep, as he was kept busy by his BGRA (Brigadier General, Royal Artillery). Several senior and experienced officers told him that, that day, he 'had witnessed one of the most brilliant episodes possible in war where perfect judgment and first-

48. Captain E.O. Mousley RFA. He survived captivity to write
The Secrets of a Kuttite.

rate discipline alone enabled us to smash the sting of the pursuit and to continue a retreat exactly as it is done on manoeuvres.'[167]

As Mousley indicated, Mesopotamia has a climate that produces extremes of hot and cold, both of which are life threatening. The Viceroy was also well aware of this and, writing to Sir Thomas Holderness on 21 October 1914, Lord Hardinge had said:

> when some weeks ago I enquired of the Commander-in-chief whether proper provision had been made for warm clothing for the troops, he told me that he was relying on private charity for this. I told him at once that I could not possibly agree to our troops being dependent for warm clothing upon private charity and I insisted upon the troops being properly clad at the expense of the Government. It is far better to have warm men in the field than men dying of pneumonia in the hospitals. It is the cheapest course in the long run.

This is an illuminating insight into the thought process of General Sir Beauchamp Duff. However, despite this interjection by Hardinge, Duff did not respond and eighteen months later, the Army was still short of blankets and clothing.

At 0400 hrs on 2 December, the trek was re-continued. Men and beasts were utterly spent. Many mules were shot as their strength gave out. The guns could move only very slowly as their teams were spent, unwatered and unfed. The painful procession wound on its way and at about 1400 hrs it halted for two and a half hours so that the stragglers could catch up. The hope was that Kut would be reached that day, but Townshend decided to halt 5 miles north of Kut because he anticipated an opposed entry to the town.

As the sun set on 2 December, its dying rays could be seen shining on the distant roofs. The pace of the column was now reduced to 1 mile in the hour and so Kut was half a day's march away.

The tired men and beasts of 6th Division rested. Some bread was delivered from Kut and Mousley shared his ration with Don Juan. The horses were tethered close together to share their body warmth; the men sought shelter from the unforgiving and persistent wind. Mousley wrote at some length about that time, saying:

> No one who has not sampled it for himself can credit the intense cold of such a Mesopotamian night. I have registered the cold of Oberhopf, where 20 feet of snow and icicles 40 feet high rendered every wood impassable. I have boated on the west coast of Scotland where the wind from Satan's antipodes cuts through coat and flesh and bone. I have felt the cold from

the glaciers of New Zealand but I have never felt cold to equal that 2 December of the retreat. Perhaps hunger and extreme exhaustion help the cold.[168]

At 0500 hrs the final leg of the journey was started, entry to Kut was not opposed and by 0730 hrs on 3 December, the vanguard entered the filthy, odorous, ill-favoured town of Kut. It was described by Barker as 'the most vile and unsanitary of all the places occupied by the British in Mesopotamia, and about the only alleviating features were the date plantations and a few gardens north-west and south-east'[169] of the hovels huddled in the bend of the river. Kut was not an attractive place to visit and certainly not the place for an extended stay.

The Mesopotamia Commission quite correctly recognised the exceptional skill and fortitude of Townshend's force, and summarised the retreat to Kut in these words:

> The Turks had ample time to prepare a strong position at Ctesiphon; but had it not been for the reinforcements, which reached them before our attack took place, it appears clear that they would have been defeated. The British Force had the utmost confidence in their leader, and the manner in which they fought did not indicate any loss of morale.
>
> Notwithstanding the deficiencies of medical equipment and of transport all the wounded were evacuated and all prisoners taken to Kut. This was a remarkable military achievement, carried out during a hazardous retreat against overwhelming odds and with lines of communication threatened and at times cut by marauding Arabs. Great credit is due to the medical officers for their devoted work in thus evacuating their wounded, but many of those so moved suffered terribly as the two prepared steamers could only accommodate a small proportion of them. The remainder had to be put in any craft that was available and so hurriedly that, as on other occasions when vessels carrying up animals were utilised, there was not time to clear them of their accumulation of filth and dung.
>
> General Townshend and his force in these exceptionally trying circumstances fully maintained their previous splendid reputation, and if for the first time defeat instead of victory attended their efforts, this was due to the exceptional difficulty of the military task imposed upon them, for the numerical odds and adverse conditions with which they had to contend were too much even for their fighting superiority.[170]

Chitral Charlie's reputation was vastly enhanced by these words, which were penned when he was, nominally, a 'prisoner of war'.

Nixon, now back at Basra, but feeling unwell, received a telegram from Chamberlain, the Secretary of State, on 4 December. It was terse and read, 'On arrival wounded at Basra. Please telegraph urgently particulars and progress.' The request for urgency fell on deaf ears because a reply was not sent until 7 December. On that date, and purporting to come from Nixon, the reply read:

> *Wounded satisfactorily disposed of. Many likely to recover in country, comfortably placed in hospitals at Amara and Basra. Those for invaliding are being placed direct on two hospital ships that were ready at Basra on arrival of riverboats. General condition of wounded very satisfactory. Medical arrangements under circumstances of considerable difficulty worked splendidly.*[171]

This travesty of the truth was a replay of the misinformation disseminated after the battle for Kut. The MC asserted that it was unable to discover who had drafted this seriously misleading and untruthful telegram. However, two staff officers asserted to the Commission that the draft was in the handwriting of Surgeon General Hathaway – although he did not initial the telegram as the initiator. Hathaway, in evidence, later admitted that he 'had assisted in the framing' of the telegram.

When called to explain this blatant corruption of the facts in this telegram Nixon, Hathaway and Cowper all assured the MC *'that it was not despatched with the object of misrepresenting the state of things.'* Nixon went as far as to say that, at the time the telegram was sent, his *'thankfulness was great at having got the wounded down safely under circumstances of great difficulty without letting them be exposed to mutilation* [by the Arabs]. *'*[172] That is all very glib and just so much nonsense.

There is enough circumstantial evidence to lay this squalid matter at the door of Hathaway. He was motivated to put a brave face on a disaster that was his responsibility and his fingerprints were on the draft telegram. Nixon may, or may not, have known about the telegram but he was fully aware of the medical debacle because he witnessed it, at Ctesiphon, and had commented upon it.

Cowper had an interest in preserving the standing of Nixon's headquarters. That was understandable, misguided and wrong. The significant casualty was the veracity of all three generals and, in addition, Hathaway's reputation was irredeemably and correctly damaged. The whole business was symptomatic of an integrity gap in Indian Expeditionary Force 'D', and the gap started at the top. The MC took a very dim view and wrote:

It is very difficult to accept these explanations [from Nixon, Hathaway and Cowper] *for whatever may have been the motive for so wording the despatch, the effect was to conceal from the authorities outside Mesopotamia the real facts as to the medical breakdown in November, gravely to mislead the Secretary of State, and through him Parliament and the public and to deceive all into a state of false security in view of future operations.*

If the full facts had been frankly reported, immediately after the battle of Ctesiphon, it would have been possible for the authorities to make strong efforts to remove or mitigate many of the defects before the next fighting took place. But this was not done, with the result that for the wounded the horrors in January 1916 equalled or even exceeded the horrors of Ctesiphon in November 1915.[173]

In Basra, the wounded were being given belated professional care, but to the north, the remnants of the 6th Division had girded its corporate loins and moved into the next uncomfortable phase of the campaign. The expectations of the 6th Division as it marched into Kut were not unreasonable: a cup of hot char and a wad, a cooked breakfast, pretty nurses, mail from home, newspapers, a decent bed raised off the desert floor, a bath and a shave in hot water. A cold beer would be the icing on the Mesopotamian cake. Soldiers are stoic fellows and ask for very little; it is just as well, because Kut offered none of the above.

This was no home from home.

It smelt appalling because Kut had no drainage system; no attempt had been made at sanitation. The whole place was indescribably filthy, owing to the insanitary habits of the inhabitants and the accumulations of refuse and filth on the thoroughfares, the riverbanks and the immediate confines of the town. Colonel Hehir, the senior medical officer, told the MC that it was the most insanitary place that the British force had occupied in Mesopotamia. Given the state of Basra, Kurnah and Amarah, that meant Kut really did plumb the depths.

However, what Kut did have to offer the new arrivals, and in abundance, was many hours of digging.

Chapter notes

152 Moberly, F.J., *The Campaign in Mesopotamia*, Vol. 2, p.107.

153 Colonel H.G. Thompson DSO, interviewed by Braddon, 1968, *The Siege*, p.101.

154 Braddon, R., p.103.155 Nunn, W., *Tigris Gunboats*, p.179.

156 In the event, both officers were admitted to the Distinguished Service Order (DSO).

157 Mant, E.J., recorded by Braddon in *The Siege*, p.109.

158 Mousley, E.O., *The Secrets of a Kuttite*, p.14.

159 Ibid.

160 Townshend, C.V.F., *My Campaign in Mesopotamia*, p.194.

161 Harden was awarded the DSO and Gray the DSM for their gallantry.

162 Nunn, W., *Tigris Gunboats*, pp.184–5.

163 Lieutenant Colonel J. McConville to Braddon, as reported in *The Siege*, p.110.

164 Kipling, R., *The Young British Soldier.*

165 Mousley, E.O., *The Secrets of a Kuttite*, p.15.

166 Moberly, T.F., *The Campaign in Mesopotamia* at p.123 specified that Turkish losses were 748. It may be that the lower figure was Turkish dead.

167 Mousley, E.O., *The Secrets of a Kuttite*, p.19.

168 Ibid, p.21.

169 Barker, A.J., *The Neglected War*, p.115.

170 MC Report, pp.29–30.

171 Ibid, p.31.

172 Ibid, p.77.

173 Ibid, p.78.

Chapter 11

The Siege – Early Days, December 1915

'Every great operation of war is unique. ...
There is no surer road to disaster than to imitate the
plans of bygone heroes and fit them to novel situations.'

(W.S. Churchill, *Marlborough*, 1933–38)

Despite the retreat to Kut, in those early days of December 1915 Hardinge still remained overly optimistic – that was, once he had got over his brief, initial feelings of disappointment at the unravelling of his great plan.

His underlying optimism was manifest in three ways. First, most importantly, he did not abandon his aspiration to take Baghdad, although he could not carry the India Office with him, which directed Townshend to remain on the defensive.[174]

Secondly, he also discounted all the reports of Turkish reinforcements as being 'unnecessarily pessimistic', and on that basis took issue with General Duff's advice that two more divisions from England were needed in Mesopotamia to counter an ever-strengthening foe. He said:

> to divert our troops from the decisive point in Flanders is to play the game
> of Germany and, in my humble opinion, this policy has been too often
> pursued during the present war to the great advantage of the enemy.[175]

Duff did not readily concede and summed up his position by saying that although the war could not be won in any of the minor theatres, it could still be lost. He further emphasised that the disposition of British forces was the function of His Majesty's Government, not that of Simla. Notwithstanding that firm position, he went on to counter-argue that in order to allow HMG to focus on the principal theatre of operations in France, 'I think we should take on ourselves a responsibility which does not rightly belong to us.'[176] Duff's convoluted thought process, illustrated here, speaks volumes.

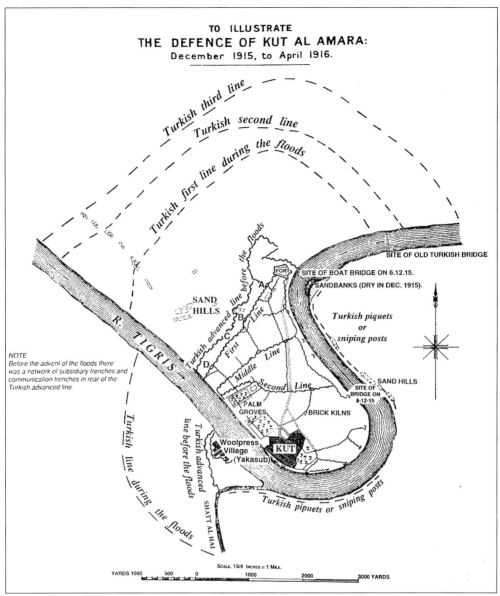

49. Plan of the 6th Division's stronghold of Kut. *(Prepared by the historical section of the Committee of Imperial Defence. Ordnance Survey 1924)*

The third of Hardinge's positions was that his confidence in Nixon remained strong. Hardinge did concede that Nixon 'may have made a mistake as a result of faulty intelligence but he is not a fool.'[177] The reality was that the intelligence was sound, Nixon was a fool to ignore it and the appraisal of Nixon's merit, by Hardinge, is open to challenge.

Relations between Hardinge and Chamberlain were now being adversely affected by the Viceroy's resentment of any suggestion made by his superior, Chamberlain, in the India Office. Chamberlain did not share the Viceroy's high opinion of Nixon and advised the Prime Minister, Asquith, that his 'confidence in Nixon's judgment is seriously shaken by his complete miscalculation as to the changes in Baghdad.' He added that Kitchener (War Minister) also thought that Nixon should be replaced.[178]

There was no meeting of the minds away from the battlefield. Political command and control of the theatre was fuzzy at best and, in the case of Hardinge, dangerous. He had an enviable track record as a pragmatic and effective administrator; the appointment of the Viceroy was not lightly bestowed, but the management of a military campaign was proving to be challenging new ground for him to plough.

On 3 December 1915, Chamberlain wrote to Hardinge and urged him to send someone to review the medical arrangements and report on the health of the troops. 'I beg you,' he warned, 'not to be content with easy assurances … we shall have no defence if all that is possible is not done.'[179]

Notwithstanding the undoubted experience and diplomatic skills of Hardinge, in mid-December he wrote foolishly that Ctesiphon was, 'a blessing in disguise'. It had given the Expeditionary Force the opportunity to inflict 'a good beating upon the Turks. Present talk that Townshend was trapped at Kut was total nonsense.' He went on to explain to Sir Percy Cox that:

> when the Commander-in-Chief and the General Staff talk of the relief of Townshend, I simply ridicule the idea that he should want relief, for with his 9,000 men he is supposed to be surrounded by 10,000 Turks and can break through whenever he chooses. It is really like one man surrounding another.[180]

Thus spoke the Viceroy, giving a view so divorced from reality as to be absurd. He was many miles from the theatre of operations and depended on Nixon for information. One can only presume that he had been fed, in army parlance, 'duff gen', and had based his opinions on entirely false premises.

The position of 6th Division in Kut was not good and getting worse. By 4 December, the Turks were intent on throwing a cordon around the town but, as yet, the encirclement was incomplete. Townshend still had the opportunity to evacuate to the south and he did, briefly, consider withdrawing further to the line of Es Sinn. He rejected that because he realised, not only did the defences there face the 'wrong way', but also, with massive forces at his disposal, Nureddin could outflank him. As the Turkish build-up developed and the Turkish commander moved 45,000 men into the area, breaking out became a diminishing option for Townshend. By 7 December, the investment was complete, the opportunity to break out had been missed and siege conditions now prevailed.

* * *

Charles Townshend had made his name and earned his nickname in 1895 right up on the North-West Frontier of India. There he commanded a small fort and withstood a large enemy force for forty-nine days before being relieved. His plight, and that of his garrison, attracted headlines all around the world, and the relief of Chitrál had a political impact that outweighed its military significance.

At the time Townshend was a captain in the Indian Army, aged thirty-four. Ambitious to a degree that set him apart from his fellows he had, nevertheless, demonstrated ample leadership skills and personal courage. He was an officer who could reasonably expect further advancement.

His appointment as a Companion of the Bath (CB) in 1895 changed his life forever. The CB award was almost without precedent to an officer of his rank and service. He became a national celebrity, dined with the great and the good and was feted wherever he went.

It all went to his head.

It fed his unhealthy conceit and fuelled the driving ambition that completely dominated his life. In the next twenty years he advanced from captain to major general. He was a middle piece officer who was judged by his superiors to be competent but not quite as talented as he thought he was.

Charles Townshend's undoubted scholarship in military history, strategy and tactics should have been factors in his advancement, but a propensity to lecture his seniors on these topics did not win him many friends. Nor did the persistent way he sidestepped the military chain of command to press his demands for new appointments and, by inference, promotion. Thus far in the campaign he had performed in an exemplary manner, and the withdrawal to Kut was, in its way, a minor military masterpiece. For Charles Townshend, the scene was set and he recorded in his diary that, 'I intend to defend Kut, as I did Chitrál.'

These were brave words; however, there was a vast difference between the two situations. In the first, ill-armed and uncoordinated tribesmen had besieged the fort at Chitrál. Food there was rationed but starvation level was never reached. Casualties among the defenders numbered about fifty, most of which were incurred on the first day. Two British relief columns, although opposed, brushed aside their adversaries in order to lift the siege.

The second case was different; a very large, well-coordinated army besieged Kut. The quality of that opposition and the magnitude of its forces make any parallels drawn with Chitrál valueless, other than the mindset of the commander. The quote that heads this chapter underscores that very point.

* * *

The man on the Clapham omnibus had been told of the triumphant march of the 6th Division and had basked in its successes. The capitulation of Baghdad was thought to be inevitable and so public expectation was high. When British forces 'retired' (a much more acceptable word than 'retreated') from Ctesiphon, it came as a shock and a scapegoat was urgently needed. Lord Crewe, speaking in the House of Lords on 8 December, said:

> The early capture of Baghdad would have been a great stroke from the military and political point of view … it was a complete error to suppose that this was a rash military adventure undertaken by General Townshend on his own initiative. The advance to Baghdad was contemplated some months ago … a sufficient force had been collected to carry out the whole operation, the whole proceedings having been thought out by the Commander-in-Chief, General Nixon.[181]

There was no mention of the fact that HMG and the Indian Government had both endorsed Nixon's plans. Although ownership of the strategy was not entirely that of Nixon, he was, nevertheless, being carefully eased into the firing line. It reflected no credit on the great panjandrums of Whitehall.

The upside of the debacle of the siege situation was that it finally dawned upon both governments that the campaign in Mesopotamia could no longer be run 'on the cheap'. India scraped together two infantry brigades and three batteries of artillery and, by mid-December, they were on the high seas heading for the Gulf. The War Office ordered the diversion of two divisions, previously promised to Egypt and France, to Basra. Hardinge asked London to provide a third division and for river transport – this latter request was about a year too late; the lead-time to design, build and despatch the ships was not far short of a year.

The perceived advantage of holding Kut was control of the Tigris and of the Shatt-al-Hai. The thinking was that the British sitting in Kut prevented

130

the Turks from using either river to attack Basra or Nasariyeh. Although the rivers were under British control, the reality was that Kut could easily be outflanked in the vast deserts that surrounded the town.

Kut was originally intended only as a staging post and supply point; accordingly, only sparse defences around the town had been built after its capture. The current situation called for comprehensive defence works, so Townshend's men had to start from scratch.

The neck of the bend was about 1,700 yards wide and it was this line to which most assets were directed. At the eastern extremity of that line was a mud-walled building dignified with the appellation 'Fort'. It was incorporated into the defence plan and from the fort to the river, on the west, a line of trenches was constructed. The depth of the entrenched camp from the first line to the loop in the river was 3,200 yards.

The men were utterly exhausted when they arrived at Kut on the morning of 3 December; many simply lay down and slept. As a result, it was twenty-four hours before a start could be made on building defences. It was backbreaking work but the imminent arrival of the Turks was a strong motivation to dig and lay out as much barbed wire as was available.

The map on page 127 shows that on the right bank (looking downstream) was Woolpress Village, in which was located a liquorice factory. The benefit of holding this position was that possession of both banks controlled all movement of river traffic. That said, the Turks' riverine assets were very sparse indeed and a thrust downriver was unlikely. In December, the Tigris was about 300 yards wide and sufficiently shallow that it could be waded. At the same time, the Hai River was a dry watercourse and of no navigable use.

The decision to occupy Woolpress Village was uncharacteristic of Townshend, but he was probably influenced by the presence there of a large stock of grain. Barker said that, 'Coming from such a brilliant tactician this seems an odd conclusion. The factory was on the 'wrong' side of the river and while it was necessary to hold it until the grain had been removed, it is difficult to understand why it otherwise had any advantage over many other areas on the right bank.'[182]

The weakness of the 6th Division's position was that its front line was critical. If the garrison failed to defend that first line it would be driven further into the 'loop', into an area about 800 yards wide by a similar measurement deep. It would then be exposed to close-range, all-round fire. Those first-line defensive trenches would also impede the obvious axis for any exit in force that Townshend might undertake. At this early stage Townshend was anxious to maintain bridges across the river so that he had an option to sally out and conduct 'an active defence'.

To Townshend's credit, he was fully aware of 'the fate which in history is generally reserved for the force that shuts itself up in an entrenched camp or fortified place. … If the relieving army is unable to reach the besieged force military history offers hardly any examples of the self-deliverance of an army once invested.'[183]

The Turks, on the other hand, had all manner of advantages, and not least of these was the very favourable ground for defence against any British relieving force. On the left bank, from Sannaiyat to Hanna, 25 miles downriver, there was only a narrow strip of land between the Tigris and very extensive marshland. This was the ground that Townshend turned to his advantage when he took Kut in September. See the map on page 147.

On the right bank, the ground was broken by old irrigation ditches, dried-up watercourses and further marshland. The Es Sinn banks taken by the British would be much more heavily populated and reinforced to face a second assault. In dry weather this was difficult going, but in the wet season it was impossible. When the Tigris broke its banks, as it had done every spring for thousands of years, the flood covered tens of thousands of square miles of desert. These floods were the most effective form of defence and any attack on the forces surrounding Kut had to be initiated before the anticipated flood.

Elsewhere, the expedition to the Dardanelles was failing in its aim and the Turks were inflicting frightful casualties on the British, French, Australian and New Zealand armies, which had barely got off the beaches. Losses at sea had also been heavy and the writing was firmly on the wall. A retirement from the Dardanelles might resolve one issue but would free a multitude of battle-hardened Turks who could, and almost certainly would, be redeployed to Mesopotamia. It was a worrying prospect.

It could be argued that in a siege situation it is the attackers who are at a disadvantage because delay gives relieving forces more time to achieve their aim. However, in this case, as in so many over recorded military history, the Turks had at hand a potent weapon.

It was – hunger.

The inevitable, forthcoming spring floods were a strategic bonus.

The first of these had engendered any number of generals to burst forth. For example, 'The General achieves the most who tries to destroy the enemy army more by hunger than by force of arms,' opined the Emperor Maurice in AD 600.[184] He was not alone in that view, and 200 years earlier, Flavius Vegetius Renatus had commented that, 'Famine makes greater havoc in an army than the enemy and is more terrible than the sword.'[185] There is any number of similar quotations but the point does not need to be laboured.

Townshend, from his studies, was fully aware of the starvation issue and surprisingly he did not do what would have been prudent and expected of him. He did not measure his food stocks and nor did he calculate, accurately, the endurance of his command. The key word there is 'accurately'. This oversight was to have serious consequences.

Townshend reported, on 4 December, that the parade state showed that within the confines of Kut there were 10,398 combatants, of which 1,505 were the Cavalry Brigade. There was little that the Brigade could contribute and there was insufficient fodder for its horses and so, sensibly, Townshend sent it back to Basra. That left 8,893 defenders; 7,411 of these were infantry. Townshend's calculation was that there were 2,700 yards of trench that had to be manned and defended, and at 'the scale of three to five men per running yard'[186] he was undermanned. Defence of Woolpress Village would absorb one infantry battalion and the town had to be garrisoned in order to control the indigenous population.

Later, when Colonel Hehir gave evidence to the Mesopotamia Commission, he provided a comprehensive summary of the population of Kut on 8 December. Hehir's numbers differ from Townshend's, but this was just a snapshot and the status and strength of the population varied on a daily basis as people were wounded or died.

Effectives

British officers	*206*
British rank and file	*2,276*
Indian officers	*153*
Indian rank and file	*6,941*
Followers (about)	*3,500*
Total	***13,076***

Sick and wounded

British officers	*12*
British rank and file	*258*
Indian officers	*22*
Indian rank and file	*1,176*
Followers	*42*
Total	***1, 510***

*Military ration strength **14, 586***
Civilians

Men	*1,538*
Women and children	*3,803*
Woolpress Village	*504*
Mahiellah (boat) men	*316*
Coolies	*64*
Total	***6,225***[187]

The figures above do not include Turkish prisoners and wounded, conservatively estimated at about 1,500. Thus there were a total of over 22,000 people, of one status or another, penned into the unsavoury salient formed by the Tigris. In addition there were 1,000 horses, 2,000 mules and ponies, and 100 bullocks.[188]

The cavalry brigade had decamped, but nevertheless 1,000 horses remained. This seems to be a high figure, but it has to be presumed that these were, in the main, pack animals that towed guns and carts. Officers' mounts, say 200, were included in this number.

Men and beasts – all had to be fed and watered.

Townshend had no illusions about the resident Arabs, many of whom were openly hostile. They were a fifth column in his midst and one that, almost certainly, had concealed weapons. His first thoughts were to expel the lot. Sir Percy Scott urged restraint, pointing out that women and children would perish in the desert, either at the hands of other barbarous Arabs or from starvation. On the basis that 'there was easily enough food for the 700 householders to last about three months', Townshend relented and only ejected non-householders. However, he took twenty hostages as surety for good behaviour from the balance. Today, such an act would be condemned. Similarly, some might not approve of the trial of twelve men, by a military court, caught in the act of looting. They were shot – *pour encourager les autres.*[189] War and death at Kut was all around.

The 'Kuttites', as they now termed themselves, settled down and waited to be relieved. Sniping and persistent shelling was the order of the day and Turkish musketry skills soon started to exact a price from those foolish enough to expose any part of their person. Edward Mousley recalled December 1915 when he wrote:

> To get from [our] dugout to the town we had to cross a shell-swept zone.
> Every few yards there was a splash of smoke and flame. This was, of course,
> at the beginning of the siege. Our dugouts were near several brick kilns,

themselves sufficient target without our gun flashes. We had a battery of 18-pounders on one side, 5-inch on the other and howitzers behind. So we came in for all the ranging. It was out of the question to leave any cooking utensils above ground, for they were certain to be perforated within minutes.

General Mellis, breathing fire and bluntly expressing encouragement, was a regular visitor to the first line, which was not his area of responsibility as he commanded the 'main force' that was held to the rear and poised to reinforce any part of the first line that was threatened. His robust personality and personal courage were an example and his soldiers would have followed him to the ends of the earth. Townshend, whose visits to the front were infrequent, reached out to his soldiers by means of his communiqués. These documents have to be read in the context of the setting but, since then, have been the subjects of considerable analysis. His first one was straightforward and ran as follows:

> I intend to defend Kut-al-Amara and not retire any further. Reinforcements are being sent at once to relieve us. The honour of our Mother Country and the Empire demands that we all work, heart and soul, in the defence of this place. We must dig in deep and dig quickly and then the enemy shells will do little damage. We have ample food and ammunition, but commanding officers must husband the ammunition and not throw it away uselessly. The way you have managed to retire some 80 or 90 miles under the very noses of the Turks is nothing short of splendid and speaks eloquently for the courage and discipline of this force.

Field Marshal von der Goltz, the 72-year-old German, had by now taken his place in Mesopotamia, accompanied by a cadre of his staff officers. The Kuttites faced a particularly adept and ruthless opponent. Christmas beckoned, but from 7 December the cantonment was subjected to constant artillery fire and casualties started to mount. The encirclement was complete, as the Turks sealed off Kut with its 35th Division. Hard on its heel were the 38th, 45th and 51st divisions. At a conservative estimate, that was 45,000 men, possibly more. The British had to defeat this host if the 6th Division was to be saved.

Nureddin wrote to Townshend, pointing out that the British position was hopeless and that surrender would save many lives. He added that exposing the civilian population to danger was counter to the customs of war. Townshend replied, courteously, rejecting the offer, but did point out that Nureddin's German comrades were expert practitioners in the matter of involving civilians in military affairs and that the reputation of von der Goltz preceded him.

The following day, news was received that the Cavalry Brigade had reached the safety of Ali al-Gharbi and that 28th Infantry Brigade had been despatched to join them there. So far so good, but the MC commented:

> *In anticipation of the arrival of two divisions from overseas Sir Fenton Aylmer* [previously] *the Adjutant General of the Indian Army was sent to take command of a force designated as the 'Tigris Corps' in which were to be incorporated the two expected divisions, the troops located at Ali al-Gharbi and ultimately other reinforcements. The two divisions, the bulk of which was still on the high seas, were gradually arriving at Basra, but their piecemeal embarkation and disembarkation were very detrimental to their efficiency as fighting units; the whole organisation was upset by the methods of their transmission and disembarkation, and there was no time for their proper reorganisation before advancing. The available transport in Mesopotamia was not sufficient even to carry the men and ammunition to the front and it was in these disadvantaged circumstances that military operations commenced.*

That extract re-states the longstanding deficiencies at Basra where, twelve months after the arrival of the Indian Army, there were still no port facilities and the gaping void in the transport inventory had not been filled.

Aylmer was an officer of the Royal Engineers and a capable and brave man. Charlie had been engaged in the same battle in which Lieutenant Fenton Aylmer RE won his Victoria Cross in November 1891. They were both members of the Hunza-Nagar Field Force attacking the fort at Nilt on the North-West Frontier.

* * *

The minor Victorian wars of which Hunza-Nagar is typical are now, at best, footnotes to history but, nevertheless, they were vicious, uncompromising affairs. There was as little compassion on the frontier as there was in the Mesopotamian desert twenty-five years later.

In the latter stages of the assault on the fort at Nilt, Aylmer and a small party of sappers found that access to the walls was barred by a series of abattis.[190] Aylmer found his way through these obstacles to a small door set in the curtain wall of the fort. The door was forced, with the loss of only one man, despite persistent enemy fire. Aylmer found cover and was able to prepare a demolition charge that he planned to place against the main doors of the fort. He lit his fuse and, under fire, ran to his target and laid his charge. After a wait it became clear that the fuse had failed. Aylmer ran back to the target doors, was wounded, but the fuse was reignited. The enemy was now fully alerted to Aylmer's intentions and he was wounded a second time. The charge blew and the two great doors to the fort collapsed. Aylmer charged through the smoke and was at once engaged in hand-to-hand fighting.

He was wounded a third time. A company of Gurkhas arrived, stormed the breach and the fort was taken after a battle that had lasted only twenty minutes. British losses in the engagement were six killed and twenty-seven wounded; the enemy had eighty killed. Aylmer won a well-merited Victoria Cross. Four years later, Aylmer was part of the force that relieved Townshend at Chitrál. The two men were near contemporaries and knew each other quite well.

* * *

The arrival of fresh troops at Basra was to be welcomed, but their organisation thereafter was hasty. There was little time for theatre training and acclimatisation. The haste was generated by Townshend's estimate of the time he could hold Kut and the big issue was food. On 3 December, and before a detailed inventory could be made, the commander sent a signal saying that he only had food for one month for British soldiers and two months for Indians. Relief was needed by early January 1916.

This estimate had the effect of generating a great sense of urgency but, until the divisions arrived, nothing could be done. On 7 December, Townshend revised his estimate and claimed food enough for sixty days for both ethnic groups. He could hold until early February. A further amendment on 11 December advised Nixon that he had sufficient for fifty-nine days – other than for meat. He could hold until 8 February. From there on, the British relief plan was based on an absolute requirement to take Kut by that latest date. The urgency with which relief operations were put in place impacted directly on their effectiveness, or lack of it. The artificial urgency was manufactured by Townshend for his own ends.

The one thing Aylmer lacked was time. Although it was no substitute, he was to have regular messages from Townshend emphasising the plight of his garrison and offering patronising, gratuitous advice on how to conduct his operations.

Aylmer's Tigris Corps, when it was fully assembled, would be composed of the 7th (Meerut) Division, commanded by Major General Younghusband CB,[191] and 3rd (Lahore) Division, commanded by Major General Henry D' Urban Keary DSO.[192]

On 7 December there was a major Turkish artillery stonk. This damaged

137

the defences of the fort, inflicted thirty casualties and softened up the British first line, which faced a major assault the following afternoon. Then the Turks made a frontal attack across the flat desert. There was no guile but lots of raw courage; the Turks paid a high butcher's bill but did not breach the first line. The combined German/Turkish generalship did not excel.

Townshend was alert to the mixed blessing of the boat bridge shown on the map (page 127 with the date 8.12.15). That bridge was moved from its original position (6.12.15) because of its vulnerability near the first line. Initially, the GOC viewed the bridge as an exit from his confinement that allowed him to strike out at his besiegers, and to that purpose he had established a bridgehead with a double company of 67th Punjabis under the command of a Captain Gribbon. The Turks responded by sending a large detachment across the dry Shatt-al-Hai to capture or destroy the bridge.

On 9 December, Gribbon led an assault on the Turks who were positioned on some adjacent sand hills. He was successful but, when counter-attacked, was forced to retire back over the bridge. In the process the officer was wounded three times, and he fell and died on the right bank.

General Mellis, at his aggressive best, would have none of this and he at once re-crossed the bridge and took possession of the far end, where he established a small beachhead. However, he quickly realised that his position on the right bank was neither tenable nor supportable and reluctantly ceded control to the enemy. The Turks now established themselves at the water's edge and commanded that end of the bridge, where they dug in. This change in fortunes raised the possibility that the Turks might mount an assault across the bridge into the very heart of the garrison. Hitherto, Townshend had identified the bridge as his route to offensive operations and had not perceived it as a potential danger.

The acceptance of its commander that the entrapped 6th Division could only be defensive was a watershed in this campaign. Hereafter, Townshend paid only lip service to the possibility that he might break out and assist those trying to relieve him. He contrived to construct a scenario in which he appeared to be prepared to break out, but by presenting sufficient difficulties, he was ordered by Nixon *not* to attempt a break-out. This deceit and his inaccurate forecasts of food stocks, in combination, were to cost thousands of lives. Chitrál Charlie deceived his soldiers; he gave them false hope and they believed him. Charles Townshend was a well-read student of warfare and knew full well that the writing was on the wall. He was well aware that 'an army, which thinks only in defensive terms, is doomed. It yields initiative and advantage in time and space to the enemy … it loses the sense of the hunter, the opportunist.'[193]

In the new circumstances he decided that the bridge had to be destroyed at the mooring point on the right bank so that, when freed from constraint, the remnants of the bridge would be swung by the current on to the garrison's left bank. The Turks had swiftly dug trenches overlooking the bridge and any sally against the far side of the bridge would be very hazardous. Two volunteers came forward and offered to place demolition charges at the Turkish end of the bridge on the right bank. Lieutenants Alec Mathews RE and Roy Sweet 2/7th GR took on the task of leading a mixed party of Gurkhas, miners and sappers. Chitrál Charlie wrote (p. 223) that:

> this was a most gallant affair, the two officers going to the enemy's side of the river across the bridge, which had sagged in places under the swift–running current owing to waterlogged pontoons and laying the saucisson,[194] while the others stood by to cut the anchor cables. With the explosion the bridge broke up. The enemy were for some time too dazed to open fire and the whole party escaped. I recommended the two British officers for the Victoria Cross[195] and the men for Indian Order of Merit.

Fenton Aylmer signalled Townshend on 10 December, saying, 'Have assumed command Tigris line. Have utmost confidence in defender of Chitrál and his gallant troops to keep flag flying till we can relieve them. Heartiest congratulations on brilliant deeds of yourself and your command.' Townshend replied, saying he was proud to serve under Aylmer. He may have said it but it is unlikely that he meant it.

That same day, Chamberlain wired to ask Townshend for a 'sitrep'. He was promptly given the facts, such as '199 casualties yesterday and 800 sick at present'. Chamberlain was also given a short essay on siege warfare in which Hannibal, Charles XII and Napoleon all got a mention.

10 December brought with it a further serious frontal assault. It was repulsed and again the Turks suffered heavy losses, but it was not all one way; the garrison had 202 casualties. The fighting strength was further reduced and a prodigious amount of ammunition had been used.

The Indian battalions had lost a disproportionate number of their British officers, and Townshend offered a commission to any of his 2,700 British soldiers who might like to apply. W.D. Swan was one of those invitees and he recalled a conversation with a fellow Norfolk, a man called Ormiston. They agreed that the Turks gave especial attention to the Caucasian officers of an Indian regiment, and that made the offer a deal less attractive. Nevertheless, Ormiston applied, was selected and emerged as an instant second lieutenant.[196]

Several accounts make mention of a camel that wandered across no-man's-land and paid the penalty. Its rotting carcass produced the foulest of odours and added to the discomfort of both sides for some weeks.

This pattern of Turkish attacks was repeated and on the 13th, the enemy again sustained dreadful losses but did establish trenches, never more than 600 yards from the first British line. The position of the defenders was that with every success there was a reduction in ammunition stocks that could not be replenished, and an increase in the load of the medical staff. Equally, the Turkish soldier's lot was not a happy one. The officers ruled by fear and physical violence, medical support was minimal and a serious wound was tantamount to death. Even a minor wound became serious when it was inexpertly treated – or not treated at all. Food was at subsistence level and the supply chain was creaking as it sought to sustain a major force overland on unmade roads. Those trenches at 600 yards now became the base for energetic 'sapping' as the Turks zigzagged across no-man's-land. However, the fort at the north-east corner of the first line was the priority target for the Turkish guns. This area was in the aegis of Brigadier General Hoghton's 17th Brigade. He had under his command 103rd Mahrattas, 119th Indian Infantry, fifty 'bombers' (grenadiers) of the Oxfordshire and Buckinghamshire Light Infantry, two 15-pounders, a battery of six Maxim guns and a company of sappers and miners.

During the night of the 23rd, an artillery stonk was focussed on the fort and lasted without respite until the following morning. By then the two 15-pounders had been knocked out and most of the mud walls had been demolished, all the telephone lines were cut and the occupants of the fort withdrew to nearby trenches. When the expected Turkish assault, by their 52nd Division, was launched, its serried ranks faced the blistering fire of the remaining four Maxim guns commanded by Captain C. Stockley. The execution was dreadful but the Turks pressed on and, despite the fifteen rounds a minute discharged at them by the Indian infantry, they reached the first line. Edward Mousley recalled:

> The Turk was evidently merely demonstrating on our sector and intended to attack through the fort. All our available guns in turn switched on to their Fort lines i.e. for a barrage already prepared, just over the walls of the Fort.
>   We increased our range and searched, getting in among the Turkish reserves all piled up and awaiting ready to support.[197]

Grenades were hurled into the Turkish ranks at only 10 yards' range, but the savage fighting became hand-to-hand. Both sides used grenades, bayonets and knives. Shovels were put to a different use. The ferocity of the fight matched that at Ctesiphon and a breakthrough here could have swung the siege in the Turks' favour. To their utmost credit, the Indian soldiers gave no ground and exacted a very high price from their adversaries. The intensity of the fighting and the carnage that ensued could not last and, after a frantic thirty minutes or so, the Turkish ranks had been reduced to small knots of men who, seeing that the day was lost, ran, leaving piles of their dead heaped in front of the British first line and all across the plain.

Among the British dead was Second Lieutenant Ormiston.

It was alleged that von der Goltz himself had planned this unsophisticated attack. If this were the case, he would have learned the same lessons as those learned by generals on the Western Front. Bravery is simply not enough in the face of machine guns.

The day was not done and shelling continued until about 2000 hrs, when the Turks tried again – this time led through the dark by 'bombers'. The first line was breached and more murderous hand-to-hand followed. The battle was not going well and ground was being lost until, just after midnight, reinforcement arrived in the shape of the Oxfordshire and Buckinghamshire Light Infantry. They turned the tide and, very badly bruised, the Turks withdrew.

Came the dawn and 907[198] Turkish corpses littered the ground. Back in Turkish lines there must have been 2–3,000 wounded. It was a major defeat, but at a cost; British/Indian dead amounted to 315, and the bravest and best were among them. The 103rd Mahratta Light Infantry and the 43rd Ox and Bucks LI drew especial praise in the *Official History* for the part they played in this particular conflict. The British casualties since 3 December now amounted to 1,625 and the hospitals were overrun.

The battlefield was a gruesome sight; the Turkish wounded cried for help and when men went forward, Turkish snipers engaged them. The mercy missions ceased until dark. About twelve hours later, those Turks who could be moved without a stretcher were helped in; the remainder had to be left where they lay – and there they died, in the dark and the biting cold, abandoned by their comrades and now by their reluctant enemies.

This was to be the last major assault of the siege and the Turks now put their effort into sniping, at which they were very proficient. With their excellent optical sights they achieved kills from up to 700 yards and in one case 1,000 yards. Major Booth of the Army Signal Company organised a counter-sniping detachment, and his energy and the skill of his small body of men helped to restore the balance. Many Kuttites developed a stoop as a consequence of their exposure to Turkish sniping. But even a stoop was no

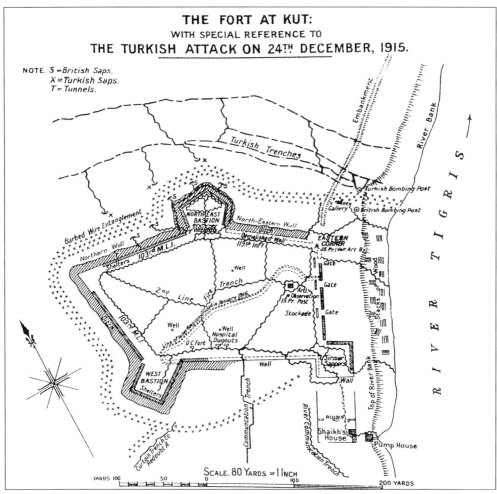

THE FORT AT KUT:
WITH SPECIAL REFERENCE TO
THE TURKISH ATTACK ON 24TH DECEMBER, 1915.

NOTE. S = *British Saps.*
X = *Turkish Saps.*
T = *Tunnels.*

**50. The fort at Kut – the scene of savage hand-to-hand fighting
in December 1915 and held at great cost.
*(Prepared by the historical section of the Committee for
Imperial Defence. Ordnance Survey, 1924)***

defence against enemy artillery and there was daily attrition from the
sporadic artillery fire.

Unsung heroes of this siege were the *bhistis* (water carriers). These were
Indian labourers/porters whose function was to fill vessels with water at the
riverbank and deliver it to the soldiery. Any number of these people were
killed as they went about their unglamorous but very dangerous business.
Turkish marksmen showed them no mercy, nor did they spare the civilian
women and children, sent out by their craven menfolk to draw water. The
British soldiers found it difficult to admire the Arab men with whom they
were incarcerated.

The weather was now brutally cold and Sergeant Munn of the Ox and Bucks LI said that he habitually wore a pair of long trousers over his puttees and shorts, a British warm[199] around his body, a balaclava cap and a scarf around his head, mitts and woollen gloves – then he wrapped himself in two blankets. Quite how he could 'stand to' if needed, he did not explain.

Chapter notes

174 Minutes on Viceroy telegram to Secretary of State, 30 November 1915, L/P&S/10/524. Reg no. 4388 and Cabinet meeting 25 November 1915, Cab 42/5/22.

175 Hardinge to Duff and reply, both 17 December. Enclosed in Hardinge to Chamberlain 24 December, Chamberlain papers, 63 2/2.

176 Ibid.

177 Hardinge to Chamberlain, 7 January 1916, Chamberlain papers, 62/2.

178 Chamberlain to Hardinge, 9 and 16 December 1915, Chamberlain papers, 62/2.

179 Chamberlain to Hardinge, 3 December 1915, Hardinge papers, 121/No. 70, Secretary of State telegram to Viceroy, 17 December 1915, Hardinge papers, 99/No. 835.

180 Hardinge to Chamberlain, 31 December 1915, Hardinge papers. To Cox, 28 December 1915, Hardinge papers, 94/No. 155.

181 Hansard, 8 December 1915.

182 Barker, A.J., *The Neglected War*, p.119.

183 Townshend, C.V.F., *My Campaign in Mesopotamia*, p.211.

184 The Emperor Maurice, *The Strategikon*, AD 600. Translated by George Dennis, 1984.

185 Flavius Vegetius Renatus, *Military Institutions of the Romans,* c. AD 378.

186 Townshend, C.V.F., *My Campaign in Mesopotamia*, p.213.

187 MC Report, p.169.

188 Moberly, F.J., *The Campaign in Mesopotamia 1914–1918*, Vols. 1–4, p.140.

189 Townshend, C.V.F., *My Campaign in Mesopotamia*, p.227.

190 A barricade of felled trees with branches pointing towards the enemy, sometimes laced with barbed wire. A well-constructed abattis was impassable.

191 Later, Major General Sir George Younghusband KCMG KCIE CB (1859–1944).

192 Later, Lieutenant General Sir Henry Keary KCB KCIE DSO (1857–1937).

193 General Sir David Fraser, *And we shall shock them*, 1983.

194 A saucisson is a sausage-shaped demolition charge.

195 Both officers were awarded the DSO. Townshend wrote later, saying, 'I am convinced that never has the VC been more fairly and squarely won than in the case of these two young officers. They volunteered for what appeared to be certain death and waited all day in cold blood to carry out the operation under cover of darkness.'

196 Swan, Mr. W.D., as recorded by Braddon, p.144.

197 Mousley, E.O., *The Secrets of a Kuttite*, p.40.

198 Barker, A.J., *The Neglected War*, p.124. Some unfortunate was obviously detailed to count the corpses.

199 A British warm is a very heavy, camel-coloured Crombie woollen overcoat, usually worn by officers both in uniform and in mufti.

Chapter 12

January 1916
The Battles of Sheikh Saad
and the Wadi River

'Without supplies no army is brave.'
(Frederick, the Great, *Instructions to his Generals*, 1747)

In Kut, the dearth of firewood was an increasing problem. Edward Mousley wrote that, 'there is only enough available to cook one meal a day for the men and provide hot water besides for breakfast. Sometimes there is not even that. Theft of wood is punishable with death.'[200] On New Year's Day there was an unpleasant incident when a sentry of the 103rd Mahratta Light Infantry not only deserted his post but shot at an officer. He missed and, as he tried to get to the Turkish lines, was captured. The miscreant was swiftly tried by court martial, found guilty and summarily shot.

The weather broke on 3 January. It started to rain and the desert 'sand' slowly turned into a morass of glutinous consistency. It was to get a great deal worse in the weeks ahead.

General Aylmer's task had become immeasurably harder as he strove to impose order on his troops, who were arriving piecemeal. Aylmer was under pressure from and being driven by Nixon to commence operations at the earliest possible date. This haste was the direct result of:

> the succession of telegrams which General Townshend despatched from Kut during December. In these he urges, as reasons for his immediate relief, the dangers of enemy reinforcements and of determined onslaught by superior numbers, the impaired morale of his troops, heavy losses in British officers, anxiety as to ammunition, etc., etc. But it is noteworthy that throughout he never, except on 5 December, puts forward deficiency of supplies as a reason for accelerating relief.[201]

It is extraordinary that a soldier of Townshend's experience and grasp of military history did not call for a complete inventory of his food stocks until late in the siege. Similarly, there was an abundance of horsemeat available for all, except for those Indian soldiers whose religion proscribed horsemeat. Mellis and Delamain both urged Townshend to order the Indians to eat horsemeat, assuring him that they would comply, but he refused and, as a consequence, until late in the siege the Indian soldiers had little or no meat.

Turkish shelling caused a steady stream of casualties, and in an attempt to eliminate Townshend's headquarters the hospital was hit. 'Casualties now varied between 26–36 daily.' There were a total of about 2,000 men who were incapacitated in some measure, a number added to by Turkish snipers using hollow point ammunition, 'of the fashion and calibre of the Snider', which caused soldiers and Arab civilians to suffer horrible wounds.[202]

1916 brought with it any number of changes. General Nixon was ailing, and had been for over a month. His ill health made him more irascible and unapproachable, but he was determined to see the campaign through to a successful conclusion. Unfortunately his judgement, sometimes questionable, was further adversely affected. He should have been cheered by the arrival of Sir George Buchanan, a civilian, who had hitherto been the official in charge of the major port of Rangoon. He was a man with a wealth of experience in Port Management and, on the face of it, a valuable new asset on Nixon's staff. The intention was that he should become Director General of the Port of Basra, with the task of reorganising the facilities and traffic flow. It was not quite like that, and the Mesopotamia Commission Report observed:

> It was unfortunately left to Sir John Nixon to arrange exactly what the duties of his position were to be. Differences naturally ensued. Sir George Buchanan's powers were so limited by Sir John Nixon that the former considered that his services were not put to their proper use. After a short stay he returned to India.

It is not difficult to imagine the interface between these two men. Nixon was not temperamentally suited to the receipt of unwelcome advice and Buchanan was a subject matter expert who did not expect his advice to be disregarded. Nixon decided to limit Buchanan's role to that of 'survey, conservancy and dredging work'.[203] The management of the port was not to be in his aegis, and Captain Huddlestone of the Royal Indian Marine retained that responsibility. Buchanan was not a man to trifle with; he promptly returned to India, where he drafted a report on what he had seen in Basra. Predictably, his report was damning. In it he said:

I found it difficult to realise that we had been in occupation of Basra for a year, as the arrangements for the landing and storing of goods and stores of every description were of the most primitive order and in the absence of roads, the whole area was a huge quagmire. To a newcomer appearances were such that troops and stores might have been landed, for the first time, the previous week. ... The military expedition to Basra is, I believe, unique, inasmuch as in no previous case has such an enormous force been landed and maintained without an adequately prepared base.[204]

On the river, things were getting better, at least in offensive terms, and Captain Nunn's command had been much reinforced by the arrival of *Butterfly*, *Cranefly*, *Dragonfly* and *Gadfly*. Later in the year, *Grayfly*, *Greenfly*, *Mayfly*, *Sawfly*, *Snakefly* and *Waterfly* would also join the flotilla. These Fly class ships were 126 feet long with a 20-foot beam and they drew between 2 and 3 feet of water. They mounted a 4-inch gun, a 12-pounder and four Maxim guns. They were crewed by two officers and twenty ratings.

January 1916 was a black month for the British and Indian armies. The MC observed sadly that, *'the history of the attempts to relieve Kut is melancholy reading enough – a record of prolonged struggle carried on with inadequate means under abnormal conditions of atrocious weather and terminating in failure.'[205]*

History reveals that the fate of Kut and its garrison was really settled in January 1916. A series of small but costly actions were to be fought in that month, marked only by the appalling losses and the suffering of the British and Indian soldiers who were engaged. The betrayal of this army was not yet complete.

The first optimistic move of the Tigris Corps to relieve Kut was an advance up both banks. This commenced on 4 January, in heavy rain, over muddy ground, and was the precursor to the Battle of Sheikh Saad. The bad weather had prevented any aerial reconnaissance and Aylmer had no accurate intelligence as to the size of the force opposing him. Townshend had signalled that he had seen two Turkish divisions, bypassing Kut and heading downriver. Further signals advised Aylmer of major Turkish troop movements. Despite these omens, Aylmer was not inclined to change; he went ahead with his plan and decided that Major General G.J. Younghusband,[206] in command of the advanced 7th (Meerut) Indian Division, would lead the Corps.

Younghusband took passage in *Gadfly* with Nunn. Contact with the enemy was not established that day and 7th Division camped for the night

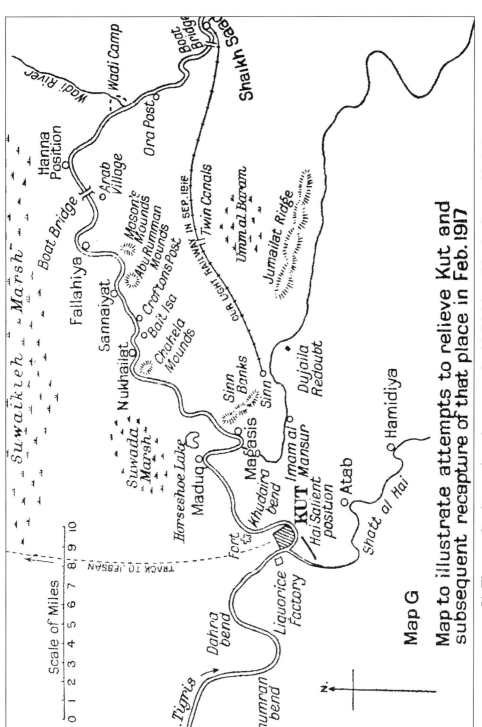

Map G

Map to illustrate attempts to relieve Kut and subsequent recapture of that place in Feb. 1917

51. The area fought over in order to save the 6th Division. (*Map by Geographia Ltd*)

147

about 5 miles from the village. The weather temporarily cleared and aeroplanes could operate; they supplemented further intelligence reports that indicated that Nureddin had 30,000 men and forty guns around Kut, and that he intended to defend Sheikh Saad with about 10,000 men, who were entrenched on both sides of the river.

The settlements along the river are no more than reference points, as in themselves they had no strategic or tactical value. They provided no defensive advantage to the occupying force.

Aylmer's instructions to Younghusband were not entirely clear, and nor was visibility the following morning when a thick mist enveloped the area. 35th Brigade (Rice) was to move up the left bank and 28th Brigade (Kemball) up the right bank. The GOC would follow in *Gadfly,* heading a flotilla bearing stores, ammunition and food. The earlier rain had exacerbated the quagmire and, for the infantry, it was very hard going.

The protective mist suddenly cleared and, about 2 miles away, both brigades could just discern what appeared to be a line of Turkish trenches. The infantry moved into extended line and marched resolutely towards the foe. It was very brave, but foolish; the Turkish artillery soon came into play. As the lines, now with many gaps, got closer, the enemy engaged them with small arms and the casualties started to accumulate. At 500 yards from the trench line it was clear that enough was enough, and the survivors went to ground and tried to scrape a hole. If they were successful, the hole filled, quickly, with water.

Younghusband's orders had been 'to hold the enemy in their positions'. But, by his unsophisticated march to contact and the exposure of both brigades to heavy fire and severe casualties without effective response, he had committed Aylmer 'to a course of action from which there was no turning back'.[207] This was the first of Younghusband's professional errors but by no means the last.

A British asset was a boat bridge that, correctly used, would allow the British force the flexibility of switching its thrust from one bank to the other. As bridges go it was a pretty poor specimen but, in a theatre where nothing much worked, beggars could not be choosers. Aylmer told Younghusband to do nothing until the following morning, 7 January, and to meet him at the bridge.

It was an unpleasant morning, very humid and hot; more heavy rain seemed likely. The men of 7th Division had tried to rest but nocturnal thunderstorms and torrential rain had precluded sleep. The generals conferred, but the sole product of the conversation was a decision to resume the attack at noon.

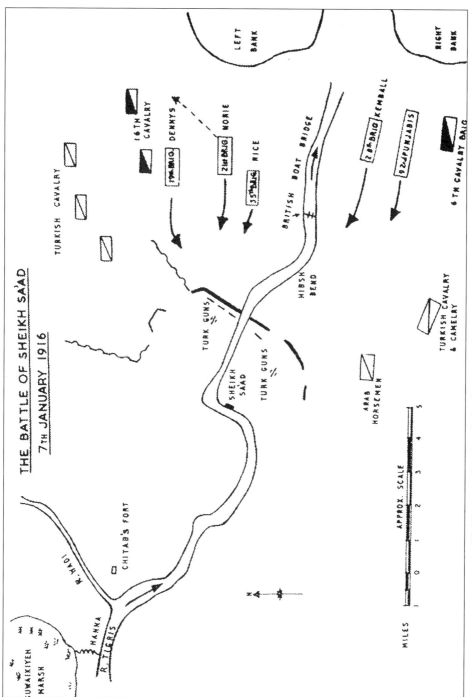

52. The opening battle in the campaign to relieve Kut. *(A.J. Barker)*

Rice would hold his position with 35th Brigade while 19th Brigade (Denny) would sweep around Rice's right and, supported by 16th Cavalry, roll up the Turkish left flank. 21st Brigade (Norrie) would follow Denny and act as a reserve. That was the plan, and Younghusband's men were to move across open country with visibility now hampered by mirages.

When the attack went in on the left bank, 28th Brigade (Kemball), with the addition of 92nd Punjabis, was to advance 'vigorously' on the right bank. In the rear of 28th Brigade was the Corps reserve under the direct command of Aylmer, the GOC-in-C. Unfortunately, the objectives for the attack were difficult to identify, as the Turks were very skilled in concealing their trenches. They did not throw the spoil up to form a parapet, so in a flat landscape the only sign of the enemy might be their heads and, at 500 yards, that is difficult to spot. The ever-present mirages made it impossible.

19th Brigade (Denny) started at noon as ordered, and led by the Seaforths, headed out into the desert. Their enthusiasm, however, took them too far north and a large gap opened up between 19th and 35th Brigade. Norrie's 21st Brigade, the reserve, had stopped to eat when a mounted staff officer galloped up and invited the Brigade to close up to the 35th.

The attack now went in. The objective was a line of Turks who were busy digging. When they sighted the British they dropped their shovels and disappeared from sight. Soon thereafter, the advancing British infantry came under fire from two directions. The attackers were exposed on a flat, featureless plain, they had no artillery support and the only option was to sprint for the enemy. The Black Watch had just been shipped in from Marseilles and in their journey to this war had marched 22 miles from Al Gharbi the previous day. The Jocks doubled forward, as did the Jats. The Seaforths too, but they were all halted about 300 yards short of the objective when they reached the killing ground.

The slaughter was immense.

The Seaforth Highlanders lost twenty officers and 380 men, and of the 485 6th Jats who had gone into action, only 150 were unwounded. The Black Watch had losses of similar proportions. Nothing had been gained, other than temporary possession of a few square miles of useless morass.

The Turks took advantage of this situation by making an attempt to get right round the British right flank; they had a large body of mounted Arabs in support. To counter this, Denny committed his small reserve and called on Norrie's 21st Brigade for assistance. 41st Dogras and 9th Bhopals extended the British line to thwart the encircling movement and finally, but far too late, the British field artillery came into effective action, as did the

4-inch gun of HMS *Cranefly*. The effect was to halt the Turkish/Arab movement, and the Arabs turned tail and fled the scene. The Turkish infantry dug in about 400 yards from the hastily established British line and did not threaten further. They probably did not need to do so because aerial reconnaissance revealed that a new, large, mixed force of Turks and Arabs was massing out to the British right. The situation was temporarily stable, but there was no doubt as to the danger to the British right on the left bank.

Kemball's 28th Brigade had enjoyed some success on the right bank. By 1600 hrs he had carried the forward Turkish positions, and the Indian soldiers of 92nd Punjabis, 51st and 53rd Sikhs had performed with great dash and commitment. On the far left of his attack, the 2nd Battalion, the Leicestershire Regiment, excelled; but at day's end, sixteen officers and 298 men did not answer to their names. '28th Brigade suffered more than 1,000 casualties in the day's fighting. Six hundred prisoners were taken and more than 350 Turkish bodies were buried.'[208] Given the circumstances and the extreme fatigue of the men, the burial of enemy dead seems to be a laudable but unnecessary gesture.

Night fell, it got very much colder and, of course, it rained. Life for the Tommies and sepoys was grim and there was even the possibility of a painful death tomorrow.

The next morning was as hot as expected, with great mirage activity. The British dug to improve their trenches and received sporadic small-arms fire. At about the time any civilised gentlemen would be thinking about a cup of coffee, Kemball signaled Aylmer and said the Turks were withdrawing. Aylmer received the news with caution as he estimated that he faced 7,500 enemy on the left bank and 4,500 on the right bank.

While the generals were busying themselves planning the next move, water and food were brought forward. The walking wounded had struggled down to the riverbank, where a Red Cross flag hung limply. The hope was that there, at the very least, they would be tended by skilled doctors and crisp, sympathetic nurses. A hot meal and change of clothes would be wonderful. That was all but a pipedream.

The post-battle situation at Ctesiphon had been awful and a disgrace – this was worse, much worse.

7th Division had five field ambulances; unfortunately, they were still aboard ships heading for Basra, so only three doctors were available to deal with the 250 casualties anticipated by Nixon/Aylmer and their staff. The reality was that there were about 3,000 men in need of urgent treatment. The medical staff were overwhelmed. Only the most serious cases could have attention – and those likely to die were left to do just that. The wounded lay, under the sun, in rows:

> Pathetic bundles of humanity lay on the riverbank clutching at the feet of anyone who walked past imploring, 'Sahib, Sahib, the blood will not stop … a blanket Sahib … water …' in the manner of the beggars who roamed Bombay and Calcutta. As they waited for treatment their wounds became septic, gangrene set in and many died even before they could be carried to the boats that were to evacuate them, downstream, to the already congested hospital at Amara.
>
> Eleven days after the battle, a field ambulance hospital unit from Meerut on its way to the front found nearly 200 British and 800 Indians still lying on the muddy ground behind Sheikh Saad. Only a few had the first field dressing, applied on the battlefield, changed. Over 100 were suffering from dysentery: there were no proper sanitary arrangements and those unable to walk lay in their ordure, past caring and without hope. Sacks of food had been dumped in the open for their sustenance, but much of which was perishable had been ruined by rain; what was edible was hardly enough to go round. As there were only one or two cooks, and only few of the miserable casualties could help themselves, its [the food] availability was of little consequence.[209]

Aylmer decided that with the balance of his battered force his next attack would be at night. He brought forward those units that had not been overly exposed and Denny's brigade was to lead the march. As they set off, a strong cold wind, accompanied by heavy rain, kept them company. The night march was a shambles. The guides lost their way and after hours spent trudging through clinging mud, 21st Brigade arrived at the location of 35th Brigade. The men were exhausted, cold and wet. As it happens, all the effort was unnecessary as the Turks were withdrawing. On the morning of the 9th it was discovered that the Turks had moved about 10 miles upriver to a position near the Ora ruins on the left bank of the Tigris and behind the modest Wadi River.

Sheikh Saad was occupied – for what it was worth.

This Turkish withdrawal, ordered by Nureddin, cost him his job; he was summarily sacked by von der Goltz and was unexpectedly replaced by his aggressive second-in-command, Khalil Pasha. This incident illustrated the relationship of the senior Turkish officers with von der Goltz. He was firmly in command and the campaign was to be fought on his terms.

The river was mined at Sheikh Saad, but the weapon was dismissed as 'a somewhat amateur home-made type, which the enemy had used before

Kurnah'[210] the previous year. The so-called Battle of Sheikh Saad had been one of attrition. Command and control was weak, the tactics lacked any form of subtlety, the fighting was ferocious and it was a portent of things to come. At this point, enemy losses during the three days of the operation, including prisoners, was estimated at about 4,500.

The downside was that British losses were 4,007, and it can be assumed that up to 1,000 of these were killed. 'The results of the premature advance with a hastily collected force were becoming very evident. As regiments arrived in the country they were being hurried to the front, thrown into brigades often not their own, to find themselves within a short while in action with lack of guns, munitions etc., while the Turks had command of the air.'[211]

It was Nixon's extraordinary decision that, as units arrived at Basra, the fighting men were dispatched to the front, and their equipment followed by their 'first-line' transport. The third priority was medical provision, ambulances, medical staff and their specialist equipment. 'Second-line' transport carried the soldiers' blankets, tents and camp essentials. This second line was the lowest priority and, in practical terms, this meant that in the face of severe weather conditions, the men spent several weeks without anything as basic as a blanket. An old soldier's first rule is, 'never get separated from your bed roll'. In this case, old soldiers or not, they were all widely separated and for far too long.

The very first duty of a British officer is the well-being of his soldiers, and that is a priority that overrides all else. Nixon, and the Staff he directed, had clearly forgotten that, and emphatically did not do their duty. As a result of this dereliction, the men (and their officers) endured miserable life-threatening conditions, even before they went into action. Once again, the medical arrangements were utterly unacceptable.

This had been an inauspicious start in the quest to relieve Kut, and Captain Wilfred Nunn RN, a sailor fully engaged in these actions, was able to watch a debacle unfold and engulf his soldier comrades. Although the reader may find this litany repetitive, even depressing, Nunn deserves to be quoted in full. At page 204 of his book, he wrote:

> The units of 3rd and 7th divisions had arrived at Basra in no regular order. When they left France it had been understood that they would be reorganised in Egypt – which they certainly were not. They had merely been packed into steamers as steamers became available. Some units were incomplete. There was a lack of staff officers, as some of the Staff had not come with the troops from France while others had not yet arrived. The

deficiencies had to be filled by any officers available on the spot and from India. In addition, many of the units had been trained on different lines.

The inadequate river transport resulted in units going upriver at odd times, sometimes without their full equipment. Then, again, land transport at the front was lacking: the Supply and Transport Corps [Army Service Corps] were under their establishment [planned strength]. High explosive shell was scanty; aeroplanes were far too few to allow regular artillery observation; there were, for a long time, no proper anti-aircraft guns; while many of the guns and howitzers were of old patterns and the telephone equipment was both ancient and inadequate.

The force was short of sappers and miners; the bridging train material was inefficient. Medical personnel and equipment was short and sadly restricted. The generals represented these matters most strongly in the right quarters but felt bound to expedite the advance, relieve Townshend without delay and take the risks involved.

It was little wonder that morale was low. It was lowered further when an anonymous jobsworth decreed that the special allowance paid to Indian soldiers in France and hitherto drawn by the Indians of 3rd and 7th divisions should be discontinued on the irrefutable basis that Mesopotamia was not France.

The single trigger of the precipitate, ill-considered action by the Tigris Corps and the loss of 4,000 men so far, was Charles Townshend's inaccurate estimate of his food stocks. Early on in December he had ruthlessly played the starvation card, and in so doing manipulated Aylmer and induced him to proceed in undue haste. Townshend's estimates of his survivability were made in December. On 5 December, he estimated fifty-five days, on the 7th he raised it to sixty days and said he could hold out until early February. On 16 January, he endorsed his earlier estimate and said he had twenty-one days' worth of rations left for British troops, seventeen for Indians. This confirms that he would run out of food on or about 7 February. The actuality was that the siege lasted until 29 April – 147 days, and well over twice Townshend's estimate. The MC Report remarked:

It is strange that neither General Nixon nor General Aylmer seem to have thought of asking General Townshend how long his supplies would hold out; nor did General Townshend himself definitely ascertain this most important fact till several weeks after he was shut up in Kut. No doubt he had received positive assurances that he would be relieved within two months at the outside, and as he was satisfied that his supplies would easily last for that period he did not attach as much importance to the food factor as he ought to have done. However, this may be, telegrams from General Aylmer on 25 January and General Lake on 29th indicate the neglect of General Townshend to intimate his true position as regards supplies was one of the main factors in the hurried advance.[212]

The reference to *'one of the main factors'* is inaccurate. It was indisputably *the* main factor. However, when the MC took evidence, Townshend was comfortably housed as an honoured guest of the Turkish Government and so he was unavailable to explain himself.

The new Turkish defences behind the Wadi River were 3 miles in front of the Hanna Defile – that easily defended narrow piece of ground between the Tigris and the Suwaikiya Marsh. The Wadi operation was carried out from 12 to 14 January 1916 (see map on page 156). The British would be advancing over the same ground that Townshend had taken back in September 1915, but now facing a much more formidable foe; one that was certainly not going to allow a repeat of previous British tactics. This engagement was fought in extreme conditions of cold, rain, mud and poor visibility.

This second engagement is justifiably described as the Battle of the River Wadi. Success at the Wadi depended upon the British being able to outflank the Turkish left on the left bank (as always, looking downstream) but the Suwaikiya Marsh was a major feature, quite impassable and a factor to be carefully considered (see map on page 156). Aylmer had massive naval superiority and his gunboats were expected to inflict damage on enemy positions in the Hanna Defile.

The Turks, having withdrawn from Sheikh Saad, had established themselves behind the high-banked but shallow Wadi River, which flowed into the left bank of the Tigris. It was a modest obstacle for infantry and pack animals but of significance to wheeled vehicles, and in particular, the guns. The Turkish position was alongside the river and provided an obstacle to the British on their route, via the Hanna Defile, to Kut.

The weather was a negative factor and Aylmer's soldiers had to cope with the worsening conditions. Nixon's attitude was a further factor. This was not a man with flair, imagination or tactical awareness. He held the enemy in low regard and believed that the courage and training of the Indian Army were sufficient to ensure success. He was hopelessly out of date, logistically illiterate, and the stern lessons learnt on the Western Front were lost on him. His replacements from France well knew the folly of charging into the maws of machine guns, and readily dug in when an advance was suicidal. To Nixon, this was a manifestation of being what he termed 'trench-minded',

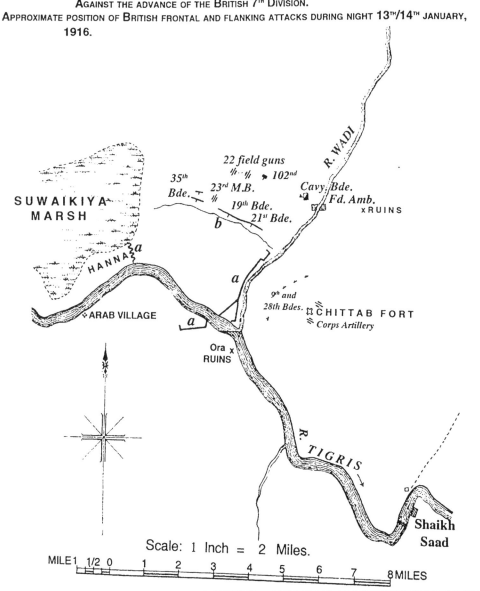

MAP
TO ILLUSTRATE THE ACTION OF THE WADI.

a = Turkish positions according to British information at 10 p.m. 12ᵗʰ January, 1916.

b = Approximate line of hastily entrenched watercuts held by Turks on 13ᵗʰ January, 1916, against the advance of the British 7ᵗʰ Division.

Approximate position of British frontal and flanking attacks during night 13ᵗʰ/14ᵗʰ January, 1916.

SUWAIKIYA MARSH

HANNA

ARAB VILLAGE

R. WADI

22 field guns

35ᵗʰ Bde.

23ʳᵈ M.B.

19ᵗʰ Bde.

21ˢᵗ Bde.

102ⁿᵈ

Cavy. Bde.

Fd. Amb.

x RUINS

9ᵗʰ and 28th Bdes.

CHITTAB FORT

Corps Artillery

Ora x RUINS

R. TIGRIS

Shaikh Saad

Scale: 1 Inch = 2 Miles.

MILE 1 1/2 0   1   2   3   4   5   6   7   8 MILES

53. The Battle of the River Wadi.
(Map was prepared for the Historical Section of the Committee for Imperial Defence and Ordnance Survey, 1924)

156

the implication being that the troops lacked an offensive spirit. Unfortunately, Nixon was firmly in command and his writ still had time to run.

Younghusband realised that, if he crossed the Wadi, he had an opportunity and the space to outflank the Turkish line and seize the Hanna Defile. Accordingly, he based his plan on that premise but, unfortunately, there were several deficiencies. The first of these was the unavailability of accurate maps and, this being the case, he had no idea what hazards or features his troops would face. Secondly, Younghusband had insufficient men to effect his plan to envelop the position, and thirdly, there was to be that aforementioned difficulty of getting wheeled vehicles across the Wadi.

Kemball and his 28th Brigade were deputed to make a frontal attack and, by so doing, hold the Turks in position. 19th, 21st and 35th brigades were to be the encircling force. The Cavalry Brigade was to 'operate' beyond the infantry brigades in open country, but it was not given an objective and, without an aim, the Brigade contributed nothing to the battle. This was another of Younghusband's errors.

Reconnaissance on 12 January yielded little in the way of firm intelligence on the lay of the land, which spread like beige carpet to the horizon. Old watercourses, canals and natural folds in the landscape were not obvious. What was obvious was that these modest features, wherever they were, could be exploited and would assume disproportionate value. They say that 'In the land of the blind, the one-eyed man is king', so in this flat, apparently featureless land, the concealed soldier was king.

Under cover of darkness, the three infantry brigades, led by the 35th, moved up to the line of the Wadi as part of the plan to extend the British right flank. There were 1,000 yards between the formations, which moved in columns. The approach to the 'start point' took most of the night and, when dawn broke, visibility was severely limited by mist. This was better than a smokescreen, but Younghusband did not take advantage and actually delayed his operation until the mist had cleared.

It was another serious error of judgement.

It was 0900 hrs before the cavalry splashed through the shallow water of the Wadi and climbed the steep opposite bank. 21st Brigade followed, but it was only now that the difficulty of getting wheeled vehicles across the river was appreciated. Ramps had to be constructed on both banks and these were dug by hand, from the unpromising local material. Delay was inevitable.

The need to get the artillery across the Wadi has been questioned by earlier historians, and the sketch map on page 156 shows why. Younghusband might well have sited his guns on the left bank of the Tigris

River and short of the Wadi River with no significant increase in range, with minimal effort, and the attack could have been made earlier. As it was, Younghusband made his third poor decision of the day and, as a result, it was past noon before the gunners were able to join the infantry.

Meanwhile, Norrie's 21st Brigade had set its sights on the Hanna Defile and headed in that direction, led by 1st/9th Gurkhas. At about 1100 hrs, while ramps were still being constructed behind them, the Gurkhas came under artillery and then small-arms fire. They halted and dug in about 200 yards short of what appeared to be the main Turkish position. The remainder of the Brigade and the 19th coming up behind changed direction and moved over to the right. The outflanking movement was still viable if the impetus was maintained. It was not.

21st and 19th brigades were in position to assault the enemy but then Younghusband made his fourth error – and it was still only early afternoon. He ordered both brigades to stand fast until the artillery was ready to provide support. The pause gave the Turkish commander time to reorder his defences and prepare for the attack.

Eventually, and when Younghusband had all of his force deployed to his liking, the two brigades advanced into a veritable torrent of fire and another expensive attritional battle ensued. Some Turks were seen to be withdrawing, and the conclusion was drawn that now was the time to commit 35th Brigade to sweep in from the far right and catch the enemy between the 35th and 28th brigades.

It came as an unwelcome shock when, as 35th Brigade moved in, it came under heavy fire from an unsuspected Turkish position. The assault was checked but, by late afternoon, 35th and 19th brigades had linked up.

There were countless acts of extreme bravery during this engagement, many of which went unnoticed and unrewarded. Sepoy Chatta Singh, of the 9th Bhopal Infantry, was the epitome of soldierly conduct. *The London Gazette* recorded in a citation that his award of the Victoria Cross was:

> for the most conspicuous bravery and devotion to duty in leaving cover to assist his Commanding Officer who was lying wounded and helpless in the open. Sepoy Chatta Singh bound up the officer's wounds and then dug cover for him with his entrenching tool, being exposed all the time to very heavy rifle fire. For five hours, until nightfall, he remained beside the wounded officer shielding him with his own body on the exposed side. He then, under cover of darkness, went back for assistance and brought the officer into safety.[213]

54. A representation of Sepoy Chatta Singh winning his Victoria Cross.
(Internet source)

The Turks were proactive and, in the face of the move to encircle them, they pushed their left flank deeper into the desert towards the Suwaikiya Marsh. By unhappy chance, they found an old irrigation channel that provided a readymade defensive position. The British cavalry brigade, who could and should have influenced affairs, did nothing and its members were little more than interested spectators.

Nightfall brought the fighting to a close, and what should have been a decisive victory turned out to have been an unsatisfactory and expensive day for the 7th Division. It had suffered 1,600 casualties, of whom 218 were killed. 28th Brigade had accepted a disproportionate share of the casualties. Initially, its role was to hold the Turks in place but, later in the day, it was committed to a frontal assault over open ground. The apparently flat terrain concealed not only a larger force than anticipated but also one particularly well placed, lining the steep bank of the Wadi. Just in front of the Wadi and parallel to it, was a dry watercourse. When men of the 28th Brigade reached this obstacle it slowed the assault, confused the attackers and they were easy pickings for the Turks concealed along the riverbank.

During the night, von der Goltz withdrew his force to the formidable Hanna Defile and, on the 16th, allegedly visited the Turkish positions in front of Kut. His party was observed and a gunner officer called down fire on the party. The first and, as it happens, only round was well directed, but Townshend recorded:

> I was very annoyed with the officer who ordered the gun to be trained on the Field Marshal and fired without my orders for I had great respect for the man whom I considered to be the leading strategist in Europe; I ordered the fire to cease at once.

This episode is beset by a series of different accounts. Major General G.O. de R. Channer, who was present, said that multiple guns opened fire. Braddon asserts, on the evidence of Captain H.S.D. MacNeal, that von der Goltz was not actually present and the target was Khalil. The significance of the incident is Townshend's reaction to it. He compared his chivalrous gesture to ceasefire with that at Torres Vedras. There, a warning shot was fired to warn off Massena, who was reconnoitring the British position. The reality is that to spare the life of the man dedicated to the killing or capture of Townshend and all his soldiers is absurd, and in sharp contrast to a further incident that followed several days later.

Lance Corporal John Boggis recalled that he was with the GOC on his rooftop observation platform, and both were peering through slits in the steel plates that offered some protection from small-arms fire. They looked out over the Turkish lines, which by now ringed Kut with about 30 miles of trenches. In the distance, a solitary Turkish soldier was at the river drawing water.

'Boggis,' called Townshend.

'Sir,' replied his orderly.

'Rifles! See that man over there?' The General pointed out the distant figure. 'We'll have a go at him.'

Both men seized weapons and squinted over their sights. Townshend, with a borrowed and un-zeroed weapon, fired first. The man dropped, and his can, of no further use to him in this life, leaked its contents into the desert sand.

'Mine,' exclaimed Townshend exultantly, and Boggis was disinclined to argue in the face of the evidence. Boggis recorded that the General was a good shot and as he left the rooftop he was in high spirits and singing a music hall hit of the day: 'When I was single my pockets would jingle. I long to be single again.'[214]

Townshend was to make it a continuing practice to snipe at Turks squatting by the river, with remarkable success, but not with the unanimous admiration of his officers. One commented to the other members of his mess that it was 'very unsporting – shooting sitting Turks'.

The lives of everyone involved in this campaign were dominated by one thing, and that was the ubiquitous Tigris River. It was the means of movement to battle and the means of evacuation of the wounded; it provided water to drink and was life-giving. It provided water in which to shave and so was an aid to strong morale. For those incarcerated in Kut, its dark brown waters were a protection, but when they rose they were a menace. It was a possible escape route, but it was also a barrier to freedom. It was variously too shallow, too sinuous, too fast-flowing. It presented opportunities and threats. It was never neutral and always a factor in military planning. For the Arabs and Turks it provided a route into Kut for spies, and was their convenient sewer. Accordingly, it posed a health risk to all, and especially to those on the bank and in Townshend's sights.

It was a nightly occurrence for Arabs to slip into the water, buoyed by an inflated goatskin, in an attempt to get to the Turkish lines. A few deserters tried the same tactic. On their arrival the welcome was not just warm; it was red hot. Most arrivals were shot out of hand; any surviving sepoys were issued with black uniforms that served to identify them. Few made old bones.

In Kut, lice had taken their place alongside the bloody flies as objects of unbridled hate. They were the product of dirty clothes on dirty flesh. They were the heralds of disease and death for many.

A tentative probe of the Hanna line showed that the Turks were as obdurate as ever and that the path to Kut would have to be forced. In the besieged town, Townshend ordered a re-evaluation of his food stocks and on 16 January he signalled Aylmer that he had food enough for twenty-one days for British troops and seventeen for his Indians; he added that in addition, he had fodder for five days, tinned meat for three, meat on the hoof for seventeen and tea for eight. On this basis he could survive beyond his earlier 7/8 February deadline. Townshend's latest forecast should have reduced the debilitating urgency that so far had been at the centre of Aylmer's endeavours. However, Nixon, by now right at the end of his period in command, was determined that the Tigris Corps should press on regardless, and signalled to that effect.

Aylmer's Corps licked its wounds and regrouped. It found that burying the dead presented a challenge in the morass. Reconnaissance of this next daunting objective brought home to Aylmer the magnitude of his task and

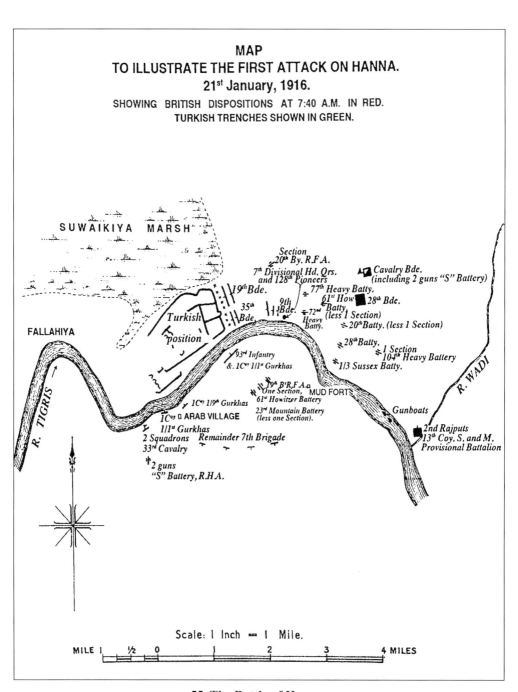

55. The Battle of Hanna.
(Prepared by the Historical Section of the Committee for Imperial Defence)

the impossibility of a successful operation on the left bank. On the night of 16/17 January, he telegraphed to Generals Nixon and Townshend as follows:

> The position of affairs must be frankly faced. The enemy is blocking the entrance of the Wadi–Nukhailat Defile with very strong works and, judging of his dispositions within them, they have been designed to resist a heavy bombardment from across the river as well as attack in front. His bivouac shelters seem to indicate that he may have with him the whole 52nd Division and two regiments of the 35th and 38th divisions, but of course I cannot be certain of this. Emplacements for nineteen guns have been seen, eleven of which are designed to fire across the river. Behind, in defile, there is a single line of entrenchments ... between marsh and river, probably 1½ miles long. Behind, again, is the Es Sinn position. It is impossible, in my opinion, to take the first position by a *coup de main* from this side alone without losing half the force. ... I do not think that our progress as an entire force can be anything but very slow.[215]

This is a very gloomy but probably reasonable judgment by Aylmer, given the experiences of the previous two weeks and the intelligence he had to hand. He held the view that the best way to proceed was for Townshend to break out, cross the river on to the right bank with the largest force he could muster and then march around the Turkish position at Es Sinn. Aylmer would then send one division across the river with an additional cavalry brigade to meet him.

That is not quite as easy as it sounds. Although Townshend had fifty *mahailas* besides other river craft available for the crossing, he would have to abandon his sick and wounded, and his artillery. Any river crossing would be contested and success was not assured.

Nixon put a stop to this outline plan immediately, saying, 'I do not in any way agree with your appreciation. ... The course you now propose for Townshend in your telegram would be disastrous from every point of view – to Townshend's force, to the whole of the forces in Mesopotamia and to the Empire, and I cannot sanction it.'[216] He went on at some length and provided his estimation of enemy forces at 5,000 between Aylmer and Kut. This, the latest and final of Nixon's estimations, was no more valid than any of those that had preceded it. However, it was to be his last.

We will return to Aylmer and his tribulations, but other significant aspects of this campaign were being enacted elsewhere.

* * *

163

Finally, on 19 January 1916, Nixon left India. The reason was the ill health that had affected him from early December. He was not sacked but had asked to be relieved. In a final message to Townshend he said that he had (as requested) recommended Charlie for command of the Tigris Corps and promotion to lieutenant general.

Both recommendations were most unlikely to come to fruition as promotion was dependent on the command of a corps and, given his domestic circumstances, Townshend was not available to command anything other than the garrison in Kut.

Duff appointed Lieutenant General Sir Percy Lake KCB KCMG, his 60-year-old chief of staff, to replace Nixon in command. Duff had only a small pool to pick from as the most talented of his generals had all been sent to France. Lake was probably the least bad choice, although Hardinge regarded him as 'an old woman'.

Duff had written to the Viceroy on 6 January 1916 on the subject of Nixon's replacement, and the following day Hardinge replied, saying that

56. Lieutenant General Sir Percy Lake KCB KCMG.

the appointment 'did not inspire me with any confidence' since, in his view, Lake was 'indecisive, easily biased and too old for active duty'.[217]

The Campaign in Mesopotamia, the *Official History*, in dealing with this very important change of command, said of Nixon's service:

> By his ability, determination and the confidence he inspired in his force – and after overcoming very great difficulties with limited means – General Nixon had achieved unbroken success during his first six months' operations in Mesopotamia. ... At the end of this period General Nixon had found himself with his advanced force well on the road to Baghdad and with only the broken remnant of a frequently defeated Turkish force to bar his further progress. He was aware that the capture of Baghdad was deemed to be politically desirable and it appeared to him that he would be to blame if he missed the opportunity, which circumstances appeared to offer him.
>
> He failed.
>
> On the one hand it has been said that his plan was based on political and military miscalculations and attempted with tired and insufficient forces and inadequate preparations. On the other hand there are those, who were on the spot and in a position to judge, who say that it was only through sheer bad fortune that he failed to achieve his object. War is not an exact science; no commander has ever achieved great military success without incurring risks and committing mistakes.[218]

That is a very generous summation of Nixon's performance, and the writer made every effort to be even-handed and to limit criticism of Nixon. In fact he attributed to Nixon a quality of generalship he clearly lacked, and this despite having had the benefit of the MC Report, published in 1917, and Townshend's memoir, published in 1920. Moreover, in implying that the neglect of Nixon's soldiers might have been the product of 'sheer bad fortune', F.J. Moberly damaged the authority of his otherwise excellent *The Campaign in Mesopotamia 1914–1918*, published in 1924.

* * *

The incompetent, culpable Nixon was being replaced by another general of doubtful quality, and it did not auger well for the fresh troops now arriving at Basra to face, first, the trillions of flies, second, the unbridled chaos of the inadequate port, and next, the rigours of soldiering in the ill-named 'Garden of Eden' in order to bring relief to the denizens of Kut.

On 8 January, the British evacuated the Dardanelles. By so doing, they released Turkish divisions for service in Mesopotamia, and there was credible intelligence that from two to five divisions would soon join the Kut theatre.

As the year turned so, in Simla, Hardinge and Duff were the recipients of unwelcome reports of a medical debacle in Mesopotamia. Duff did not at first respond, 'knowing from experience that in unsuccessful operations, carried out under difficult conditions, hardships must occur and that complaints were often unduly exaggerated.'[219]

On this basis Duff did nothing.

Aylmer's reasonable attempts to involve Townshend, to some degree, in assisting in his own (Townshend's) salvation, had been firmly squashed by Nixon, and that left the Corps Commander with very few other options. Townshend had estimated that only 4,000 men could be ferried across the Tigris in one night, twenty hours would be needed to get the guns over and seventy-five hours for the animals. In addition to these difficulties, the Turks were solidly ensconced behind their well-built defences in the Hanna Defile.

Although a breakout by the 6th Division or any part of it was a non-starter, nevertheless, in Kut a plan had been prepared and codenamed Project 'E'. A main body commanded by Townshend and composed of two weak brigades, each of 2,500 men, was to cross to the right bank and seek to cooperate with Aylmer's relieving force. Meanwhile, Kut was to be defended by about 4,000 – a number that included the sick and convalescents.

Previously, Townshend had declared his strength as being 12,400, so there is a discrepancy of about 3,000 men who are unaccounted for. This is of no practical consequence as Project 'E' was never activated, but it does cast doubt on the authenticity of the plan.

Nixon, sick man that he had been, nevertheless made major decisions without viewing the ground over which he expected his soldiers to fight. Aylmer had been defeated twice and his confidence had taken a frightful blow. He was only too aware that unsuccessful generals get the sack and knew that unless he was able to take the Hanna Defile and open the path to Kut, his career was facing oblivion. To add to Aylmer's difficulties, Sod's Law came into play. A boat bridge had been built across the Tigris and this would provide him with the means of switching his troops from bank to bank as required. Just after its construction was completed the bridge was struck by one of the steamers in gale force conditions. The component parts of the bridge that were not destroyed drifted off downstream. Repairs could be made, but the bitter cold and driving rain made it testing for the sappers who were called forward to assist.

The persistent bad weather was affecting not only the morale and efficiency of the troops, but also their health. The unremitting exposure to the elements was taking its toll before Hanna but in Kut as well, where men stood up to their waists in flooded trenches.

Townshend's senior doctor, Colonel P. Hehir, advised his commander that scurvy had broken out among his non-meat-eating Indian troops. Their gums exuded pus, their teeth had loosened in their sockets and their breath was foul.[220] Sick lists were growing daily.

There were still in Kut 3,000 horses and mules. They were being slaughtered routinely and the Christian element of the garrison lived on unpalatable but welcome horse stew. Townshend, despite protestations to the contrary, did not hold his Indian soldiers in much affection, but it was now clear that he had to address the matter of their diet. The perceived wisdom was that those Indian soldiers who ate horseflesh would be damned in their villages at war's end. No girl would take such a man as a husband and he would be unwelcome in the family home. In a phrase, it was social suicide to eat horseflesh; well, the reality was a little different.

If Townshend, an officer of the Indian Army, had been closer to his men, he would have known that Sikhs were not overly concerned over the issue, Gurkhas were entirely pragmatic and it was only the Muslims who were immoveable on the matter. Townshend asked Simla to obtain religious dispensation for his Sikhs, Dogras, Rajputs and Gurkhas. This was swiftly obtained, and just as Mellis and Delamain had been counselling for weeks, once given this dispensation and ordered on 21 January to eat horse, most of the soldiers readily complied. Only the most devout of the Muslims did not.

A German aeroplane made an appearance and, although unskilled, its capacity to drop small bombs added to the trials of the garrison.

Battle casualty replacements had to march up the long river line from Basra in the dreadful weather and were obliged to halt at Kurnah and Amara on the way. The weather, and in particular the strong winds, affected the river steamers. The ships, with their high profile, were unable to steer an accurate course up the winding river and their sailings were interrupted or postponed.

Aylmer, who was, by now, an older and wiser man, realised that he had to make better use of all his assets and determined to move some of his artillery across to the right bank in order to enfilade the Turks. The master plan was not sophisticated and, apart from a more comprehensive artillery programme, a frontal attack was all that the General could muster. The ground was firmly to the Turks' advantage. An attack from a flank was quite impossible. There was only one approach, so deception was not on the menu. The Turks had the river on their right and the now flooded marsh on their

57. Pack animals and soldiers make their way across the Mesopotamian 'desert'. Note the depth of mud. *(Henry Weaver)*

left. Their trench line was only about a mile wide but it was defended in considerable depth. The ground over which the British were to attack was already a muddy morass, and the proposed artillery bombardment would make the ground even more so.

It was going to be a tough nut to crack.

In order to spot for the guns, observation ladders or scaffolding were necessary. The slightest fold in the ground concealed everything behind it and in the forthcoming battle the artillery carried a great responsibility. Aylmer had forty-six guns and the firepower of the two gunboats *Cranefly* and *Dragonfly*. In total, Aylmer's available artillery bore no comparison with the support available to a division on the Western Front, where hundreds of guns, firing for several hours, would precede a divisional operation.

The intention was that, on 19 January, the Turkish line would be bombarded, from two directions, the wire destroyed and a frontal assault would sweep forward and take the enemy position. How simple is that? In the event, the weather was so appalling that the operation was delayed. The Turks kept on digging and they put the respite to good use.

British intentions were signalled to the enemy on the 20th when a brief artillery strike fell on the front line. This served to identify the British objective if anyone was at all in doubt. The following day the dose was to be repeated as a precursor to the infantry attack; nevertheless, this planned artillery programme was far too small to be effective.

On 21 January, the weakened 7th Division prepared for its test. The Division was only at brigade strength, and of the established strength of 9,000, only about 4,000 men were fit. In the face of the manpower deficiency 21st Brigade's battalions had been dispersed among the 19th and 35th brigades. This was an entirely logical measure but was not without its problems. These battalions were now working with complete strangers at every level. Younghusband deployed his two brigades, with 19th on the right and 35th on the left. He had planned his assault meticulously but much depended upon the efficacy of the preliminary bombardment by those forty-six guns.

There was a carefully calculated, timed programme: after the cessation of the bombardment and when a foothold had been made in the first line of Turkish trenches, 'bombers' were to move along the Turkish position clearing out survivors. In the plan, provision was made to deal with prisoners.

Townshend reported that he had seen about 3,000 Turks moving back towards Kut, complete with guns; this message was taken by Aylmer at face value. This was a serious error and Townshend's veracity, always doubtful, should not have been relied upon. The conclusion was incorrectly drawn that the preliminary bombardment, on 20 January, had been so effective as to cause Khalil/von der Goltz to withdraw. Aylmer's conclusion was strengthened when Turkish artillery did not reply. The assault planned for the 21st looked likely to be a walkover.

A mist that covered the defile delayed the dawn attack; this prevented the gunners registering their guns. This registration should have been unnecessary after the 'stonk' of the previous day. Nevertheless, Younghusband waited (again) for the mist to clear and this, of course, was much to the benefit of the Turks, who had clear line of sight of their attackers. The advantage that the mist had offered to the British infantry had been spurned and, when the guns finally came into action, any initiative had been surrendered. The bad news was that the Turkish wire was not destroyed.

The infantry was launched at the Turks across a muddy swamp. The pace of the assault was slowed by the conditions. The Black Watch, on the left, covered the first couple of hundred yards, but the Turks, far from sheltering from the British guns, were in a position to respond with small-arms fire. The kilted warriors started to take severe casualties. Together with some Jats, a small group of Scots got into the front line and did sterling work driving their opponents back to their second line. It did not last, and well-organised counter-attack retook the Turkish front line and saw the death of the occupying Scots and Jats.

Only two officers and fifteen men of the Black Watch survived this attack and a fine battalion of an outstanding regiment had been reduced to company strength. It was no longer a viable fighting unit. This repulse on the left of the British line was repeated right along the front. Over on the right, two battalions of Dogras, brave men that they were, got about twenty-five men into the Turkish front line.

There they all perished.

Communications between the Divisional Commander and his brigades broke down and Younghusband, who had established his headquarters about a mile behind the British line, was unaware of the disaster unfolding to his front. The telephone line was cut and the conditions underfoot made nonsense of the word 'runner', on whom all communications now depended. Any movement on this battlefield attracted fire and runners had a low life expectancy. The attacks of the 7th Division petered out in the deep mud of the Mesopotamian desert. Captain F.W. Page-Roberts was a witness to the aftermath, and wrote in a letter:

> Some of the wounded drowned; some died of cold; many were picked off by the watchful Turks; all suffered agonies. One of them shot through the leg lay all day in no-man's-land. As bullets began to splash around him, once the battle had stopped, he scooped a wall of mud around his head, and then around his shoulders, and then around his legs, until he lay in a sort of mud coffin, lacking only a lid. The water inside it getting deeper with the rain and redder with his blood.
>
> Most of that night he lay there too. He was found by two stretcher-bearers, who carried him for more than three hours – dropping him twice as they fell into holes, to the ambulance point. Here he was given rum and lay for another three hours in the rain. Then onto a cart, to be wheeled to the river, where, sardine-like, he was packed onto the open deck of a boat – which reached Basra six days later.[221]

The man whose dreadful experience is described above was actually and incredibly one of the fortunate ones. As night fell it became possible to try to bring in some of his comrades. Even the unwounded suffered in the extreme conditions, and according to contemporary accounts the night of

21 January 1916 exceeded in misery, horror and pain anything previously seen in this God benighted campaign. The medical staff strove manfully under an impossible burden; 2,700 men (of 4,000) needing medical aid, and the surviving 1,300 could not cope with the responsibility of caring for their comrades lying in deep mud out in the darkness. Gallant, willing soldiers who had given of their best went to their Maker in the ghastly wind-lashed night as wounded men, suffering from shock, died of exposure.

Medical arrangements that had failed at Ctesiphon, Kut, Sheikh Saad and the Wadi failed again, but this time it was, *'the most complete breakdown of all'* (MC Report). Tents had been erected in the casualty clearing centre in ankle-deep mud. Wounded, bleeding men, under the brutal light of hurricane lamps, were laid in this saturated tract as the two sections of five field ambulances gave of their inadequate best. HMS *Julnar* had been designated as a hospital ship and patients, if they were lucky, were carried in the infernal army transport carts to the riverbank and on to the ship. Many others spent the night in the rain and wind in an AT cart. This text has repeatedly reported on the grievous medical situation, and the fact that it has been repeated again here serves to underscore the crashing, ongoing incompetence of a command structure that betrayed those it directed.

After the event, not unreasonably, Aylmer criticised Younghusband for not following his quite specific instructions, which were to 'hold the enemy and not commit himself'. The latter admitted receiving the order and said in his defence that he advanced and 'felt the enemy hard on both banks.' So be it, but he had clear instructions. Later giving evidence to the MC, Aylmer said that he had *'fought the action on the Wadi against his better judgement, acting under superior orders and that he had proposed another plan of attack, which was not accepted by Headquarters.'*[222]

Aylmer had a direct and personal responsibility to ensure that his force was, in all respects, ready to fight an intractable foe. The unavailability of doctors, nurses and equipment must have been known to, in ascending order, Younghusband, Aylmer, Nixon and now Lake. All of these senior officers are culpable. Their men deserved very much better.

The torrential rain continued unabated and trenches filled with water. The Tigris broke its banks and both sides now focused on surviving the weather. The Turks, too, were cold, wet and thoroughly miserable. However, their wounded were spread across a smaller area and more easily recovered.

Aylmer decided to ask for a six-hour truce, not a suggestion to which the Turks readily agreed. Eventually, under a white flag, both sides made a start on burying the dead – very difficult in a flooded landscape – and collecting more of the wounded. At this point, on to the battlefield appeared 'Arabs' or perhaps Turkish soldiers. These people set to work killing the wounded and stripping the dead. It was monstrous behaviour, and white flag or not, British and Indian soldiers ran to help. Belatedly, Turkish officers intervened and the murder ceased. Barker, no great admirer of the Arab in any of his forms, concluded that these murdering jackals were in some way allied to the Turks, who were ashamed of the association (p. 177).

On the morning of 22 January, Aylmer signalled to his new commander, General Lake, and to Townshend that he had to cease his attack because of the parlous state of his troops and the atrocious weather. He commented on the added obstacle that the rapidly increasing floods presented. With this message the odds on a relief of Kut lengthened considerably.

Historians, among them A.J. Barker, have concluded from the comfort of an armchair that the Battle of the Hanna Defile should never have been fought. With 20/20 hindsight, it is evident that the 7th Division was on a hiding to nothing. Younghusband's leadership was consistently poor; he had still not factored in the quality of his opposition or the impregnability of its bunkers. The employment of his limited artillery was flawed and his inflexible approach gave the Turks advance warning of his intentions. The weather conditions were dire and, if anything, favoured the defence.

Colonel Barker was right.

The worsening situation in Mesopotamia, of which this debacle was the latest in a series, was kept under wraps by a comprehensive censoring process, and the letters that soldiers wrote home went through a fine censorship filter. The despatches of war correspondents were also very closely controlled and no criticism of either the political direction of the campaign or the military leadership was permitted. The means of communication were severely limited, and they too were under government control. The official position was that all was well; only the blandest reports were permitted to leave the country. This thoroughly unhealthy and dishonest official attitude gave blanket protection to those who were failing miserably in their duty.

However, in Kut, Townshend had control of the telegraph system and used it fully for his personal use. He sent copious messages to his many theatrical friends and to his family. To his discredit, he prevented any of his soldiers using the same facility, and one signalman who did seek to reach his family had his message intercepted by a ship of the Royal Navy, at sea. He was reported to Townshend and referred for trial by court martial – the outcome of that is unknown.

Political correctness was not invented in the twenty-first century, because it was alive and well in Mesopotamia in 1915–16. The expression 'friendly

58. The GOC and staff officers of the besieged 6 Indian Division. Captain Clifton ADC, Major E.E. Forbes DAD Transport, Colonel Annesley ADS & T, Colonel U.W. Evens GSO 1, Colonel P. Hehir ADMS, General Townshend (Braddon). This is a rare image of Colonel Hehir, perhaps the only senior medic to emerge from Mesopotamia with his professional skills recognised.

Arab' was proscribed[223] on the basis that it inferred that there were unfriendly Arabs – of whom there were a multitude. All manner of euphemisms were employed to describe these people, such as 'marauder in Turkish pay' and 'Kurds and others'. The myth was propagated that food was plentiful, morale very high, the health of the troops could not be better, and 'Medical problem? What medical problem?' In the years since and in the countless campaigns that have been fought over the last hundred years, nothing much has changed – today the 'spin' is more sophisticated but no less dishonest.

On 26 January, in besieged Kut, Townshend was aware of the failure at the Hanna Defile and he issued a communiqué to his troops. The style is unmistakably Charlie. He addressed his remarks to his soldiers and said:

The relief force under General Aylmer has been unsuccessful in its efforts to dislodge the Turks on the left bank of the river, some 14 miles below the position of Es Sinn, where we defeated the Turks in September last, when their strength was greater than it is now. Our relieving force suffered severe loss and had very bad weather to contend against. They are entrenched close to the Turkish position. More reinforcements are on their way upriver, and I confidently expect to be relieved during the first half of the month of February.

I desire all ranks to know why I decided to stand at Kut during our retirement from Ctesiphon. It was, because so long as we hold Kut the Turks cannot get their ships, barges, stores and munitions past this place and so cannot move down to attack Amarah. Thus we are holding up the whole Turkish advance. It also gives time for our reinforcements to come upriver from Basra and so restore success to our arms; it gives time to our allies, the Russians, who are overrunning Persia, to move towards Baghdad. I had a personal message from General Baratoff, commanding the Russian Expeditionary Force in Persia, the other day telling me of his admiration of what you men of the 6th Division and troops attached have done in the past two months and telling me of his own progress on the road from Kirmanshah, to Baghdad.

By standing at Kut I maintain the territory we have won in the past year at the expense of much blood, commencing with your glorious victory at Shaiba, and thus we maintain the campaign as a glorious one instead of letting disaster pursue its course down to Amarah and perhaps beyond.

I have ample food for eighty-four days and that is not counting the 3,000 animals, which can be eaten. When I defended Chitral some twenty years ago, we lived well on atta[224] and horseflesh, but I repeat, I expect confidently to be relieved in the first half of the month of February.

Our duty stands out plain and simple. It is our duty to our Empire, to our beloved King and Country, to stand here and hold up the Turkish advance as we are doing now, and with the help of all, heart and soul with me together, we will make this defence to be remembered in history as a glorious one. All England and India are watching us now and are proud of the splendid courage and devotion you have shown. Let us all remember the defence of Plevna, for that is what is in my mind.

I am absolutely calm and confident as to the result. The Turk, although good behind a trench, is of little value in the attack. They have tried it once, and their losses in one night in their attempt on the fort were 2,000 alone. They have also had very heavy losses from General Aylmer's musketry and guns, and I have no doubt that they have had enough.

I want to tell you now, that when I was ordered to advance on Ctesiphon, I officially demanded an army corps, or two divisions, to perform the task successfully. Having pointed out the grave danger of doing

174

this with one division only, I had done my duty. You know the result and whether I was right or not; your names will go down to history as the heroes of Ctesiphon, for heroes you proved yourself in that battle.

Perhaps by right I should not have told you of the above, but I feel I owe it to all of you to speak straightly and openly and to take you into my confidence. God knows I felt our heavy losses, and the suffering of my poor brave wounded, and I will remember it as long as I live. I may truly say that no general I know of has been more loyally obeyed and served than I have been in command of the 6th Division.

These words are long, I am afraid, but I speak straight from the heart, and you see I have thrown all officialdom overboard. We will succeed; mark my words. Save your ammunition as if it is gold.

This lengthy document did no more than express Townshend's aspirations. His first sentence was a not very subtle comparison of his stunning victory at Es Sinn and Aylmer's failure against a weaker enemy in the same place.

The reality was that he held his Indian soldiers in ill-disguised contempt. He made very few visits to his wounded, languishing in hospital, and then only to the British soldiers. The tenor of his remarks is inappropriate for a general officer. That said, Townshend did enjoy the affection of his soldiers. He was an extrovert, positive personality and he was pushing on an open door because a soldier *wants* to like and respect his senior officers. It is the 'factory setting', in computer terms. However, the closer one served to Charles Townshend, the less effective were the rose-tinted spectacles and the more one was likely to be critical of him.

General Sir Percy Lake, in his previous appointment in India, as Chief of the General Staff, had been privy to all the countless signals that had flowed between Basra and Simla and, not unreasonably, thought that he had a handle on matters in Mesopotamia. Little did he know of Nixon's long-term manipulation of the facts and the depth of his deceit. Nevertheless, in that earlier appointment, Lake had wide-ranging responsibility for the conduct of the campaign and the logistic support, or lack of it. He cannot be excused for his failure to identify all the problems and resolve them.

By any yardstick, and although duped by Nixon, he had failed.

However, it was only on his arrival in mid-January 1916 that he quickly discovered just how bad the situation was and the extent to which Nixon had misled him. He was appalled by what he found. Lake made a start on sorting out the mess, but this was not going to be a quick fix and he was not the man best equipped to tackle the deep-rooted issues. Although Nixon had left Lake a dreadful legacy, Hardinge still, surprisingly, gave his unqualified approbation to the erstwhile commander-in-chief.

Major General M. Cowper CB CIE, the officer responsible for 'in-theatre' logistics, warned Simla that the paddle steamers that were now being provided were unsuitable for use on the Tigris, and the square-ended barges that were arriving did not meet the specification and were also unsuitable. Cowper drew the conclusion that these were factors that would adversely affect attempts to relieve Kut. General Duff reacted very badly and wrote back to Lake, saying:

> Please warn General Cowper that if anything of this sort again occurs or if I receive any more querulous or petulant demands for shipping, I shall at once remove him from the force and will refuse him further employment of any kind.[225]

Cowper's duty was to raise these issues and although his precise form of words is unknown, he did not deserve such an unvarnished threat in response. This shows Duff up to be a foolish bully and is probably indicative of his attitude to the whole campaign. Duff's anger washed off on Lake, who, of course, he had only just selected. Duff was Lake's superior, but the two would have had a long professional and social relationship.

Lieutenant General Sir Percy Lake KCB KCMG was sixty years of age and his appointment was intended to be temporary until a War Office nominee could take up the job. He was very closely acquainted with all the senior officers serving in the theatre. For example, he knew Townshend very well and, in 1913, he had had to rebuke him for stepping over the line (again) when Charlie was commanding a brigade. Lake had supported the appointments of Barrett, Nixon, Townshend, Aylmer and Younghusband. Inevitably he had a personal relationship with all of these officers and it is the nature of an army that he would have felt a sense of comradeship towards them all. Aylmer, for example, had only months previously been Adjutant General of the Indian Army, and his office had been in close proximity to that of Lake.

The new Army Commander boarded a steamer on 24 January, and journeyed upriver to consult with Aylmer and to see for himself the conditions facing his front-line soldiers. He left behind an abject shambles in Basra and found a different shambles above the Wadi River when he arrived on 27 January. The medical debacle of the week before had still not been fully resolved, the wounded had not been cleared, nor had all the dead been buried.

Lake now commanded about 63,000 men – a vast force, of which 15,000 were British and the balance Indian. However, of his 63,000, no less than

59. An illustration of how barges were used to increase the capacity of river steamers. *(IWM)*

8,000 were hospital cases and a further 15,000 were in some way unable to take their place in the line. His effective strength was of the order of 40,000 and so, numerically at least, he was about as strong as von der Goltz.

Aylmer could only muster 14,000 at best, although 11,000 reinforcements were en route, weather permitting. As recently as 20 January, intelligence sources advised that 36,000 Turks had left the Dardanelles to confront the British. It became clear that Lake's priority remained the relief of Kut. He had the opportunity to take command in the field himself but, after some blunt discussions, Lake returned to Basra on 29 January, leaving operations in the unsteady hands of Aylmer. Lake's insurance policy was in the shape of Lieutenant General Sir George Gorringe, whom he appointed as Aylmer's chief of staff. Gorringe, at forty-seven, was a generation younger than Lake or Nixon, and noted for his ruthlessness.

Lake returned to the chaos of Basra. The Indian Government, recognising that all was not well, had overreacted to Lake's initial request for three months' reserve of 'materiel' in all its varied forms. Ships hurried to Basra and there they lay at anchor for weeks waiting to be unloaded as there were still no wharfing facilities. Utter disorganisation was the order of the day. The dearth of trained and specialist staff officers added to the problem and poor Lake had, unknowingly, exacerbated existing problems.

Aylmer regrouped, was reinforced, considered his options and worked to maintain his corps in the bleak desert. The month of February 1916 saw no further serious fighting, but in Kut the privations of the siege were manifest. Edward Mousley was one of many whose health was starting to fail. He recorded in his diary that:

> The horse rations have fallen way to very little; we give them pieces of palm tree to gnaw on. The rheumatism is much worse. It is bleak and cold in the observation post. One can only psychologise viciously on the point of view between a full man and an empty one. Eating maketh a satisfied man, drinking, a merry man, smoking, a contented man. But eating, drinking and smoking maketh a happy man.
>
> It is not far from the truth to say I have today none of these. For by *eating* one cannot mean a slice of chaff bread, nor by *drinking* a water-coloured liquid like our siege tea, nor yet by *smoking* a collection of strange dried twigs and dust. Man, it has been most excellently observed, cannot live by bread alone. How much less, then, can he live on half chaff and half flour? [Mousley's italics.][226]

In the early spring of March 1916, it finally became clear to the myopic IG that things had gone very badly wrong in Mesopotamia and a day of reckoning was not too far distant. General Duff recognised that it was time to try, at this very late stage, to ameliorate at least some of the damage. In London, disquiet over the management of the campaign in Mesopotamia had come to a head. Kitchener, the Minister for War, and Lieutenant General Sir 'Wully' Robertson, Chief of the Imperial General Staff, agreed that enough was enough. The War Committee called for a comprehensive evaluation of the situation and the upshot was that, with immediate effect, the Imperial General Staff in London would assume responsibility for operations in Mesopotamia.

This was a hugely important, completely correct decision – because it prised the hands of Hardinge and Duff off the levers of military power. If it was perceived to be a severe, if veiled, administrative rebuke, that is because it was.

It was the closing days of the tenure of Charles Hardinge as Viceroy, but urged by Chamberlain in early December 1915, he had caused Duff to initiate an inquiry to report on the medical arrangements in the theatre of his concern. The first attempt at an investigation, in January 1916, had gone off at half cock and failed miserably. Later, and when all the chickens had come home to roost, Hardinge sought to give the impression that the abortive mission was quite independent of any advice, instruction or action from London.[227]

The two worthies selected to look into the matter were Lord Chelmsford and Surgeon General MacNeese (soon to replace Babtie). Chelmsford had already been named as the successor to Hardinge and so he did not appear. MacNeese, a weak personality, was 'got around'[228] by Nixon and consequently produced a report so unsatisfactory that it was scrapped.

By now, news was filtering back to Britain, and even the King and Queen let it be known that they were disturbed by what they had heard.[229] Austen Chamberlain, Secretary of State for India, was fully aware that things were going seriously wrong. Despite that, General Sir Beauchamp Duff was decorated with the Grand Cross of the Star of India (GCSI) in March. This can only have been with the agreement of Hardinge and Chamberlain, and possibly with the acquiescence of the King Emperor, in whose name the award was made. Lord Curzon wrote privately to Chamberlain expressing his disgust, saying of the decoration, 'What for the Lord only knows – hardly for Mesopotamia.'[230]

Meanwhile, valuable time had been lost. In March 1916, a new commission was formed and Sir William Vincent, a senior Indian civil official, and Major General A.H. Bingley, two of the members of this commission, began their duties. They were subsequently joined at Basra by the third member, Mr E.A. Ridsdale, a Red Cross Commissioner.

This group became known as the 'Vincent-Bingley Commission'. The report of this commission was swiftly compiled and was signed on 29 June 1916. It was not published, but was utterly damning, and dismayed Duff and the acolytes around him.

The three members of the Commission did not pull any punches and, having visited Mesopotamia, they had taken evidence first-hand from participants on all sides of the medical scandal. They named those whom they judged to have failed in their duty, and if Duff had ever thought that Vincent-Bingley would ease the pressure, he got that very, very wrong. The Report threw graphic, specific, fresh fuel upon the fire and inflamed the opinion of those who read of the grotesque deficiencies of the medical service in Mesopotamia.

Duff, faced with that uncompromising and bleak report, then complained bitterly about the very enquiry he had instigated. Much later, when giving evidence himself to the MC, he claimed weakly and unconvincingly that Vincent-Bingley had exceed its brief and delved into matters not of its concern. It was too late for Duff; he had shot himself in the foot – well, both feet, actually.

A flavour of Vincent-Bingley is this extract from its Report:

The absence of any river steamers equipped for the transport of sick and wounded, and of any separate medical establishment for such vessels ... has had more prejudicial results than almost any other defects in the organisation. It has constantly delayed evacuation, dislocated medical arrangements and caused great suffering and injury. So long as operations were confined to the immediate vicinity of Basra there was no need for any such transport but directly columns advanced up the Tigris, Euphrates and Karun the necessity of some means of speedy evacuating the sick and wounded by water became apparent.[231]

That report and all its repercussions lay in the future. Meanwhile, deep in the desert, Aylmer was convinced that the key to success was for Townshend to attack the Turks from the rear, and he lived in hope that at some stage this concept would find support.

On the face of it, Townshend's message on 23 January to Aylmer and Lake was supportive. Townshend suggested that there were three possible courses open to him in the event that Aylmer could not reach him. These courses were: first, to attempt to break out of Kut by crossing the Tigris to the right bank and then to make straight for Sheikh Saad, being met halfway if possible by a column sent by Aylmer; second, to hold Kut to the last; and finally, for him to open negotiations with the enemy seeking terms for surrender.

Townshend had no intention of breaking out, but he raised the matter confident that it would be rejected. Holding Kut 'to the last' had the required and expected heroic ring but raised the spectre of defeat. Townshend had a pipe dream that von der Goltz and Khalil, filled with admiration for his brilliant advance to Ctesiphon, his masterly withdrawal to Kut and his tenacious defence of that town, would allow the garrison to march out to freedom bearing its weapons.

It was never going to happen, but Charlie had plans for his own salvation and an element of that was his intention of establishing a relationship with his adversaries. Braddon argued that the anger Townshend displayed when the artillery fired on Goltz was indicative of his undeclared aim. Later events added credence to this theory.

Nixon had vetoed a break-out and now, just as Charlie expected, Lake did the same. The only other highly unattractive option was a further frontal assault by Aylmer. The stumbling block was the well-defended – and formidable – Dujaila Redoubt.

Chapter notes

200 Mousley, E.O., *Secrets of a Kuttite*, p.50. There are no recorded instances of anyone being tried, found guilty and executed for this offence.

201 MC Report, p.31.

202 Townshend, C.V.F., *My Campaign in Mesopotamia*, pp.235–6.

203 Moberly, F.J., *The Campaign in Mesopotamia*, p.281.

204 MC Report, p.56.

205 Ibid, p.31.

206 Major General Sir George Younghusband KCMG KCIE CB (1858–1944).

207 Barker, A.J., *The Neglected War*, p.153.

208 Ibid, p.156.

209 Ibid, p.157.

210 Nunn, W., *Tigris Gunboats*, p.203.

211 Ibid, p.204.

212 MC Report, p.31.

213 LG Supplement, 21 June 1916.

214 Mr J. Boggis in an interview with Braddon, *The Siege*, p.161.

215 Moberly, F.J., *The Campaign in Mesopotamia*, p.261.

216 Ibid, p.261.

217 Duff to Hardinge, 6 January 1916, and reply, 7 January. Hardinge papers, 103/No. 2075 & 1528.

218 Moberly, F.J., *The Campaign in Mesopotamia*, p.264.

219 Ibid, p.351.

220 Eato, H., interviewed by Braddon, R., quoted in *The Siege*, p.188.

221 Page-Roberts, F.W., quoted by Braddon, *The Siege*, p.170.

222 MC Report, p.32.

223 Barker, A.J., *The Forgotten War*, p.176.

224 Atta is the hard wheat flour commonly used in South-East Asia to make a dense bread. Atta is not only the flour but also the name of the bread it produces.

225 Wilcox, R., *Battles on the Tigris*, p.105.

226 Mousley, E.O., *The Secrets of a Kuttite*, p.82.

227 Gould, D., 'Lord Harding and the Mesopotamia Expedition and Inquiry', *The Historical Journal*, December 1976.

228 Hardinge to Chamberlain, 10 March 1916, Chamberlain papers, 62/2. Chamberlain note of 17 July, Crewe papers, M/15(2).

229 Stamfordham to Chamberlain, 28 February 1916 and E.W. Wallington to Chamberlain, 29 February, Chamberlain papers, 46/2/65,67.

230 Curzon to Chamberlain, 17 March 1916, Chamberlain papers, 23/1/2.

231 Vincent–Bingley Report, absorbed into the MC Report at p.64.

Chapter 13

February–March 1916
The Battle of the Dujaila Redoubt

'Judgement and not headlong courage,
is the true arbiter of war.'
(Count Belisarius, c. AD 505–506)

In Kut, March 1916 got off to a grim start. All twenty-one of the Turkish guns were employed in a major 'stonk'. Three German aeroplanes dropped a total of fifty bombs. They hit not only the hospital but also Arab housing and the mosque. Nine soldiers were killed and twenty-eight wounded.[232]

Townshend ordered the issue of respirators as, from some unidentified source, it was rumoured that the Turks were going to use gas. The respirators were widely seen as an 'enbuggerance' by the soldiers of Mr G. Roff. He said that his men's response was, 'Fancy this place having respirators. Fancy respirators being a bit of flannel you pissed on and then wrapped around your mouth and nostrils. No food: but respirators you pissed on. Typical army.'[233]

The sappers laboured to construct the elements of a flying bridge and three recalcitrant Arabs observed them closely. On the night of 4 March, the three men swam the river and reported to the Turks what was taking place in Kut.[234] Immediately, the Turkish piquets were strengthened and the possibility of a surprise river crossing, never a high probability, now became a total non-starter.

The following day, the sappers constructed a mine and it was their intention to launch it into the river where it would float downstream and blow up one of Khalil's bridges. The launch point was to be the Woolpress Village. The mine was sent on its way and was last seen dancing away on its mission of destruction. Shortly afterwards, it exploded and deposited a layer of mud all over the adjacent geography. E.W.C. Sandes[235] was more specific and commented that it created a crater in the bank of the Shatt-al-Hai.[236]

On 5 March, Townshend sent, by wireless, his despatches from Ctesiphon. As is the norm, he named individuals who had distinguished themselves and recommended some for decorations. Then, in a typically gauche manner, he added that his division had:

> suffered professionally in comparison with our comrades in the European theatres of war who, in many instances, are being promoted over our heads simply because the despatches of their operations were promptly published and promptly rewarded. I know in my own case that several major generals junior to me in the Army have been promoted to lieutenant general over my head although these officers had not had an independent command nor such responsibilities as I had.[237]

This ingenuous final paragraph encapsulates the ambition and feeling of self-worth that were the dominant characteristics of Charles Townshend.

In Basra, Lake had gripped the parlous administrative situation that he obtained in the port, but the problems were so deep-rooted and fundamental in nature that he was starting from scratch. Progress was being made but it was slow, and the turn-round time for ships was still measured in weeks and not days. Inevitably, the resupply of the divisions at the front remained inadequate.

The 13th Division was on its way to reinforce Aylmer, but the continuing sense of urgency had not abated despite the extraordinary message from Townshend that he had found 'great supplies of barley'. He also averred that by killing and eating all his 3,000 animals he could resist for a further eighty-four days. Townshend and the truth were not always bedfellows, and this sudden windfall and the new estimate of survivability placed further strain on his credibility in Basra, Simla and London.

Completely unacceptable losses had been incurred at Sheikh Saad, the Wadi and the Hanna Defile and, despite a trickle of reinforcements coming upriver, the Tigris Corps was not fully up to strength, although the arrival of the 13th Division would alter the balance – if it arrived in time. In the meantime, Aylmer kept the Hanna Defile under fire and held Turkish troops in place. The only practical effect of that was that the Turks were encouraged to dig their fortifications deeper. On 13 February, General Townshend, expressing anxiety on account of the reports of the imminent arrival of two fresh Turkish divisions, urged that General Aylmer should advance as soon as possible.[238]

Townshend's urging, not for the first, second or third time, was a goad that Aylmer did not need. The annual and entirely predictable spring floods were on time. The Tigris continued to rise throughout February, as did the water in trenches and previously dry watercourses across Mesopotamia. The Shatt-al-Hai was now navigable and General Lake recognised that that could provide the Turks with a route to Nasariyeh and from thence to Basra. It was sufficient reason for him to insist that Townshend continue to hold Kut and command the confluence of the Hai and the Tigris. By now it appeared that unless Kut was relieved by around 15 March, the probability was that the water table would accomplish what the Turks had so far failed to do.

Aylmer was under great pressure and decided to launch his attack on 6 March; however, the ground over which his soldiers had to advance was, as ever, a complete swamp. In the forlorn hope that conditions would improve, he delayed until 8 March. This was the same day that the first two battalions of the 13th Division arrived in Sheikh Saad. The remainder were strung out all the way back to Basra. Clearly, the Division was neither organised nor deployable, and certainly not battle ready.

Aylmer, having been worsted at Hanna, looked for another solution. He decided to switch his force to the right bank and by so doing bypass the Hanna position on the left bank. He would keep the Turks in position on the left bank and not allow them to decamp to the right bank.

It was not ideal and the terrain was much to the advantage of the defenders, but there was a possibility of outflanking the Es Sinn ridge. Although this was little more than a substantial bank within sight of Kut, it was elevated above the flat desert and provided line of sight and, in consequence, line of fire. Aylmer's objective was the Dujaila Depression and its associated redoubt. The depression was not a large feature, being only about 150 yards wide, but, more usefully, some 6 feet deep. It afforded cover from sight and cover from direct fire. To its front it was flat terrain with a thin cover of thorny scrub and the two defendable Nasifiya and Maqasis canals. To the right of the depression and on the extreme right of the Turkish position was the Dujaila Redoubt, and this defence work was key to the battle that was to follow.

The master plan was to seize the redoubt and spin around it, mopping up the Turks from their now unprotected flank. Defeating the Turks on the right bank would destabilise their position on the left bank and open the door to Kut.

It gives the reader a sense of the scale of this operation if the composition of the British force is identified. The order of battle is below:

Column 'A' (Brigadier General G. Christian)
36th Brigade
37th Brigade
9th Brigade (from D'Urban Keary's 3rd Division)
22,000 men, six guns

Column 'B' (Major General Kemball with Column 'A' under command)
28th Brigade and logistic support
8,000 men, twenty-four guns

Column 'C' (Major General D'Urban Keary)
7th Brigade
8th Brigade
6,500 men, thirty-two guns.

The Dujaila Redoubt was some 5 miles distant from the river and had no water supply. It was lightly held and the bulk of its nominated defenders bivouacked on the riverbank. A night march with superior numbers could be moved across the Turkish front so as to arrive at daybreak and mount an assault before the redoubt could be fully manned.

The key elements in this plan were the accurate timing of the approach march and the maintenance of surprise. The Mesopotamia Commission observed:

A night march is far from being an easy operation at any time. The difficulties vary with the nature of the ground, the distance to be traversed and the number of troops engaged. It requires good march discipline and first-rate staff work especially when, as in this case, an attack is to follow immediately. To Major General Kemball was entrusted the task of turning the flank to be attacked in cooperation with a column on his right.[239]

A realistic speed of march was estimated to be 1 mile per hour and the model for such an operation was that at Tel-el-Kebir in 1882, when Lord Wolseley marched 13,000 men 3½ miles over easy going. His troops arrived in the right place at the right time and his attack was a crashing success.

This case was different in both scale and scope. To outflank the Es Sinn bank, about 20,000 men would have to move between 12 and 16 miles, together with wheeled vehicles, field ambulances and pack animals. Concentrating this force before the start was, in itself, a test of coordination and required skilled staff work. Some of the units had to march several miles to the concentration area to rendezvous by 2030 hrs.

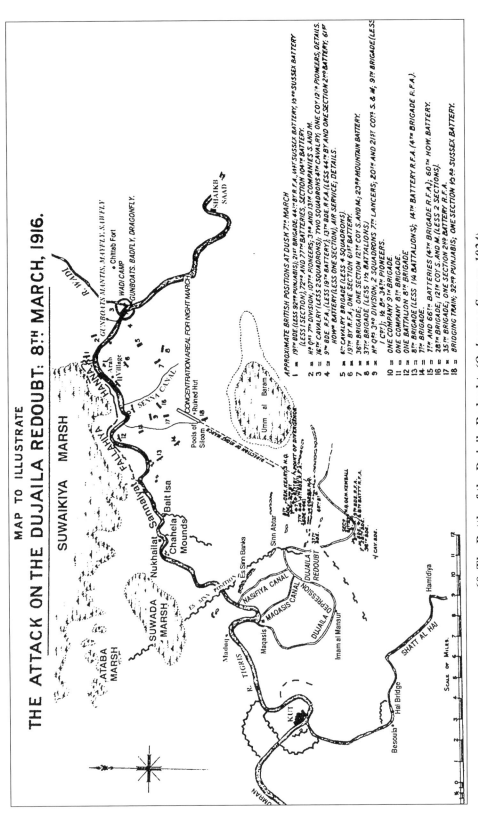

60. The Battle of the Dujaila Redoubt. (*Ordnance Survey, 1924*)

2100 hrs was the time of departure and only one hour had been built into the programme to cater for contingencies. The MC commented shrewdly that:

> *Lord Wolseley had had a marked advantage. His small army was entirely composed of well-trained British troops with a most efficient staff. General W. Aylmer's force was heterogeneous, British and Indian troops being mixed up together and he and other generals make many complaints about the 'scrappy' character of their staffs. This army was expected to march about 14 miles* [or more] *in rather less than nine hours.*

Aylmer had drawn up his plan for the advance and assault only after discussion with his formation commanders and a weighing of all the factors. The Corps Commander intended to exert complete control over the operation and accordingly his plan was very detailed. Much more significantly, he left little to the initiative of subordinate commanders. This determination to retain iron control was probably a by-product of his defeats at Sheikh Saad, the Wadi and the Hanna Defile. In those actions he had delegated the initiative and his subordinates had not served him well.

At 1400 hrs on 7 March, General Aylmer held a coordinating conference. General Gorringe was in attendance and the latter, in addressing the principal commanders, emphasised the fact that it was hoped to surprise the enemy. He concluded that, 'As delay or hesitation in the attack would give the Turks time to push in their reserve and reinforcements, it was essential that the capture of the Dujaila Redoubt should be pushed through with the greatest vigour.'[240]

Aylmer predictably endorsed what Gorringe had said and underscored the vital necessity for dash in the impending operations. General Kemball received permission to eliminate his logistic tail from his assault force in order for them to march in the rear.

In the event, Kemball's orders were issued too late and when he arrived at the rendezvous the whole of the transport and field ambulances were formed up as ordered originally. It was far too late to reorganise the order of march, so Kemball had to bite on this organisational bullet.

The night of 7 March was dry and proved to be fine, clear and starlit, with a fairly warm temperature. When Columns 'A' and 'B' under Kemball stepped off, he was at the head of a body that stretched for 2 miles over the desert. The force was led and guided by Captain K. Mason RE, assisted by a small staff that checked the dead reckoning with a bicycle wheel, three pedometers and an improvised pace-stick.[241/242]

Things had started to go wrong from the start. A number of units had been late in arriving at the concentration area and Kemball's departure was delayed until 2222 hrs. The single hour allowed for contingencies was already used up. In the dark, units were mixed and valuable time was lost restoring order.

The march was marked by the need for brief halts in the first half hour; at midnight, after ninety minutes en route, only about 3 miles had been covered. As units paused on the march, men lay down and fell asleep – some were left behind. At midnight, Kemball ordered a ten-minute halt. Up the line came a message not to continue as Column 'C' had lost contact. This was because transport ahead of it had slowed and halted – another invaluable hour was lost before Kemball got the nod to move on. At 0230 hrs, the head of the column reached the predesignated 'point of divergence', and it was from here that the columns diverted, each to their own objectives.

A problem that had not been anticipated was the degree not only to which soldiers would fall asleep, but also the difficulty of waking them. The prime offenders were the drivers of mule and camel-drawn transport.

Kemball, whose 28th Brigade had the furthest to go, had had an unsuccessful campaign so far and was hoping for better days ahead. He advanced a further 2 miles, at which point he encountered an enemy entrenchment that, happily, was unoccupied. The *Official History* said that nevertheless the position was a significant obstacle because it was:

> 5 feet deep and too great an obstacle for the column to cross. The scouts of the 26th Punjabis moved south for about 150 yards and got round it, but a gap in the trench line some 30 yards wide was found for the column to pass through. This, however, necessitated reducing the front of the column and further delay occurred before all had negotiated it. In consequence, it was not until 0510 hrs that the head of the column struck the Dujaila Depression just beyond the entrenchment, at a distance of about 1½ miles from the point of divergence. Here a short halt was necessary to make certain that it was the depression (which was very shallow here), to allow the troops in the rear to close up and to change the direction of the advance to a bearing of 238°. There still remained a distance of about 3 miles to be traversed to General Kemball's position of deployment, so it was clear that he could not reach it by the appointed time.

At about 0530 hrs, after the resumption of the advance, lights of Arab encampments were observed on both flanks, but General Kemball could not afford to delay and merely pushed out protective guards to either flank. The first signs of dawn appeared about 0545 hrs, and three-quarters of an hour later, when it was quite light, the head of the column reached what was taken to be the bend in the depression, i.e., the position of deployment. Soon, however, it was found that an embankment across the depression had been taken for the bank turning northwards, and that the head of the column was actually some 1,500 yards short of the corner.[243]

By now the sun was up and the cloak of darkness, so important in maintaining surprise, had been relinquished. The Dujaila Redoubt was plainly visible some 4,000 yards to the north-west. There was no visible sign of Turkish activity and it appeared that the Turks had not detected the presence of the British force. Surprisingly, surprise had been established.

Colonel Walton, who commanded 26th Punjabis, the leading battalion, continued to advance, advising his brigade commander, General Christian, of his intention. Christian and his brigade major came forward to see for themselves. Christian drew the same conclusion as Walton and hurried back to brief Kemball.

General Kemball, however, did not agree. In practically every action he had seen in Mesopotamia it had appeared as if the trenches were empty until the Turks actually opened heavy fire from them. Moreover, his past experience in the country had shown him that to start an attack before the brigade and battalion commanders had time and opportunity to get the bearings of their objectives was likely to lead to loss of direction and disconnected attacks. He consequently ordered General Christian to recall the 26th Punjabis.[244]

After the engagement it transpired that the Turks had not seen the British force, and they were only alerted when they came under artillery fire. Kemball was conscious of how exposed his force was to hostile artillery and moved his two columns into the depression. He sent a message to Aylmer to say that, by about 0700 hrs, his men would be fully deployed in the area of the bend (later to be called Kemball's Corner) in the depression. The force shook itself out and deployed in accordance with Aylmer's plan, and all along the British line the objectives could clearly be seen.

With more 20/20 hindsight, it is evident that an immediate attack on the unwary Turks may well have carried the day. It was a situation that an innovative commander such as Townshend might have exploited. In which case, the Dujaila Redoubt would probably have been taken, and chances are that the relief of Kut would have followed. Aylmer's night march had, for the most part, succeeded. His troops were successfully deployed and the enemy was unaware of their presence, but the inflexibility of the plan was its weakness.

Aylmer had decided that an artillery strike was to take place before the infantry made its move, and the suggestion to attack at once drew the terse reply, 'Stick to the programme.' If surprise was one of the objects, announcing an attack with a bombardment was counterproductive. None of the formation commanders were prepared to take the initiative, and indeed, if an uncoordinated attack had been launched it would probably have failed.

But then so did the carefully planned and coordinated attack that followed.

The Artillery laid down fire on the enemy positions and, thoroughly alerted, the Turkish reinforcements poured into the vacant trenches. Three thousand had moved from Magasis Fort and multitudes more were being ferried across the Tigris 'in native coracle-like *mashoofs* and on skin rafts towed by motorboats. An air reconnaissance estimated that another 3,000 came across the river during the day.'[245] The guns caught some of the reinforcing Turks in open ground, but once they had gained the deeply dug trench line they were safe. It was 1000 hrs when the British emerged from their hastily dug scrapes and made for the enemy 700 yards to their front, to be met by a hail of well-directed and effective small-arms fire. Casualties mounted quickly and Kemball's force got forward a scant 200 yards before the advance checked and the soldiers went to earth. Every man had a 'Sirhind' entrenching tool, a piece of kit introduced in 1908. It was cumbersome, heavy but heaven-sent in these circumstances.

Column 'C' (D'Urban Keary) to the east of the redoubt had planned its attack for 0530 hrs, but that was not to be as this column had been seriously delayed. On arrival at the column's start line ('point of departure' in new money), the formation was disorganised, with the infantry component mixed in with animal transport units, field ambulances and the like. Both Aylmer and his Chief of Staff, Gorringe, had travelled with D'Urban Keary, so were able to see for themselves the parlous situation of Columns 'A' and 'B'. There was a gap in the Turkish line in front of Column 'C', but the opportunity offered was not taken. Aylmer was present, but he directed that there must be no deviation from 'the plan'. On that basis he must take direct responsibility for the inertia that was to spell disaster.

The British artillery bombardment was wholly inadequate. In the planning of the operation it had been accorded an entirely false value. It was the PBI – 'the poor bloody infantry' – who suffered as a result of artillery inadequacy. These soldiers had marched all night, carrying weapons, packs laden with ammunition, two days' rations, water and an entrenching tool. By now, as the sun rose in the sky, many had already consumed the water they had been able to carry and they were faced by an obdurate, tenacious, skilled and well-concealed enemy. They depended as never before on good generalship.

They did not get good generalship and they paid with their lives.

By 1630 hrs, the columns led by Kemball were no longer a viable fighting force and Aylmer, with extraordinary optimism, decided that success could be achieved if the 8th Brigade of D'Urban Keary's column was to strike at the east side of the redoubt, some 3,000 yards ahead. The 1st Battalion, the Manchester Regiment and the 59th Rifles were to be in the van, with 2nd Battalion Rajputs in support. Those 3,000 yards were of flat, featureless desert and the British infantry was to be exposed to fire all the way as it plodded forward. Incredibly, and despite small-arms and then artillery fire from Turkish guns, a fragile foothold was gained in the Turkish line. The Manchesters and the 59th had excelled, but their success was brief and a violent counter-attack threw them back. The survivors retreated, still under fire, those same 3,000 yards.

This was another painful and costly defeat. The 8th Brigade had been devastated and taken a 50 per cent loss. It was reduced to a head count of only 1,127. In all, thirty-three British officers and twenty-three Indian officers did not return. 2nd Rajputs lost all of their British officers and twelve of their sixteen Indian officers. 1st Battalion/2nd Gurkhas, which had joined the assault, was, for practical purposes, wiped out. The butcher's bill for this affair was about 3,500, including 123 British officers. Turkish losses were about 1,200.

The Cavalry had played no part in the operation and, as at previous battles, it was uninvolved and non-productive. These mounted soldiers could and should have been put to better use. Aylmer's plan for his Cavalry was for it to guard the left flank, but, as the battle developed, it could have been used to sweep right around the Dujaila position and the Hai to stem the movement of Turkish reinforcements.

Townshend and his garrison could hear the sounds of the battle taking place on the right bank. However, Kut was firmly on the left bank and the practical difficulty of breaking out in support of Aylmer has to be acknowledged. Project 'E' was no more than an aspiration, not least because an opposed river crossing to the right bank would be slow, difficult and costly. To break out on the left bank would require the breaching of at least three lines of Turkish defences. The probability of Townshend emerging on either bank in a condition to affect the outcome of the battle was nil. Any breakout should have been made in very early December the previous year, and four months later in March, it was no longer a viable military option.

During the night of 8/9 March, as many of the wounded as possible were recovered, but by no means all. The British force withdrew to 'Kemball's Corner' and hundreds of their wounded remained out in the desert at the hands of the merciless Arabs. They were butchered where they lay, stripped of their clothes and boots. Their bodies were mutilated. British casualties on 8 and 9 March totalled 3,474, and most of these occurred on the 8th. The 9th Infantry Brigade had lost 23 per cent of its strength, three battalions of the 28th Brigade from 24–32 per cent, the 36th Brigade, 24 per cent, and the 8th Brigade, 33 per cent. The Manchesters and 2nd Rajputs suffered a high proportion of those losses.[246] In the morning, Aylmer ordered the move back to the place from which this sad expedition had started and withdrew, a chastened and disappointed man. His personal future now hung in the balance.

The MC took evidence from many of the participants and observed:

> *Our opinion is that the chances of 'A' Column being up to time were slender: that the operation ... was the nature of a 'gamble' in which the odds against success were high, but whether they were too high to justify the action cannot be stated in terms of certainty.*
>
> *General Kemball said that in spite of their severe losses, he had full confidence in his men ... and was anxious to try again. Headquarters did not accept this offer, and it can hardly say that they were wrong. The other reason given for not renewing the attack was the deficiency of water. General Kemball asserts that there was plenty where he was, and very likely there was enough for his men, but it is not clear that there was for the whole force.[247]*

Kemball's judgment has to be called into question. He had been badly mauled again but was content to put the remainder of his force at serious risk despite there being, at best, a question mark over the matter of water provision. Kemball had not been a successful commander in the battles to relieve Kut – but then he was not alone in that. In the future, the failure at Dujaila became a tactical football kicked around by the participating generals in order that 'blame' could be correctly attributed.

Now that the War Office and His Majesty's Government had taken control of the campaign, it was the War Office, in the shape of Kitchener, who sacked Aylmer. He handed over command of Tigris Corps to acting Lieutenant General Sir George Gorringe. On 12 March, Aylmer wrote to his old friend Townshend and his letter has been reproduced in most of the books written concerned with this campaign. He wrote:

My Dear Townshend,

The War Office say that my conduct of operations has been unfortunate, and have ordered my suspension. I need not tell you how deeply I grieve that I have not been able to relieve you; but I have every confidence that my successor will be able to do so very soon.

I have had a harder task than most people realise. It all looks so easy when you sit in an armchair in the W.O.! The business a few days ago very nearly came off. I cannot tell you how much I admire the splendid way in which you are defending Kut.

I heartily pray that you will gain your reward in speedy relief. Give my best wishes to Dalamain, Mellis and Hamilton. Goodbye and God Bless you all, and may you be more fortunate than myself.

Yours ever,
Fenton Aylmer

These are the words and sentiments of a gallant gentleman, but a mediocre general. With his career in ruins he turned to his right, saluted and marched off the military stage into obscurity and retirement in 1919.

Townshend had known Aylmer for years and may have been saddened by his fall from grace, but he was immeasurably more distressed at the promotion to lieutenant general, albeit 'acting', of George Gorringe.

John Boggis recounted how, on hearing the news, Townshend expostulated to those about him, 'But he's *junior* to me.' This was Charlie's darkest nightmare; he had been 'passed over'. Later that same day, Townshend wept on the shoulder of one of his officers.[248] 'Twas not a pretty sight, and in combination with his most recent communiqué it was enough to erode the respect that, hitherto, he had commanded.

Townshend was all the more aggrieved because, as recently as 5 March, he had once again raised the matter of his promotion with Lake. The fact that he was not in a position to exercise the authority of a lieutenant general, as he was, effectively, a prisoner, seems to have escaped him. Cracks were starting to appear in the demeanour and style of Chitrál Charlie. Mention was made of his recent communiqué. That was issued on 10 March and it read as follows:

as on a former occasion, I take the troops of all ranks into my confidence.

We have now stood a three-month siege in a manner which has called upon you the praise of our beloved King and our fellow countrymen in England, Scotland, Ireland and India, and all this after your brilliant battles of Kut-al–Amara and Ctesiphon and your retirement to Kut, all of which feats of arms are now famous.

Since 5 December 1915, you have spent three months of cruel uncertainty, and to all men and all people uncertainty is intolerable. As I say, on top of all this comes the second failure to relieve us and I ask you to give a little sympathy to me who have commanded you in those battles referred to, and who, having come to you as a stranger, now love my command with a depth of feeling I have never known in my life before.

When I mention myself I would also mention the names of the generals under me, whose names are distinguished in the Army as leaders of men.

I am speaking to you as I did before straight from the heart, and as I say, I ask for your sympathy for my feelings, having promised you relief on certain dates on the promise of those ordered to relieve us. Not their fault, no doubt. Do not think that I blame them; they are giving their lives freely, and deserve our gratitude and admiration.

But I want you to help me again, as before. I have asked General Aylmer for the next attempt to bring such numbers as will break down all resistance and leave no doubt as to the issue.

In order then to hold out, I am killing a large number of horses so as to reduce the quantity of grain eaten every day, and I have had to reduce your ration. It is necessary to do this in order to keep our flag flying.

I am determined to hold out, and I know you are with me heart and soul.

This open letter to his soldiers hits several unfortunate notes. It is undignified and un-officerlike. Townshend may have been under great pressure but, nevertheless, no officer or commander, of any rank, should ever appeal to his soldiers for sympathy in this way. As one soldier remarked, 'If he's looking for sympathy he'll find it in the dictionary – between shit and syphilis.'

The *Official History*, *The Campaign in Mesopotamia* (p. 308), sombrely noted that the casualties of the siege up to 29 February totalled 2,927. This comprised 846 killed or died of wounds, 1,608 wounded. Thirty were 'missing' or had deserted and 443 had died of disease. It went on to say that, 'The most prevalent diseases were gastro-enteritis, diarrhoea and malaria among British troops and dysentery and pneumonia among the Indian troops. In January and early February, frostbite and trench rheumatism were also common.'

Chapter notes

232 Diary of Lieutenant Colonel L. Bell Syer, quoted by Braddon, *The Siege*, p.199.

233 Roff, G., Ibid.

234 Sherson, E., *Townshend of Chitrál and Kut,* p.318.

235 Lieutenant Colonel E.W.C. Sandes DSO MC RE survived the siege and in 1933 wrote the book *The Military Engineer in India*. This was reprinted in 2001.

236 Braddon, R., interview of 1967–68 and recorded in *The Siege*, p.201.

237 Townshend, C.V.F., *My Campaign in Mesopotamia.* p.287.

238 Moberly, F.J., *The Campaign in Mesopotamia*, p.300.

239 MC Report, p.33.

240 Moberly, F.J., *The Campaign in Mesopotamia*, p.318.

241 Ibid, p.320.

242 A pace stick was and is the weapon of choice of drill instructors in the infantry. It is rather like a man-sized compass. By skilful manipulation it is used to measure the length of the pace. RMA Sandhurst is now thought, by aficionados, to be the spiritual home of the pace stick, now that there is no longer a Guards' Depot to nurture it.

243 Moberly, F.J., *The Campaign in Mesopotamia*, p.322.

244 Ibid, p.323.

245 Barker, A.J., *The Neglected War*, p.192.

246 Moberly, F.J., *The Campaign in Mesopotamia*, p.348.

247 MC Report, p.34.

248 Harris, Major J.H., interviewed by Braddon and recorded in *The Siege*, p.212.

Chapter 14

April 1916
The Battle of Sannaiyat
and Capitulation

'Famine makes greater havoc in an army than the
enemy and is more terrible than the sword.'
(Flavius Vegetius Renatus, *Military Institutions of the Romans*,
c. AD 378, Clarke, 1776)

On 10 March, Captain E.O. Mousley, hitherto a young man with a very positive attitude, confided in his diary what was probably in the minds of many of his fellow 'Kuttites'. He recorded that:

> One would think that the lesson of Ctesiphon was sufficient to chasten the authorities out of the belief that the Mesopotamian campaign could be dallied with.
>
> By sheer brilliancy of arms a whole country had been conquered by one unsupported division. This achievement was not enough, however, and the cheap methods in vogue further required this one division to risk the whole fruits of a campaign in a single doubtful throw and against the advice of its generals.
>
> Through the same cheap methods of having insufficient forces to follow up a brilliant victory, our army was badly let down and several thousand lives flung away.[249]

The spectre of defeat had appeared and the Kuttites were beginning to see themselves as victims. It was not an unreasonable judgment by Mousley, given his limited access to the complete picture.

When it became clear that Kut could not be re-supplied by river the only alternative was to drop food from the air. However, aircraft were few in number, ill-equipped for the purpose and the pilots unskilled in the process. Small amounts were safely delivered, but frequently the bounty fell into the

61. British graves. *(Dr G. Bulger, original photo by Harry Weaver)*

river or inside Turkish lines. The pilots, in their flimsy canvas and string aircraft, were much at risk from small-arms fire and the higher they went to avoid it, the less accurate their ration drop. At this stage in the siege, any successful drop was greeted with acclaim.

Starvation was now evident and the Kuttites started to show all the signs of vitamin deficiency, about which the medics could do nothing. The horses ate the tails of their fellows and their head ropes. Anything that grew was eaten; grass and weeds were much favoured and when stewed up, described as 'spinach'. Rats, cats and dogs all headed for the pot, and this was not the time to be squeamish. It may have been coincidence but, on 12 April, Brigadier General F.A. Hoghton ate some of the 'spinach' and died soon thereafter. It seemed that the stew had contained something injurious and brought about an ignominious end for a brave and effective commander.

His comrade, Major General Sir Charles Mellis vc, was unwell, but still breathing fire and brimstone, and appeared to be indestructible.

It may well be restating the blindingly obvious but, when the Duke of Marlborough wrote to Colonel Cadogan in 1703, he remarked that, 'An army cannot preserve good order unless its soldiers have meat in their bellies, coats on their backs and shoes on their feet.' In March 1916, the Kuttites would say 'aye' to that, especially as eating their boots looked like becoming an option.

It came as a severe shock to Hardinge when he discovered that Townshend had advised strongly against the advance to Ctesiphon and that Nixon had not only ignored the advice, but had kept it to himself. Hitherto, Hardinge had been Nixon's unquestioning and greatest supporter but, by 25 March 1916, with Nixon now back in India on sick leave and his own tenure at its end, Hardinge was sadly disillusioned. He wrote to Chamberlain expressing his dismay.[250]

After the bloody affair at Dujaila, the British spent the rest of March adjusting, reinforcing, and reorganising shattered units. The heavy loss of officers made it difficult to regain the cohesiveness and rapport at unit level that is so essential to sound morale and efficiency.

On 4 April, Lord Hardinge vacated the appointment of Viceroy of India, handed over to Lord Chelmsford and embarked on a ship for the journey back to the UK, where he would be warmly welcomed back into the heart of the British establishment. There was no hint of criticism of his management of the Mesopotamian campaign. Smoothly, after some leave, he once more took up the appointment of Permanent Under Secretary at the Foreign Office. Hardinge, 'a rather cold, reserved man',[251] was now a lonely one. His wife Winifred had died in July 1915 and his son Edd had died of wounds some six months before. His public life, always important, now assumed greater importance.

In Mesopotamia, spring was in the air, it was warmer and the nights, although cold, were not life-threatening. The warmer weather signalled the reappearance of the hosts of energetic flies. However, they were not the only enemy. As the snows melted high in the Caucasus, the meltwater flowed by way of countless, previously dry streambeds to the headwaters of the Tigris and the Euphrates.

Inexorably, the river level rose.

It had risen every spring, 'even before Pontius was a pilot'[252] (Pilate). Over 10,000 square miles of the Babylonian Plain, between the rivers, flooded. The area around Kut was subject to this annual, irresistible inundation.

Troops on both sides set to, constructing bunds to hold back the waters, with only very limited success. Wheeled vehicles were immobile and the gunners in particular were hamstrung. Both sides patrolled, but with little hope of any sort of tactical success. Patrols had to wade through filthy, muddy water and sought to clear the dry ground of enemy snipers. This was very dangerous work and death by drowning was always on the cards for the man brought low in the endless water-covered landscape. Any form of large-scale operation was impossible and it was obvious to all, except General Sir Percy Lake, that the relief of Kut was becoming more unlikely, day by day.

The conditions were dangerous. Latrines were flooded and raw sewage swirled around the trenches. Sleeping was only possible above the water level; washing was an improbable aspiration and hot, freshly cooked food non-existent. The maintenance of high morale in these conditions was a herculean task.

Curiously, the sailors in HM's ships *on* the water were much more comfortable and drier than the soldiers ashore who were *in* the water.

In Basra, communications were maintained with units and one British battalion arrived at the front equipped with a Japanese invention, 'a fly-catching machine'. These were issued on a scale of one per company. The inventor and the staff officer who arranged the purchase of this absurd device clearly had no appreciation of just how many multiple millions, nay trillions of flies there were. An issue of 10,000 machines per company would probably have been insufficient. This high-tech device was described as:

> A box with a triangular piece of wood revolving on a clockwork-operated spindle and its purpose as might be deduced was to reduce the vast numbers of the fly population with which troops in the forward areas were infested. Through a cutaway opening in the box the unsuspecting fly settled on the revolving triangle, which was sticky with a fly catching material, and then slowly revolved into the box where the now thoroughly bemused fly was scraped off.[253]

The box came complete with operating instructions and helpful photographs of piles of dead flies slain by this lethal weapon. Predictably, the soldiers turned the boxes to good use and bet on the kill rate of each box. To the Staff in Basra, still utterly divorced from the real world upriver, there were records to keep, and apparently during a period of savage fighting the adjutant of one battalion received a signal to 'report how many files caught in April'. Across the signal the adjutant wrote, 'Balls', and this message was relayed back to the assiduous staff officer in Basra. By immediate response came a correction saying, 'For files, read flies.' The adjutant responded, 'For balls, read cock.'[254]

This same officer, who had just survived a Turkish bombardment, received a message from Basra asking him to comment on 'the attitude of the enemy'. He replied, 'Hostile'. An immediate return asked him to amplify his answer. He replied, 'Very hostile'.

Townshend or his senior supply officer had initiated a search of Kut for foodstuffs and had found a remarkable amount hidden in the roofs, and in one case behind a skilfully constructed and camouflaged false wall. In addition, Townshend was buying grain from the population. This accumulation in due course would allow him to forecast with confidence that he could hang out until 15 April.[255]

On 11 March, General Gorringe took over command of the Tigris Corps and advised General Lake that he intended to extend along the right bank of the river, placing his artillery in positions to dominate hostile guns on the left bank. Gorringe, like all of those who had gone before him, was tied to the river and his capacity to move on that river.

That same day, the total number of river steamers and tugs available to support Gorringe was thirty-seven. These vessels propelled the sixty-eight available barges and provided an average daily delivery at the front of 300 tons, against a requirement of 468 tons. This is assuming that no personnel were to be transported and that the full number of craft was always available.

Of course, this was never the case.

Local assets had been commandeered and 200 of the slow and unwieldy *mahailas* were employed to help fill the transport gap. Matters did improve, albeit slowly, and by 25 March there were forty-five tugs and steamers and an additional seventy-nine barges. This increased the daily lift by 38 tons, offset in part by an increase in the demand of 22 tons.

One of the ongoing difficulties was that vessels sent out to the theatre were of varying types and there was no commonality on spare parts or fittings. Barges that were to be married to these steamers were often incompatible with the power available to move them. On arrival, some steamers required a refit. Unfortunately, Basra was not a port and neither was it a shipyard.

> To have made the most of the existing steamers, six barges (two with steamer, two loading and two unloading) would have been necessary for each steamer, but owing to some misunderstanding nothing like this number were sent.[256]

The climate of Mesopotamia was always a factor; from here on it was the decisive factor. The ever-present Tigris shaped the actions of both sides as its flooding limited movement and, by so doing, negated the best-laid plans.

The newly arrived 13th Division brought the Tigris Corps up to a full strength of 30,000. The 13th Division was commanded by Major General Sir Frederick Maude.[257] He was an experienced officer, having already served in the Dardanelles and on the Western Front. Maude was to prosper in Mesopotamia like no other general officer that served in that campaign. He was the only one to win distinction, other than Townshend, although the distinction of the latter ultimately faded.

Every attempt had been made to provide Gorringe with all that he needed and all available river craft had been put to the task of carrying troops, ammunition, ordnance, medical and other warlike stores. But they could not carry everything, and so it was the food that was left behind – it was then swiftly pointed out to Gorringe that he only had 'rations for seven or eight days'.[258] He also had a further 3,000 men in transit to the front, but now rations took precedence and those reinforcements were held back and would not be available in the short term.

Notwithstanding Aylmer's bloody defeat at the Hanna Defile, Gorringe decided that he would repeat the action and he detailed 13th Division to make the attack. On 31 March/1 April, in very heavy rain, the Division started to move into the forward British trenches. The rain was so severe that the assault was delayed until 5 April, by which time General Lake was in attendance, as was a Brigadier General W. Gilman. The latter was the appointed liaison officer between Indian Expeditionary Force 'D' and the War Office in London. His presence was because Kitchener and Robertson obviously wanted their man on the spot to plug the perceived veracity gap; he would report directly to Lieutenant General Sir William Robertson.

The first objective for Gorringe on the left bank was the Turkish position blocking the Hanna Defile.

> That consisted of five entrenched lines one behind the other covering a depth of about 1½ miles, with a number of gun positions behind the third line and a barbed wire in front of their advanced line. On the right bank their forward position, just east of the Abu Rumman Mounds, ran roughly southward from the Tigris for about 2 miles.[259]

There was to be a much more sophisticated artillery programme than hitherto, but there was understandable apprehension in the ranks at the prospect of charging across the same bloody plain that had been the site of an earlier catastrophe. In the event, at 0455 hrs, the 13th Division made its assault behind a rolling bombardment and took the first Turkish line but, nevertheless, with predictable losses. For example, The Prince of Wales Volunteers lost three officers and twenty-three men from its 'A' Company alone.

The main body of the Turks had withdrawn unseen and the trenches were empty. A handful of prisoners were taken who said that the flooding had forced the hand of Khalil. He had withdrawn very skillfully and established a new position on the left bank, centred upon the Fallahiya bend and at Sannaiyat.

Maude exploited this swift success by sending his 40th Brigade forward to secure and hold a line between the river and the marsh about 2,000 yards east of the Fallahiya position. Gorringe had no intention of letting the enemy consolidate their dispositions and he determined to apply pressure as soon as possible – not least because the Tigris was rising again, and if the Turks breached the bank they could flood the area in front of their trenches and stop dead any further British advance.

At 1100 hrs, Gorringe stopped any independent actions by his subordinate commanders. The day was brutally hot and the mirage made nonsense of any attempt at observation. He realised that with the marsh and river as his two boundaries on the left bank only a frontal attack was possible. An attack in the relative cool of the evening was favoured.

Meanwhile, over on the right bank, 3rd Division had made excellent progress and, skirting some floods, it had occupied the abandoned Abu Rumman position. The nearest enemy force was at Bait Isa and, according to aerial reconnaissance, that consisted of 1,000 infantry, and there were 2,000 cavalry and six guns at Umm al Baram.

At this point Gorringe had every cause to be satisfied with the opening phase of his plan. At about 1945 hrs, General Maude's 13th Division, supported by artillery firing from both banks, assaulted Fallahiya. The ground was taken, but only after a stern, bloody fight in which 1,868 casualties were suffered. It was a surprise to find that the enemy position was not a continuous line, nor did it have any depth. All the indications were that Fallahiya was only a temporary blocking position designed to win time to build a stronger Sannaiyat position. Temporary or not, it was effective, as 1,868 witnesses would testify.

Gorringe's Corps was committed and courageous, but courage was not enough to offset the handicap of a logistics system that failed in every possible respect. The Mesopotamia Commission commented in its Report:

There is a consensus of evidence that the Force was deficient, even as late as in the spring of 1916, in wire cutters, telephones, water carts, Very lights, rockets, tents, mosquito nets, sun helmets, periscopes, telescopic sights, loophole plates, flares, bombs, hand grenades and even blankets and clothing. Our heavy casualties and reverses were in fact largely due to the lack of articles essential to the success of war carried out under modern conditions.[260]

This is not a list of sophisticated 'nice to haves'. These are low-cost, simple items that any nineteenth century army would expect to have in its inventory, and this was the state of affairs nearly two decades into the twentieth century in an army of the British Empire, upon which 'the sun never sets'.

The extreme left of the Turkish Sannaiyat position had been hard up against floodwaters that had overflowed from the Suwaikiya Marsh. However, capriciously, the water had receded and it looked as if it would be possible to outflank the Turkish left between its current position and the marsh. This was to be the objective of Younghusband's 7th Division, and the advance of an estimated 2¾ miles across a flat plain should not have presented any navigational problems, especially as there was an old Turkish communication trench that ran from Fallahiya to Sannaiyat to act as a guide. The target was the northern flank of the position, which consisted of three lines of trenches, about 100 yards apart

The attack was timed for 0455 hrs, a favoured time just before first light, but the advance of 7th Division to its assembly position was not straightforward. 19th and 28th brigades arrived in the right place at the right time – this despite them getting tangled up with elements of the 13th Division and its wounded all going in the opposite direction. 21st Brigade got into a frightful mess and the upshot was that at 0455 hrs, the Division was not ready. General Kemball asked Younghusband, his commander, to come forward and make a decision.

It is clear that the enemy were much further away than had been originally calculated; the estimate of 2¾ miles had been about a mile short – perhaps more. Younghusband decided that the attack should continue as (almost) planned, at 0530 hrs. The shroud of darkness was lost but the enemy trenches could not be discerned, so the objective was unclear. What was clear was that the driving north-west wind was having the effect of pushing surface water from the Suwaikiya Marsh and by so doing had contracted the distance between the communication trench and the marsh to about 400 yards.

The British went forward and any doubts as to the location of the enemy were quickly dispelled when they ran into 'a torrent of fire'[261] from both sides of the river. Once again, the bloodletting was horrific, and the first charge stalled, as did subsequent attempts. 7th Division went to ground 400 yards short of the Turkish wire.

The badly bruised 7th Division was extracted to fill a support role and 13th Division was ordered to make an advance on a two-brigade front, with 38th on the right and 40th on the left.

The flooded state of the Suwaikiya Marsh made a turning movement impracticable, and the frontage on which attack was possible was thus reduced to about 1,200 yards – in other words, manoeuvre was impossible, and the attackers were confined to the bottleneck of comparatively dry ground between the Tigris and the marsh.

Captain Whalley-Kelley, writing in the regimental history of The Prince of Wales's Volunteers (South Lancashire Regiment), recorded a participant's view of the events that followed:

By 2.00 am on the 9th April the [6th] Battalion [part of 38th Brigade] was formed up on its starting line in four lines of platoons in column at 50 yards distance, with the 6th King's Own [Royal Lancaster Regiment] on the right and the 6th East Lancashires on the left in the same formation. The objectives were only 650 yards away across the plain, and consequently the men had to lie down while waiting for zero.

It was a bitter night, and during the long wait everyone became numb with cold. At 4.20 am the long lines of infantry moved off silently and punctually, covering the first few hundred yards quickly and easily. When the leading platoons came within a hundred yards of their wire, however, the Turks fired a number of flares obliquely from their front, causing some confusion in the direction of march. At the same time they opened a heavy fire with machine guns and rifles, followed almost immediately by a storm of well-directed shells. The rapidity with which this defensive fire was put down seems to indicate that the enemy was well aware of the impending attack, and as our own artillery bombardment was ten minutes late in commencing it failed to synchronize with the assault – a disastrous error which, combined with the confusion caused by the Turkish flares, prevented all but the leading platoons closing with their opponents. These small parties entered the trenches and drove the enemy back to his second line, but they were unsupported and unable to get farther forward. The Turks rallied and counter-attacked, regaining their front line, although the gallant survivors of the invading platoons held their own until their bombs gave out.

Dawn was now breaking and it proved impossible to rally and reorganize units in daylight under heavy fire, and on ground devoid of any cover. Some companies of the Brigade managed to dig in where they stood, but the remainder fell back to the starting line. By dusk, however, it was clear that there was nothing to be gained by staying out in shallow trenches in exposed localities, and the forward companies were withdrawn also. Later a new line was consolidated about 400 yards from the Turkish position.

The non-success of the attack on the Sannaiyat position was not due to lack of courage on the part of the troops engaged, but their ranks now contained a large percentage of inexperienced soldiers, and owing to the casualties in the previous assaults all units were lacking in trained officers and junior leaders. Further, the difficulties and hazards of a night attack must never be forgotten, even with the most highly trained and seasoned troops.[262]

Battle casualties in this unsuccessful action amounted to 1,600, and in the two linked actions at Fallahiya and Sannaiyat, the 13th Division lost 3,600 men, or a chilling 46 per cent of its strength. Little wonder that in all that carnage and ferocious hand-to-hand fighting there were numerous acts of great courage, and five Victoria Crosses were won. On 10 April, Townshend issued another communiqué, and in it he said:

The result of the attack of the Relief Force on the Turks entrenched in the Sannaiyat position is that the Relief Force has not yet won its way through, but is entrenched close up to the Turks, in some places 200 or 300 yards distant. General Gorringe wired me last night that he was consolidating his position as close to the enemy's trenches as he can get, with the intention [of] attacking again. He has had some difficulty with the floods, which he had remedied.

I have no other details. However, you will see that I must not run any risk over the calculated date to which our rations would last – namely 15th April. As you will understand well, digging means delay, although General Gorringe does not say so.

I am compelled therefore to appeal to you all to make a determined effort to eke out our scanty means so that I can hold out for certain till our comrades arrive and I know I shall not appeal to you in vain. I have to reduce our rations to five ounces of meat for all ranks British and Indian.

In this way I can hold out until 21 April, if it becomes necessary, and it is my duty to take all precautions in my power. I am sorry that I can no longer favour the Indian soldiers in the matter of meat, but there is no possibility of doing so now. It must be remembered that there is plenty of horseflesh, which they have been authorised by their religious leaders to eat, and I have to recall with sorrow that by not having taken advantage of this wise and just dispensation, they have weakened my power of resistance by one month.

Townshend then went on to refer back to his communiqué of 26 January, extolled the manner in which the garrison had done its duty hitherto and assured them that they would be remembered in history, not unlike the defenders of 'Plevna and Ladysmith'. The probability was that not one man in a thousand had ever heard of Plevna, and only the British would connect with Ladysmith. He concluded by saying how confident he was of relief and asked again for support over 'the food question'.

This communiqué had the merit of bringing the garrison up to date but its content was quickly common knowledge in the town. Among the 6,000 inhabitants there were, without question, informants in touch with the Turks. Thus Townshend's communiqué gave Khalil the important information he required and was the genesis of his subsequent uncompromising position two weeks or so later when he declined to negotiate with Townshend.

This completely unachievable 15 April deadline applied yet more pressure on Gorringe, who had to fight a redoubtable foe and the elements as well. The water table rose again, and at this time of the year that was only to be expected. What was not expected was that, in what were impossible conditions, the British would be obliged to conduct offensive operations while building bunds to keep floodwaters at bay. On the left bank, the trenches were so filled with water that men had to swim! On the right bank, the Turks broke down the banks at Bait Aisa and Umm-al-Bahram, and by so doing exacerbated the effects of the flood. However, this was not entirely to the Turks' advantage, as they had to suffer their share of the water and the discomfort.

Gorringe was unimaginative and ruthless, but made of stout stuff. Notwithstanding the bizarre state of the battlefield, he decided that he would cause the 7th Division to hold the line on the left bank whilst he once more concentrated on taking the Es Sinn position. To get at Es Sinn, he had first to eliminate a complex of Turkish trenches that were located at Bait Aisa and in front of Es Sinn. His attack would, of necessity, make best use of what dry ground was available, but the effect of that was to channel his troops into areas that the Turks had already identified as his approach routes.

The troops were, to a man, tired and hungry. Many of them were in failing health. They had been in constant action for several months and the losses had made it necessary to reorganise units into composite battalions. Regimental cohesion was duly lost and, when that went, high morale went with it. Officers did not know their men, nor indeed did they know their fellow officers. Five thousand replacements were en route from Basra, but they were 'more jam tomorrow' and their arrival time and date was unknown.

The planned attack was put on 'hold' when yet another and especially heavy thunderstorm made any sort of progress impossible. The gale force winds drove the river water over the bund and completely flooded the country between the river and Umm-al-Bahram. The guns were unable to move into position to support the attack.

Eventually, just before first light on 15 April and in the midst of a further storm, the trudge forward was initiated. The 7th and 9th brigades waded slowly towards an objective on the far side of a massive lake. The thunder and lightning that played over their heads affected the compasses in use and, in the dark, men waded purposefully to they knew not where. Some units moved in a complete circle. Only one battalion found and took its objective. Two days later, the brigades tried again to take Bait Aisa. Shrouded by mist, they reached the Turkish lines behind an artillery barrage with only slight casualties.

What followed was a rare and very welcome, albeit brief, success. The 1st/1st Gurkhas and 1st/9th Gurkhas did particularly well, and did fearful execution with their kukris. The Turks were caught off guard. Khalil recognised that this was a critical situation and launched an overwhelming counter-attack with 10,000 men. The Gurkhas, who had advanced well beyond their objective, were cut off and the headquarters of 7th Brigade was captured and then retaken. 13th Division moved forward in support and the British established a line. During the night, the Turks made a series of frontal assaults and 8th Brigade bore the brunt, especially the 59th Rifles and 47th Sikhs. The gunners fired over open sights and the riflemen expended an average of 400 rounds each. With the dawn it became clear that many of those rounds had found a target.

The Battle of Bait Aisa raged on for several days and the balance swayed either way. The irresistible force of legend had met the immovable object of the same legend. It was a bloody and savage affair.

The battlefield was thick with Turkish bodies; the enemy had suffered over 4,000 casualties, the British, 1,650. More Turks were killed in this engagement than in Sheikh Saad, the Wadi and Fallahiya combined.[263] This was simply because, for a change, the Turks had been forced into an offensive. Despite their very heavy losses, the Turks still blocked the route to Kut and the relief of the garrison was looking more and more unlikely.

Gorringe was running out of ideas.

In London, patience with Duff and his Indian Army generals was running out.

In Kut, food was running out and men were now starving to death.

The result of all of this was that time too was running out.

It was evident to most of the participants that a disaster was imminent. The Turks had only to delay Gorringe to ensure the capitulation of Kut. In that garrison, by 18 April, life was very grim. In addition, Moberly noted:

> The weather was now becoming very hot in the daytime, and the glare of the sunlight, with dust outside the inundated areas, was very trying; and, in addition, all suffered greatly from the plague of flies, mosquitoes and sand flies. A Member of Parliament, who was in Mesopotamia at this period, describes in *Mons, Anzac and Kut* his experience of the flies. 'Nothing that I have ever seen or dreamed of came up to the flies. They hatched out until they were almost the air. They were in myriads. The horses were half mad. The flies were mostly tiny. They rolled up in little balls when one passed one's hand across one's sweating face. They were on your eyelids and lashes and in your lips and nostrils. We could not speak for them and could hardly see.'[264]

Edward Mousley recorded in his diary the demise of his much-loved horse, and noted that, 'Don Juan' had taken his last hedge. Mousley had, up until this point, managed to extend his charger's reprieve, but inevitably the order came. He gathered a last feed of grass for the horse, which salaamed most vigorously, as he had been taught. Mousley wrote:

> I asked the NCO to be careful that his first bullet was effective and to tell me when it was over. I kissed Don on the cheek; he turned and watched me go. Shortly after they brought me his black tail … Strange as it may seem, we ate his heart and kidneys for dinner, as they are reserved for owners. I am sure he would have preferred that I, rather than another, should do so.[265]

Gorringe and his troops did not give up. For the next ten days there were continuous offensive operations, all conducted in thick mud, the consistency of porridge or treacle. Weapons were clogged with mud and movement was slow, but nothing inhibited the killing.

The resupply of the garrison was now vital. Desperate situations sometimes call for desperate measures, and in this case the plan was not only desperate but also wildly optimistic. The paddle steamer *Julnar*, commanded by Lieutenant H.O.B. Firman RN, was selected to make a dash upriver to deliver sustenance to the garrison. In Amara, *Julnar* was fitted with protective steel plates and sand bags were placed to afford protection. She was then fully loaded. This activity was noted by Arab observers, who passed on the intelligence to the Turks.

There were ample volunteers to man the vessel and twelve, unmarried, naval ratings volunteered to crew the vessel. Engineer Sub Lieutenant W.L. Reed RNR gave his services as Chief Engineer. Lieutenant Commander C.H. Cowley RNVR, who had previously commanded *Mejidieh*, took the post of pilot. Cowley had been born in Baghdad, spent much of his working life on the Tigris and been employed by the 'Euphrates' and 'Tigris Navigation Company'. By dint of his birthplace he was considered, by the Turks, to be a Turkish subject. Charles Cowley realised that his life would be forfeit if he was captured but, nevertheless, he offered his services – this was particularly courageous, given the very hazardous nature of the mission.

The Tigris was at its height, sand banks were shifting and the 25-mile journey was to be made on the night of 24/25 April. It would not be easy as attempts to conceal the operation had failed. Nevertheless, in a vain attempt to confuse the Turks, all available artillery was brought into action as the ship, bearing 270 tons of supplies, slipped away in the dusk. The Turks were not at all confused; quite the reverse, they waited in ambush.

Julnar came under sustained fire as soon as she closed on the Turkish line. She passed through the Es Sinn line and was within 4 miles of Kut (8½

62. This poor quality photograph is of particular interest as it is the last image of HMS *Julnar* as she set off on her final mission on 24 April 1916. *(W. Nunn)*

miles by river) at Magasis when she struck one of several steel hawsers that had been stretched diagonally across the river. She rode over the hawser, but it fouled her rudder and she was held fast.

The ship was a sitting duck, subjected to a fierce bombardment at short range, and after being drenched with fire *Julnar* succumbed to a boarding party. The survivors of the crew were taken prisoner but Cowley was summarily murdered. Firman, who was killed in the bombardment, and Cowley were awarded the Victoria Cross. Members of the crew were also decorated for a gallant but failed team enterprise.

63. Lieutenant Commander C.H. Cowley VC RNVR, executed by the Turks on 25 April 1916. (*E. Sherson*)

64. Lieutenant H.O.B. Firman VC RN. *(Internet source)*

The attempt to succour the Kut garrison had failed, and in doing so it had signalled the end of the aggressive but very costly operations of the Tigris Corps. The Corps had stuck to its task from December 1915 until late April 1916. Tens of thousands of men had been killed or crippled and had suffered frightful privation in the process. 'These men showed grit and determination of a quality as fine as any recorded in the annuls [*sic*] of the Army.'[266] The MC concluded that, sadly:

211

There was great cause for anxiety in the state of the supplies of the relieving force. The Army was living from hand to mouth, a state of things to which the usual deficiency of transport largely contributed. ... After sixteen days [of] continuous fighting not only against the Turks but against the floods, all hope of relieving Kut had to be given up. The losses had exceeded 33 per cent and were even greater in British officers, and the fighting efficiency of the force was seriously affected.[267]

All that remained was for the British to negotiate the best terms that Khalil would grant. Townshend obtained the blessing of General Sir Percy Lake, the Army Commander, to open discussions. Lake said optimistically, 'With your prestige you are likely to get the best terms. We would of course supply food as you might arrange.'[268] Townshend's plan was to suggest to Khalil a six-day armistice, during which they could discuss terms and food could be supplied to the garrison. All troops were to hold their present position. In fact, as he recorded, 'the result was that much against my will. On 26 April, I had to negotiate with Khalil Pasha knowing that I had not a biscuit up my sleeve to argue with, knowing that Khalil knew I was *in extremis* for food. Twenty men were now dying daily from starvation.'

Khalil had, of course, a clear view of conditions inside Kut from his informants and Townshend's own recent insecure communiqué and he responded to Townshend's approach that same day. Later, the two commanders, each in his own steam launch, met on the river 'near the right flank of the Turkish entrenchments on the left bank'. Khalil was giving nothing away, and he had no need to. He declined all of Townshend's gambits, but according to Townshend:

My personal liberty was offered on condition that I did not destroy guns and material, ammunition etc. Such conditions, of course, were impossible to accept. Khalil told me that I would be sent to Constantinople and treated with the same honour as Osman Pasha with whose defence of Plevna[269] the Turks compared to mine of Kut. He said that I would be the honoured guest of the Turkish nation. My Force would be sent to Asia Minor to be interned in places in a good climate near the sea.

The final act was the occupation of Kut by Ottoman forces, which took place on 29 April when the Union flag was hauled down. Giving evidence to the MC, General Sir Percy Lake summarised the three main causes of failure. He determined that they were *'premature attacks, inadequate transport and exceptionally unfavourable weather'.*[270] This was hardly original thought on Lake's part. The last two of these factors were evident from the start of the campaign. One was never corrected and the other was predictable, God-given and unavoidable. As for *'premature attacks'*, Lake and the generals who served under him decided the timing of these operations. However, the MC did recognise that, like the curate's egg of legend, it was not all bad, and remarked:

> *This army had been put to a severe test, the 6th Division in particular. It had been almost continuously fighting or marching or moving by water for the best part of a year. It had been repeatedly short of supplies and owing to its frequent movements had felt acutely the want of adequate river transport. Nevertheless it had performed feats of fighting and endurance of which any army could be proud. The part of the advance called by the troops Townshend's regatta was an astounding piece of work.*

The Tigris Corps could do no more; the survivors had some respite but they were few in number. Twenty-three thousand casualties had been suffered since relief operations had started. 2nd Black Watch was reduced to forty-eight strong out of 842; 6th Jats, fifty of 825; 125th Rifles, eighty-eight of 840; and 1st Seaforths, 102 of 926. This was the bitter taste of defeat.

From September 1914 until May 1916, fourteen Victoria Crosses had been awarded. Tellingly, eight of these were won in April 1916 alone – all in the frantic attempts to relieve Kut, and perhaps a measure of the intensity of the fighting.

In Kut, when all were mustered, the garrison was composed of:

277 British officers
204 Indian officers
2,592 British rank and file
6,988 Indian rank and file
3,248 Indian camp followers.

This totals 13,309. However, in addition there were 1,450 sick and wounded, and of these, the worse cases, that is to say 1,136, were exchanged and despatched downriver. About three months later, the Turks released a further 345 being held in Baghdad.

During the siege, total casualties had been 3,776, of whom 1,513 had been killed by enemy action, 721 had died of disease and 1,958 had been wounded. Seventy-two men were 'missing'; some of these were from 67th Punjabis who fell at the bridge on 9 December 1915. The unmeasured balance were deserters.[271]

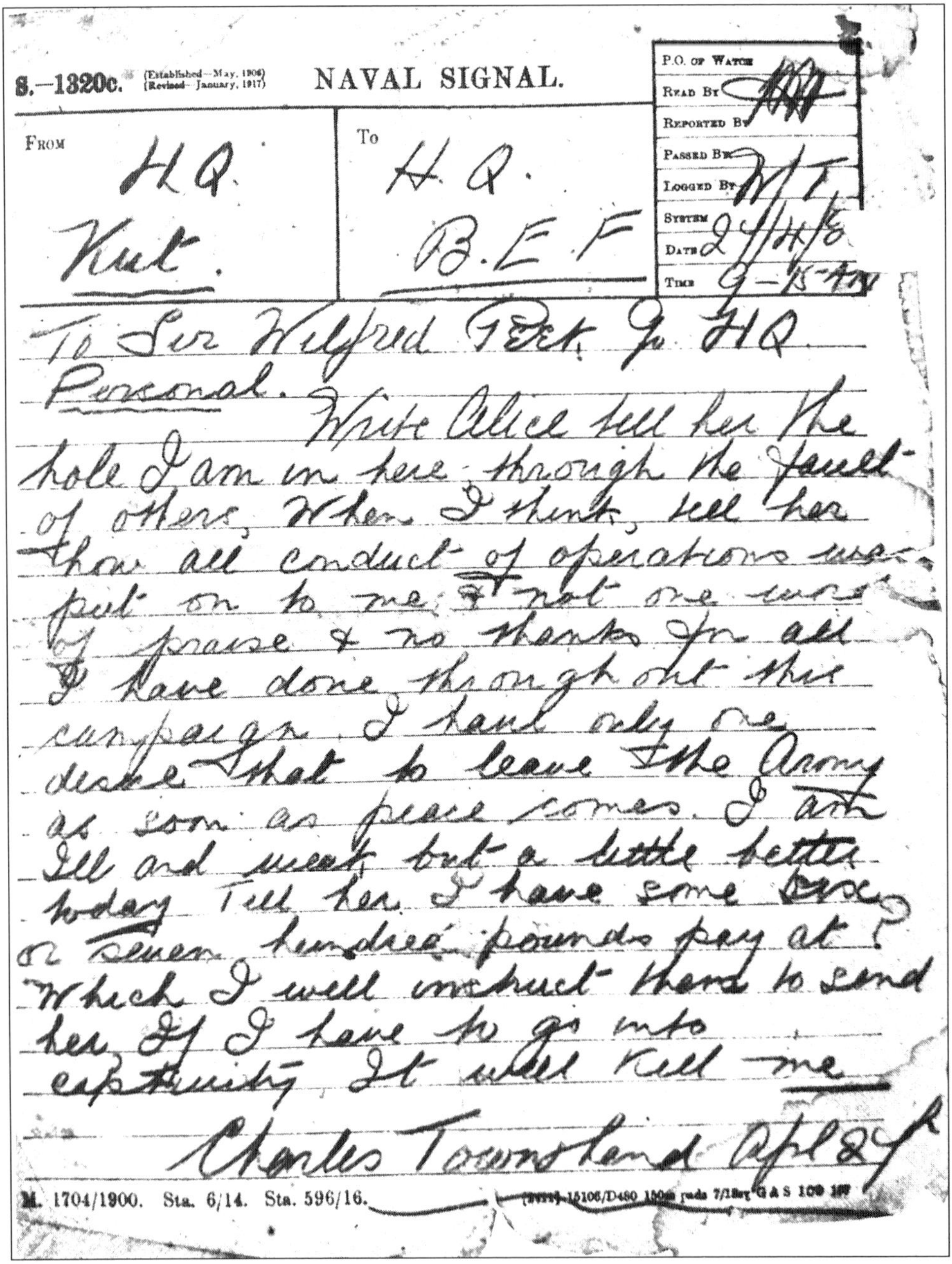

S.—1320c. (Established—May, 1906)
(Revised—January, 1917)

NAVAL SIGNAL.

FROM	To
HQ. Kut.	H.Q. B.E.F

P.O. OF WATCH
READ BY
REPORTED BY
PASSED BY
LOGGED BY
SYSTEM
DATE
TIME

To Sir Wilfred Peek. Go HQ.
Personal. Write Alice tell her the
hole I am in here through the fault
of others, When I think, tell her
how all conduct of operations was
put on to me, & not one word
of praise & no thanks for all
I have done throughout this
campaign. I have only one
desire that to leave the Army
as soon as peace comes. I am
Ill and weak but a little better
today Tell her I have some six
or seven hundred pounds pay at ?
Which I will instruct them to send
her If I have to go into
captivity It will kill me

Charles Townshend Apl 8

M. 1704/1900. Sta. 6/14. Sta. 596/16.

65. One of Townshend's last signals before his surrender. The tone is self-pitying and does not reflect well on him. *(R. Braddon)*

The civil population of about 6,000 did not get away unscathed: 247 were killed and 663 wounded. Not mentioned by any source are the Turkish prisoners. About 1,200 were taken by 6th Division at Ctesiphon and brought to Kut. However, thereafter their fate is unrecorded and it is presumed that, given the food issue, they were released. It is an intriguing loose end.

The final butcher's bill for operations in Mesopotamia from September 1914 to May 1916 was 40,000. 'All this went for nothing, not an inch of ground or any political advantage. Nothing, that is, beyond corpses and ruined reputations.'[272]

Chapter notes

249 Mousley, E.O., *The Secrets of a Kuttite*, p.91.

250 Hardinge to Chamberlain, 25 March 1916, Chamberlain papers, 62/2.

251 Busch, *Hardinge of Penshurst*, p.224.

252 This is an army expression going back generations to describe more colourfully 'a long time ago'.

253 Barker, A.J., *The Neglected War*, p.188.

254 Braddon, R., *The Siege of Kut*, p.262.

255 The papers of Mr R. Hague, as quoted by Braddon, R., in *The Siege*, p.216.

256 Moberly, F.J., *The Campaign in Mesopotamia*, p.358.

257 Major General (later, Lieutenant General) Frederick Stanley Maude KCB CMG DSO (1864–1917)

258 Moberly, F.J., *The Campaign in Mesopotamia*, p.371.

259 Ibid, p.372.

260 MC Report, p.38.

261 Candler, Edmund, quoted by Moberly, F.J., *The Campaign in Mesopotamia*, p.382.

262 Whalley-Kelley, H., *Ich Dien*, privately published.

263 Barker, A.J., *The Neglected War*, p.209.

264 Moberly, F.J., *The Campaign in Mesopotamia*, p.393.

265 Mousley, E.O., *The Secrets of a Kuttite*, p.131.

266 Barker, A.J., *The Neglected War*, p.214.

267 MC Report, p.35.

268 Townshend, C.V.F., *My Campaign in Mesopotamia*, p.335.

269 The Siege of Plevna was a series of major battles of the Russo–Turkish War (1877–78). These battles were fought by the combined armies of Russia and Romania against the Ottoman Empire. The Ottoman defence of that town held up the main enemy advance southwards into Bulgaria for five months. This had the effect of encouraging other great powers actively to support the Ottoman cause. Eventually, after the fourth major engagement in which the Ottoman forces temporarily broke out of confinement, force of arms and starvation forced the garrison to surrender.

270 MC Report, p.35.

271 Moberly, F.J., *The Campaign in Mesopotamia*, p.459.

272 Dixon, N.E., *On the Psychology of Military Incompetence*, p.95.

Chapter 15

Aftermath

'Commanders must have integrity. Without integrity, they have no power.'

(Sun Bin, *The Lost Art of War*, c. 350 BC, translated by Thomas Cleary)

The surrender of Kut was, without question, one of the greatest military defeats ever suffered by the British, and the loss of national prestige was commensurately enormous. Kut took its place with Yorktown and Kabul, and was only to be exceeded by the abject capitulation of Singapore twenty-six years later.

Colonel Nizam Bey, commanding the occupying force, was vastly discommoded, when he arrived in the British lines at the head of a Turkish force, to be told that the garrison's forty-three guns had all been destroyed.[273] The Turks swiftly took control of the town, hoisted the Ottoman crescent flag and got down to some serious looting.

The British officers assembled at the erstwhile garrison headquarters and many offered their swords to Nizam Bey as a token of their defeat – he accepted the swords and shook the donors by the hand. Other officers would have none of this and either broke their blades or cast them into the Tigris, where, no doubt under layers of silt, they remain to this day.

There were special arrangements for Townshend's surrender. Khalil Pasha came to the town, accepted Charlie's sword and revolver and, immediately, handed both back to him. This was a chivalrous gesture. However, it was in marked contrast with the conduct of a previously, generally admired enemy. The Turks now promptly and summarily hanged a considerable number of locals who they pronounced to be 'collaborators'. They may well have been, but they really did not have many other options.

Major General Charles Mellis was lying in his hospital bed when a Turkish soldier presumed to steal his boots. Mellis rose from his bed, chased and caught the thief, who was then soundly thrashed by a Turkish officer. Soon thereafter, but unconnected to this incident, a stream of Turks came to gaze at the redoubtable Mellis, whose courage and qualities of leadership were recognised. The feisty little general was the recipient of the title 'His Excellency Mellis Pasha'.

His captors treated Charles Townshend with fawning courtesy, and when he moved among his troops Mr H. Eato recalled that he said, 'I'm going to get you all released on parole.'[274] It was an empty promise that raised the expectations of the captured soldiers. There was, of course, no parole; only an order to form up and march the 9 miles upstream to Shamran. Nine miles was no test for fit, well-fed and shod infantry soldiers. But these men were starved, sick and in many cases their boots, rotted in the floods, were falling to pieces. Aggressive, hostile captors whipped the column of men along the route. It was a march that was beyond the capacity of some and they fell by the wayside – there they died.

At Shamran, initially, there was no food, only some large tents big enough to give cover to a hundred men. Later, a heap of Turkish army biscuits were dumped on the ground. These biscuits were circular, fibrous and as hard as stone. They looked like dog biscuits and tasted much worse. They contained sufficient straw and dirt to be utterly unpalatable. But to starving men they were all there was, so those who still had teeth tried to gnaw at the circumference. Some tried to break a biscuit into smaller pieces; others soaked them in Tigris water for hours and were agreeably surprised at the degree to which the biscuits swelled. They were now much more digestible but no less disagreeable.

The following morning a grim pattern emerged. Men started to froth at the mouth, their bowels loosened and their stomachs rebelled. 'A green slime' was the produce and in short order death followed. The doctors termed it 'enteritis', others thought it was an extreme form of cholera. Whatever it was, it was poisoning men who had survived shot and shell and all other sorts of privation. There was no other form of food available in the bleak wastes of the desert and the doctors issued orders that the biscuits should be soaked and then baked, 'or they will kill you.'[275]

That was no doubt excellent advice but not easy to implement. There were no facilities whatsoever to bake anything, and only camel thorn to provide a fire. For many it was all 'just too bloody difficult'. They ate their soaked biscuits and paid the price. The inhumanity of the Turks who watched this business was entirely in character. They had a track record in cruelty, well earned by the persecution of their Armenian population, starting on 24 April 1915. From that date, the Ottoman Government killed from 800,000 to 1,500,000 people. This was on much the same scale as that displayed by the Japanese and Germans some twenty-five years later in different parts of the globe. Compassion was not on offer and these captive British and Indian soldiers would need all the help they could get.

Moberly, in his *Official History, The Campaign in Mesopotamia* (p. 460), characteristically tried to rationalise the completely irrational and random manner in which the Turks treated their captives. Nevertheless, he concluded:

> of the British rank and file in captivity, 209 were exchanged, but more than 1,700, or over 70 per cent, died in captivity or have never been traced. Of the Indian rank and file about 1,300 are known to have died in captivity; between 1,100 and 1,200 escaped or were exchanged; the remainder were either repatriated or have been presumed to be dead.

In total, more than 3,000 British, Indian and followers perished 'in conditions and in circumstances which must forever form a blot on the Turkish reputation'. Long after the war, and certainly up to 1924, ex-prisoners of war were turning up in India.

Townshend was held at Kut for two days while appropriate arrangements were made on his behalf. Then he embarked in a launch with an entourage

66. One of the Indian soldiers of the 6th Division who survived a Turkish prison camp – many did not.

that consisted of Captain Morland, his aide-de-camp, Lieutenant Colonel Parr, two British orderlies, of whom Private John Boggis was one, an Indian servant, and a Portuguese cook. The vessel sailed upriver and, at Shamran, Charlie went ashore to say his farewells to Delamain, Hamilton and the newly promoted Evens, his former GSO1. The soldiers lined the bank, and as 'Our Charlie' sailed away they waved and cheered. Townshend commented in his diary that, 'I shall never forget that cheer. Tears filled my eyes as I stood to attention at the salute. Never shall I have such a command again. I loved the 6th Division with all my heart.'

He was quite right: he would never have such a command again – in fact, he would never be employed again. His behaviour, from April 1916 until the war's end, earned him the contempt of some, the dislike of others and the enmity of many more. This was because he did nothing to ease the condition of his men in captivity, despite having access to the senior levels of the Turkish Government. If 'betrayal' is an element in this book, then by his outrageous neglect of his duty and his men, Townshend takes his place among the betrayers. With his men out of sight and out of mind, Townshend was now at liberty to focus on things that really mattered – the well-being, comfort, status and reputation of Charles Townshend. All else was secondary.

Townshend was enough of a realist to recognise that the Turks would use him for propaganda purposes. The Turks 'were determined to show the British Force captured to the world.'[276] The Turkish newspaper *Tanin* was scathing when it said, 'This time they did not succeed in scuttling. This time the English who, when they cannot achieve success, consider it the greatest honour to run away, have been unable to do so as they did at Gallipoli.'[277]

When Russell Braddon published his book *The Siege* in 1969, he was forthright in his condemnation of Townshend, who epitomised all that Braddon abhorred. Braddon found few redeeming characteristics in Charlie and, as a result, his book, excellent though it is, lacks balance. However, Braddon had been able to interview many survivors of the 6th Division, so his book does enjoy a degree of authority. The book was duly published and created uproar with the survivors of the 6th Division, to whom 'their Charlie' was a hero despite his behaviour after the surrender being well documented. His surviving soldiers were vocal in his support and, fifty-three years after Townshend had abandoned them to their fate, they still thought that the sun rose and set upon him. As they say in Yorkshire, 'There's nowt so queer as folk.' To return to 1916, *The Times,* on 31 May, in an editorial thundered:

The main issue is not what General Townshend said to General Nixon, but first, who was responsible for the mad decision to advance on Baghdad. We trust Sir John Nixon will explain why he never transmitted General Townshend's objections and why he decided to disregard them.

In Baghdad, it was intended that Townshend should stay in von der Goltz's house, the Field Marshal having recently died. 'Typhus', said some, 'Poisoned by the Turks', alleged others, but the result was the same and the old German did not live long enough to see the fall of Kut. Townshend was housed in the Italian Consulate, where Khalil threw a dinner party in his honour. They sat for some hours while Townshend spoke at length about Napoleon.

Later in his journey to a comfortable billet, Townshend chanced upon a party of his soldiers and sailors led by Sub Lieutenant Reed. Some of the party were survivors of the *Julnar* episode, but the meeting was unproductive and all that Townshend could provide for his men was warm best wishes. The peregrinations and lifestyle of Chitrál Charlie, from this point on and until his death in May 1924, are not relevant to this text, but can be found in his biography of that title published by Pen and Sword Books.

Chapter notes
273 Sandes, E.W.C., *In Kut and Captivity.*
274 Eato, H., quoted by Braddon, R., *The Siege*, p.259.
275 Spackman, W.S., ibid, p.260.
276 Townshend, C.V.F., *My Campaign in Mesopotamia*, p.336.
277 Arabian Report, No. XXIa, 4 July 1916, FO/2779/152060.

Chapter 16

The Inquiry

'In the hunt for legitimate victims the Press has in
many cases been hurried into illegitimate extremes.
The demand for punishment has almost degenerated
into the witch-hunting of barbaric times.'
(Viscount Haldane, House of Lords, 13 January 1917)

In the summer of 1916 there was little to cheer about.

The abject retreat from the Dardanelles on 8 January had left a painful scar in the UK, but in Australia and New Zealand it was viewed as nothing short of a national catastrophe. Politically, the Gallipoli campaign was unfinished business. Empire casualties had been 115,000 and there were questions that had to be answered.

The Easter Rising in Dublin on 24 April 1916 had created fear of an enemy within. The surrender of Kut on 29 April so soon after was a national humiliation, and the pyrrhic naval victory achieved off Jutland on 1 June had done little to offset the loss of prestige. Lord Kitchener, the Secretary of State for War, a national hero, was lost on HMS *Hampshire* on 5 June. National morale was low and a proactive press was in pursuit of Asquith and his government.

The Vincent-Bingley Report was drafted in May 1916 after the principals had spent eight days in Bombay (now Mumbai) and a further six weeks taking evidence in and around Basra. Initially, His Majesty's Government kept the Report under wraps as its findings were nothing short of political dynamite. There were suggestions that the Report could be issued in a shortened form, but that lack of transparency was readily seen to be politically dangerous. However, by now the public was sufficiently aware of the medical debacle in Mesopotamia. Survivors and witnesses to the Battles of Ctesiphon, Sheikh Saad, the Wadi River, the Hanna Defile, the Dujaila Redoubt and Sannaiyat provided reports of the shambles along and on the Tigris. Public anger increased at the reported suffering of Indian and British soldiers, and the Press was in full cry.

The Vincent-Bingley Report was eventually completed in July 1916 but was not immediately made public. Perhaps this was as well, as the nation was reeling in shock at the recent slaughter on the Somme. In 20,000 homes, women were mourning the death of husbands, and sons; 40,000 other homes knew a loved one had been wounded.

General Sir Beauchamp Duff, who had set up the Vincent-Bingley investigation, was now firmly hoisted with his own petard. He did not voice his views publically, and little wonder. However, he wrote that it was 'of a nature calculated to encourage the enemy and give him information of military value'.[278] He thrashed around and then took the line that the reporters had exceeded their brief.

The Report was composed of 180 paragraphs, and Duff pronounced that seventy-seven of these were 'objectionable'. He placed the 'objectionable' paragraphs into four categories. These were: those dealing with operations not yet made public, those showing lack of organisation, those complaining of lack of morale, and those condemning certain officers by name. He thought that the first might be militarily important and the last three could be used as propaganda to disrupt the morale of the troops.[279]

Duff was in a quandary; that there was a report was no secret but he could not suppress it. Reluctantly, he forwarded it to Chamberlain in the India Office and to the Chief of the Imperial General Staff, General Wully Robertson. Robertson believed, and probably hoped, that the relief of the 6th Division would quell the need for commissions of inquiry.

The priapic David Lloyd George, no firm ally of the Prime Minister and an active rival for political power, had replaced Kitchener in the War Office. The Prime Minister, Herbert Henry Asquith, known always as 'H.H.', had been in post since 1908. In peacetime, he had established himself as a safe pair of hands with the skills to pursue Liberal policies in the face of Conservative opposition. He was not an attractive individual, certainly not with the ladies, as he had a reputation as a 'groper'. The stress of wartime administration was beyond him and, in any case, he was 'idle'. He clung to office for almost two years, heading a coalition government from May 1915.

In summary, Asquith was an unsuccessful war leader who devoted a disproportionate amount of time and energy to his personal comfort and affairs. His biographer, John Little, described him as 'feckless'.[280]

The Press pursued the Vincent-Bingley issue, reflected public anger and became increasingly strident in its criticism. Asquith's grip on power was slipping from his grasp but he stayed long enough to appease the Press, in part, and gained some breathing space. He achieved this because, in early

August 1916, HMG appointed a group of worthies to form the Mesopotamia Commission. At the same time a separate body was formed to examine the conduct of operations in the Dardanelles.

In the House of Commons, Sir Henry Craik, the MP for Glasgow and Aberdeen Universities, put the ball into play on 14 August 1916 when he asked the Secretary of State for India whether he had communicated with the authorities in India and obtained consent to the publication of the report by Vincent, Bingley and Ridsdale, and whether the Report 'would be laid upon the table before the recess.'[281]

Austen Chamberlain produced a lengthy answer and said that now that a further commission had been appointed (Mesopotamia), it would 'proceed with all possible expedition to inquire with regard to the provision for the sick and wounded.' In the meantime, the conclusions of Vincent-Bingley had to be considered *sub judice.*

In December 1916, Lloyd George achieved his aim when he brushed Asquith aside and became Prime Minister. The new Prime Minister, his government and, by no means least, Lord Hardinge, were under close scrutiny and the hope was that the MC might pull some chestnuts from the political fires. The Commission was charged to:

Enquire into the origin, inception and conduct of war in Mesopotamia, including the supply of drafts, reinforcements, ammunition and equipment to the troops and fleet, the provision for the sick and wounded, and the responsibility for these departments of Government whose duty it is to minister to the wants of the forces employed in the theatre of War.[282]

So, who were the men selected to conduct this inquiry? Today their names ring few bells, and even in 1916 they may not have been front-line household names, but they were all firmly 'establishment' figures. They were:

Lord George Hamilton GCSI PC (1845–1927)
Educated at Harrow. In 1864 he was commissioned into the Rifle Brigade and served in Canada. Four years later, he 'exchanged' into the Coldstream Guards, but he was a guardsman only very briefly. Disraeli, no less, invited him to contest the

67. Lord George Hamilton – the Chairman of the Mesopotamia Commission.

constituency of Middlesex on behalf of the Conservative Party; duly elected, he held that seat for seventeen years (1868–85). He moved and represented Ealing from 1885 to 1906. He held office as Under Secretary of State for India for four years, from 1874 to 1878. He was only thirty-three when he was made a Privy Councillor in 1878. He moved on to become First Lord of the Admiralty in 1885 and served in that post until 1892 (with a brief gap in 1886). In 1895, he was appointed Secretary of State for India and held the job until 1903.

Hamilton was well qualified to be the Chairman of the Commission; his experience of the India Office gave him an insight into the workings of that organisation and probably a feel for the relationships. However, his heart was not in the job, and he said so.

Richard Hely-Hutchinson, 6th Earl of Donoughmore KP PC (1875–1948)
Educated at Eton. He served briefly as a militia officer in Ireland and took his seat in the House of Lords in 1900. A Conservative politician, he was Under Secretary of State for War from 1903 to 1905 in Arthur Balfour's government.

Lord Hugh Cecil, 1st Baron Quickswood MP (1869–1956)
Educated at Eton and Oxford. He was a Conservative politician and was first elected MP in 1895; he took especial interest in religious issues. He served in the Royal Flying Corps in France and, based on his practical experience, was a staunch defender of Lord Trenchard, who had a chequered career in the First World War. He represented Oxford University from 1910 until 1937. He was an opponent of Home Rule for Ireland and a man of strong principles. He was Churchill's best man in 1908.

John Hodge MP (1855–1937)
His education is unknown but he attended the 'University of Life' and made a name for himself as a pugnacious trade unionist. He was a member of Manchester City Council from 1897 to 1901, and stood for Parliament in 1900 and 1903. He was eventually elected in the 1906 General Election. Hodge was staunchly patriotic, and the impression is that he was included on this commission by Asquith as a left-wing token.

Sir Archibald Williamson, 1st Baron Forres Bt MP (1860–1931)
Educated at Craigmont School and Edinburgh University. He was elected as the Liberal Member for Elginshire from 1906 to 1918, and for Moray and Nairn until 1922. He had been the chairman of several Home Office,

Board of Trade and Parliamentary committees, so his experience led directly to his appointment to the MC. After the war, he became Financial Secretary to the War Office from 1919 to 1921.

Commander Josiah Wedgwood, 1st Baron Wedgwood DSO PC DL MP (1872–1943)

Educated at Clifton College and the Royal Naval College, Greenwich. When war broke out in South Africa, he was commissioned in the Army and served as a captain commanding a battery of artillery. After a period spent as a magistrate, he returned to UK and was first elected as a Liberal MP in 1906. At that time he made it clear that the party whip would not bind him.

In 1914, he joined the Royal Naval Volunteer Reserve. He served in France and was later wounded in the Dardanelles, having first won the Distinguished Service Order during the landings at Cape Helles. At this time he espoused the Zionist cause and returned to the Army to command a machine-gun company in the 2nd South African Brigade. In 1917, he was appointed Assistant Director of Trench Warfare in the rank of colonel. After the war, he described himself as an 'impenitent, independent radical'. That he proved to be a 'loose cannon' on the MC probably surprised no one.

Admiral Sir Cyprian Bridge GCB (1839–1924)

Educated at Walthamstow House. He joined the Royal Navy 1853 and served during the transition from sail to steam, seeing active service in the Crimean War. Interestingly, he commanded the Osprey Class Sloop *Espiegle* in the Western Pacific (a later ship of that name has already featured in this text). He was appointed Commander-in-Chief of the Australian Squadron in 1894, and in 1898, after promotion to vice admiral, he took command of the China Station. He retired from the Navy in 1904, aged sixty-five, and was then called on to investigate the Dogger Bank Incident.[283]

General Sir Neville Lyttelton GCB GCVO (1845–1931)

Educated at Eton. He was commissioned into the Rifle Brigade in 1865. In a lengthy and very successful career, he saw action in Egypt, the Sudan and South Africa. He was Commander-in-Chief South Africa, Commander-in-Chief Ireland and, finally, Chief of the Imperial General Staff 1904–1908. In the latter post he was the professional Head of the British Army. However, the *Oxford Dictionary of National Biography* judged that he was 'feckless, malleable and failed to lead the Army Council'. That is not a ringing endorsement of his ability.

68. General Sir Neville Lyttelton GCB GCVO.

Notwithstanding Lyttelton's incapacity as a bureaucrat in his final appointment, it should not, and probably did not, dull his concern for the care of soldiers that he had had to exercise during his career.

* * *

Lord George Hamilton was by no means a neutral chairman, and later he made no secret of the fact that he had taken the job on in order to avoid a political crisis.[284] There were six members of the Commission who had military experience to some degree.

Appointment to the Commission was not a sinecure and its members were all active in public life in one capacity or another. The Commission was given the authority to compel attendance by witnesses to take their evidence on oath. It met on sixty occasions and took evidence from those witnesses *'who were either in England or could be brought home without serious detriment to the public interest'*. A hundred and eighteen senior witnesses were duly examined and some are listed at Appendix A on page 268.

The Commission decided that it was unnecessary to visit Mesopotamia because it had access to the comprehensive records of the Vincent-Bingley Report, which it incorporated into its own report. Nevertheless, the decision of the MC not to visit the theatre was later perceived to have been a mistake, and as a result its credibility was damaged.

In the meantime, Major General Frederick Maude, who had previously served on the Western Front and in the Dardanelles, and had played a part in the operations to relieve Kut in April 1916, was the rising new star. He had witnessed the surrender of Kut and he prospered at the failure of Generals Lake and Gorringe, neither of whom had been able to relieve the garrison.

Maude was promoted to lieutenant general and given command of the Tigris Corps vice Sir George Gorringe in July 1916. Later that same month, he was appointed as Army Commander vice Sir Percy Lake. The rise of Maude had been nothing short of meteoric. He was to prove to be the right horse for the right course.

General Sir Wully Robertson, the Chief of the Imperial General Staff, ordered Maude to stabilise the British line south of Kut, but Maude was more proactive than that and exceeded his brief. He reorganised his force and streamlined his logistic support, and as a result was well placed when he was ordered, on 18 September 1916, to advance further into Mesopotamia and up the Tigris. This was an entirely political decision driven through by Austen Chamberlain (Secretary of State for India) and Lord Curzon (a member of the War Council and Leader of the House of Lords), taken in the face of the opposition of the CIGS.

Maude was not an appealing personality, but he had an eye for detail and was known as 'Systematic Joe' by his officers. Heavily reinforced, Maude won the battles of Mohammed Abdul Hassan, Hai and Dahra in January 1917. He recaptured Kut in February 1917 and took the great prize of Baghdad on 11 March 1917. From Baghdad, he launched the Samarrah Offensive and extended his operations to the Euphrates and Diyala rivers.

By the summer of 1917, the British position in Mesopotamia was immeasurably stronger and more secure than when the MC was established. The port facilities at Basra had been rapidly increased and improved, and two further anchorages were established at Magil and Nahr Umar to reduce the bottleneck at Basra. Taken together, these initiatives increased the tonnage landed in the theatre from 38,916 to 100,000 tons by mid 1917. At this point fourteen ships could be attended to and cleared within three days. Maude's appreciation that modern industrial warfare required the harnessing of all resources to achieve strategic advantage set him apart from his predecessors and, in part, he was responsible for transforming Basra into a major regional east-of-Suez port.[285]

The MC published its lengthy, 188-page Report in June 1917. The Press, and the *Daily Mail* in particular, fed public indignation and gave rise to the quotation at the head of this chapter. The judgments in the Report were all-embracing and broadly critical of both the Indian Government and HMG. Lord Curzon, one-time friend of Hardinge and a former viceroy, on reading the Report, did not sit on any convenient fence. He pronounced that, 'I regret to say that a more shocking exposure of official blundering and incompetence has not in my opinion been made, at any rate since the Crimean War.'[286] Curzon was a powerful political figure and his view carried weight.

The MC Report concluded that the despatch of Indian Expeditionary Force 'D' was justifiable but that the division of responsibility between the IG and HMG was unworkable, and the scope of the expedition *'was never sufficiently defined in advance, so as to make each successive move part of a well thought-out and matured plan.'*[287] It drew attention to the fact that the commander-in-chief (Duff) should have visited the theatre and, because he did not do so, the Army headquarters in Simla did not appreciate the difficulties being experienced on the ground and, consequently, could not make adequate provision. It commented upon the advance to Baghdad in these terms:

> *The weightiest share of responsibility lies with Sir John Nixon, whose confident optimism was the main cause of the decision to advance. The other persons responsible were: In India, The Viceroy (Lord Hardinge) and the Commander-in-Chief (Sir Beauchamp Duff); In England, the Military Secretary of the India Office (Sir Edmund Barrow), the Secretary of State for India (Mr Austen Chamberlain) and the War Committee of the Cabinet.*[288]

The Report dealt with 'Supplies, Equipment and Reinforcements' and found that the expedition was provisioned with general armament and equipment on a scale intended for an Indian frontier expedition and not up to the standard of modern European warfare, and was quite insufficient. It mentioned that the diet of Indian troops lacked nutritive qualities, causing scurvy and other conditions, but it balanced the criticism by agreeing that *'since then this ration has twice been improved.'*

An illuminating anecdote that gets a telling in many histories of the period concerns the Quarter Master General in Delhi, who, when advised that the lack of fresh vegetables in Mesopotamia was causing scurvy and beriberi, allegedly responded by saying, 'That's what they all say. What I always say is – if you want vegetables – GROW 'EM.' Chamberlain recorded this ignorant and unsophisticated attitude in a note on 14 July 1917.[289]

In dealing with transport, the MC findings were predictable. At page 113, sub-paragraph (f) appears: *'With General Sir John Nixon rests the responsibility for recommending the advance in 1915 with insufficient transport and equipment. For what ensued from shortage of steamers, General Sir John Nixon must be held to blame.'* It goes on to describe the shortage of transport as *'fatal'* to the relief operations. The facilities or lack of them at Basra were said to be *'hopelessly inadequate'*.

It was on page 114 that the Report reached 'Medical' and the reader will, by now, already have drawn his or her own conclusion on this topic. However, the formal record was predictably damning. The MC said Vincent-Bingley found that:

> *A grave responsibility for that part of the suffering, which resulted from avoidable circumstances, rests with the Senior Medical Officer of the Force, Surgeon General G.H. Hathaway and with General Sir John Nixon the General Officer Commanding the Force from 9 April 1915 until 19 January 1916. General Hathaway did not represent with sufficient promptitude and force the needs of the service for which he was responsible, and in particular failed to urge the necessity for adequate transport for the sick and wounded with the insistency that the situation demanded, General Nixon did not, in our opinion, appreciate the conditions which would necessarily arise if provision for the sick and wounded of his force were not made on a more liberal scale. We endorse the finding as regards Surgeon General Hathaway, who in our judgment showed himself to be unfit for the high administrative office he held.*

The senior leadership in the Indian Army Medical Service had been unsettled during the campaign. Surgeon General Sir William Babtie was the Director of the service from March 1914 to June 1915. However, during this period he was out of station for six weeks in February/March 1915. His absence is unexplained, but no one was nominated to stand in for him, despite it being the normal practice for someone to deputise for a senior officer when he is out of station for an extended period. The six weeks that Babtie, the head of the medical service, was away saw his organisation leaderless. It was an unsatisfactory state of affairs. Surgeon General J.G. MacNeece relieved Babtie in July 1915 and followed him as Director. He returned 'home' on sick leave on 15 April 1916, just before the fall of Kut.

The Commission examined in some detail the performance of the man who headed the medical organisation. Given the dire under-achievement of the Indian Medical Service, it is little wonder that General Babtie suffered under the scrutiny. The Report considered:

> In one sense, the numerous sanitary and precautionary requisitions of Colonel Hehir are a measure of Sir William Babtie's omissions. We have seen that during the first months of the campaign Colonel Hehir was forced to wire to India for sun glasses, anti-toxin, mosquito-nets, spine pads etc. etc. Though it is true Sir William Babtie was not technically responsible for the actual provision of all of these requisites, yet it is quite clear that they were essential to the maintenance of the health of the troops, and in our opinion Sir William Babtie should have made it his duty to have impressed upon the Quarter Master General's or other departments concerned the necessity for providing well beforehand, these and other medical ancillaries in which the expedition is proved to have been deficient. He did not do this, with the result that many of these essentials did not reach the troops in sufficient time and sufficient quantities.[290]

The evidence adduced by the Commission showed that the dietary needs of the soldiers were not satisfied, despite an early warning from Colonel Hehir on 8 April 1915 in which he gave clear warning that 2 ounces of potatoes and only 28 ounces of fresh meat per week was insufficient to prevent scurvy, unless supplemented by additional vegetables. Babtie said, in his defence, that he had raised the question of rationing at the Commander-in Chief's conference and an additional ration was sanctioned. The Commission was unimpressed and sceptical about the implementation of this supplement because, nevertheless, Indian troops suffered from scurvy – an entirely preventable disease. This was an indictment of not only the medical establishment but the supply system as well. In May 1916, 7,500 men were lost to the force for nineteen weeks suffering from scurvy directly attributed to deficiencies in the Indian ration.

General Babtie came in for further criticism over the non-provision of medical personnel in that he 'despatched Force 'D' 1,800 miles from its base, with medical personnel short even of the authorised scale. When reinforcements were sent he took, or acquiesced in, measures that even further reduced the exiguous scale ... so that each division was supplied with only twelve sections of field ambulance instead of the proper complement of twenty.'

Babtie, a soldier by profession but, more importantly, a doctor by discipline, was sufficiently senior that his responsibilities ranged well outside the detailed treatment of the sick and wounded. For example, at its base the scale of provision of hospital ships was dependent upon his advice.

Later, the well-documented dearth and inadequacy of these vessels was laid at his door. He defended himself by saying that he was not in the 'command loop' and that Nixon had not made clear to him the extensive campaign up the Tigris that was planned. His medical arrangements were accordingly limited to the conquest and retention of Basra and the oil fields. He advised the Commission that, *'if he had had a hint of Baghdad the arrangements would have had to be absolutely put into the melting pot.'*[291]

Notwithstanding the litany of medical issues and their associated failings, Sir William Babtie, a distinguished and gallant officer, impressed the Commission as *'an officer of ability and knowledge'* when it took his evidence. But, it concluded, he did not bring his qualities to bear upon the task before him and *'he accepted obviously insufficient medical provision without protest and without adequate effort to improve it. He cannot therefore be held blameless.*[292] *Having regard to all the circumstances, we desire to say that the faults of his administration were not in our judgment, such as to prove him unfit for important responsible administrative posts.'*

Major General MacNeece, who replaced Babtie, was willing and desirous of leading his service to the best of his ability, but rather crushingly the MC described him as *'a man of advancing years and diminishing strength, unequal to the position he was called upon to fill'*. His administration of the Indian Medical Service covered the worst of the medical disasters, but he had inherited a bag of worms and quite reasonably he escaped any formal censure, particularly as the medical situation had, by now, improved.

Lord Hardinge, however, was judged to be generally responsible as he was the head of the IG and had been entrusted with the management of the expedition, medical provision included. He may have shown the *'utmost goodwill'*, but given the magnitude of his authority he was *'not sufficiently strenuous and peremptory'*. However, Duff earned *'a more sever censure ... for not only did he, as Commander-in Chief of the Army in India, fail closely to superintend the adequacy of medical provision but he declined, for a considerable time, to give credence to rumours which proved to be true and he failed to take measures, which a subsequent experience shows would have saved the wounded from avoidable suffering.'*

There were more general criticisms made of the IG, but on perusal those criticisms are aimed at the only two people with the executive power to effect change and to improve the *'cumbrous and inept military system of administration'*. That is to say, Hardinge and Duff.

Generals Townshend, Aylmer, Younghusband, Gorringe and Lake did not feature in the Report in any negative sense, but Hathaway, Hardinge, Duff and Nixon attracted frequent criticism.

The tenor of life in the theatre was addressed by the Report and it commented upon the attempts made by Colonel Hehir to assist and advise Surgeon General Hathaway (on the instructions of General Babtie), which fell on stony ground and were clearly resented. The Report noted with disfavour the treatment meted out to Major Carter, the first to bring to the notice of the authorities the medical difficulties, and whom Generals Cowper and Hathaway then threatened with professional sanctions for his trouble. The Report also noted the later threats made to Cowper by Duff, via Lake, when Cowper, in turn, presumed to comment negatively on the provision of river transport. The Report concluded that, *'Such incidents as these indicate the atmosphere of repression of complaints which permeated Indian officialdom, and do much to explain the unfortunate suppressions of truth.'*[293]

The Report drew attention to the absurd dual chain of command that was in place in 1914, the various authorities that had to be consulted and who had a voice in the direction of affairs. It said:

> *We will enumerate the various authorities; first the General Officer Commanding on the spot in Mesopotamia, then the Commander-in-Chief in India, then the Viceroy, followed by the Secretary of State for India with his Military Secretary, then the War Council with the Imperial Staff and finally the Cabinet. It was under this dual system that the administrative failures took place during 1915 and early in 1916 and it was not until London took over the sole charge that there was any marked improvement in the management of the campaign.*[294]

The members of the MC were not as one in the production of its Report, and Commander Josiah Wedgwood took a different view to his colleagues. He had served during the war and insisted on producing a minority report. He took a very robust line with the two most senior people who were considered to have a case to answer. He said, writing of the attitude of the IG towards the expedition to Mesopotamia and to the war as a whole:

> *It is precisely Lord Hardinge and Sir Beauchamp Duff who I cannot merely charge with human error. They, and they alone … formed and were the Indian Administration during that part of the war under consideration. <u>Throughout their conduct of the war they seem to have shown little desire to help and some desire to actually obstruct the energetic prosecution of the war.</u>* [Author's emphasis] *As a reason for this obstruction they gave – the situation in India; and I for one feel no sense of obligation to them for placing 'risks' in India above the dire necessities of the British Empire, and the welfare of their own troops in Mesopotamia.*[295]

**69. Commander Josiah Wedgwood MP – the author of the Minority Report
and outspoken critic of Hardinge and Duff.** *(Internet source)*

In June 1917, the MC published its findings and, initially, these were only
circulated in government circles – causing consternation, as very senior
government servants, both military and civilian, were named in the most
uncompromising terms. For example, Wedgwood had, in effect, accused
Hardinge and Duff with conduct tantamount to treason. The body of the MC
was less aggressive when it said:

> *To Lord Hardinge of Penshurst, as Viceroy, belongs the general
> responsibility attaching to his position as the head of the Indian
> Government, to which had been entrusted the management of the
> expedition, including the provision of medical services. In regard to the
> actual medical administration he appears to us to have shown throughout
> the utmost good will, but considering the paramount authority of his office,
> his action was not sufficiently strenuous and peremptory.*

233

Wedgwood did not end with that first blast, and a little later in his report he added, *'To charge two high officials with "little desire to help and some desire to actually obstruct the energetic prosecution of the war" is a serious accusation and one difficult to accept.'* He went on to say that he had accumulated a body of evidence from cables, letters and extracts from the protests made by such as Lord Kitchener and Lord Crewe. He then made it clear that Hardinge and Duff had served the Empire best by leaving their posts. He observed:

> *I have felt it advisable to back up the extracted evidence with a list of measures for helping the Empire that India has adopted since the departure of Lord Hardinge and General Duff, many of them having been previously waved aside as impracticable by these same officials in written evidence before the Commission. Such a list will confirm my findings.*

Wedgwood's 'evidence' fills many pages of the MC Report, and if nothing else it certainly highlights the unfortunate attitude of 'India first at all costs', an attitude that was emphatically confirmed when Lord Crewe, General Sir Edmund Barrow and Major General Maurice (Director of Military Operations) gave their evidence.

There is no profit in pursuing the campaign of Josiah Wedgwood, but suffice it to say he was clearly angered by what he had heard and was anxious that retribution should fall on those guilty of culpable incompetence. He was not alone. The publication of the MC Report, and Wedgwood's addendum in particular, was inflammatory; the Government looked to limit the damage and the first step was to debate the issue in the House of Commons.

The MC Report had identified and censured in approximately descending order of culpability the following: Lord Hardinge, General Sir Beauchamp Duff, Lieutenant General Sir John Nixon, Major General H.G. Hathaway, Lieutenant General Sir William Babtie, Mr Austen Chamberlain, General Sir Edmund Barrow and the War Committee of the Cabinet.

The extraordinary, convoluted and grossly inefficient administrative system that managed the Indian Army was fully exposed and dissected by the Commission. The decision-making process, compounded by geographic constraints and inadequate funding, combined to inhibit the effectiveness of the Army. The Commission's very strong recommendation for immediate reform and reorganisation was a positive outcome of its labours.

The MC, its work done, stood down and left it to HMG to decide how to play a very volatile document that simply could not be ignored.

Hardinge's reaction at the time was predictable. The document was, in his view, 'unfair and narrow minded, leaving the impression that Mesopotamia was India's sole effort, criticising everybody and giving credit to nobody in the process'.[296]

The Cabinet's concern, however, was how it was to deal with the Report. Pigeonholing it was not realistic and would certainly anger the House; the suggestion that there be courts martial for the civilians mentioned, like courts martial for officers, would, as a priority, require the drafting of specific charges. Neither would it be easy; as in Hardinge's case, although the Commission had been censorious, it had nevertheless not specified any crime.

Lloyd George was in a quandary and recognised that the MC Report was a volatile document likely to blow up in his government's face. There was a need to be decisive. The Prime Minister ducked the issue and took refuge in the safe haven of politicians – he appointed a committee to advise him.

But first there was to be a debate in the House of Commons.

Chapter notes

278 Hardinge to Chamberlain telegram No. M39 0554, 18 July 1916.

279 Davis, P.K., *Ends and Means*, p.177.

280 Little, J.G.H., *H. Asquith and Britain's Manpower problems, 1914–1915*.

281 Hansard, 14 August 1916.

282 MC Report, p.3.

283 On 21/22 October 1904 the Russian Baltic Fleet mistook forty-eight British fishing trawlers as torpedo boats of the Imperial Japanese Navy and opened fire. Fortunately, the Russian gunnery was appalling and only one trawler was sunk, with the loss of two men. The incident almost led to war with Russia.

284 Barker, A.J., *The Neglected War*, p.375.

285 Memorandum on *India's contribution to the War in Men, Material and Money: August 1914 to November 1918*, India Office Library, L/MIL/17/5/2381.

286 Curzon, memo of 4 June 1917, Cab 1/24/5, Chamberlain to Curzon, 5 June, Chamberlain papers, E/6/3.

287 MC Report, p.111.

288 Ibid, p.112.

289 It also features in the Crewe papers at M/15(2) and also in *Tragedy of Mesopotamia* by George Buchanan at p.69 in his book, which was written in 1938.

290 MC Report, p.71.

291 Ibid, p.74.

292 Ibid, p.114.

293 Ibid, p.88.

294 Ibid, p.117.

295 MC, Wedgwood, p.121.

296 Busch, B.C., *Hardinge of Penshurst*, p.268.

Chapter 17

The Debate

'It was Hardinge who had failed, not merely
as a viceroy but as a man, half a whine and half
an attempt to shift the blame and had just been
made a Knight of the Garter in spite of the
gathering protest about his competence.'

(*The Morning Post*, 13 July 1917)

The debate in the House of Commons, held over 12/13 July 1917 and faithfully recorded in Hansard, amounts to about 80,000 words. To put that into perspective, this book is about 100,000 words. The extracts from Hansard can do no more than give a flavour of the debate, in which there were few references to the officers and men who were so shamefully treated in Mesopotamia. In contrast, warm tributes were paid, during the debate, to the public service given to all of those who were censured in the Mesopotamia Commission Report. The only exception to the eulogising was Surgeon General Hathaway; he was the most junior of those named and attracted unanimous scorn.

On 12 July, Mr S. MacNeill addressed the House and challenged the status of Lord Hardinge. He quoted the cases of Lord Tenterden and the Earl of Iddesleigh who, on succeeding to peerages, did not apply for writs of succession to the House of Lords, on the grounds that a seat in that assembly would disqualify Lord Tenterden for the position of Permanent Under-Secretary of State for Foreign Affairs and the Earl of Iddesleigh for the position of Chairman of the Board of the Inland Revenue, of which they were respectively holders. He went on to ask, in one very long sentence:

> What is the reason in Lord Hardinge's case for the rupture of a hitherto unbroken constitutional usage, that a Member of either House of Parliament should not be a member of the permanent Civil Service; and whether, having regard to the fact that the Report of the Mesopotamia Commission is likely to shake public confidence in Lord Hardinge's administrative ingenuity and the withholding of information from the public of foreign

affairs, and the lack of effective control by Parliament of foreign policy, he will consider the desirability of removing Lord Hardinge from the Foreign Office in the public interest?

Mr Bonar Law[297] the Leader of the House of Commons, replied on behalf of the Government, saying that, in his opinion, it was clearly open to the Government to allow a civil servant who is a peer to make a statement in the House of Lords on a particular occasion, provided that this course does not conflict with the duties of the office, which he holds for the time being. However, very significantly, he said he would not even consider the desirability of removing Lord Hardinge from his post.

That afternoon, Sir Fredrick Smith, the Attorney General (more popularly known as F.E. Smith), formally opened the debate and dealt at very great length with the authority, standing and legal issues arising from the MC and its Report. As a lawyer, he spoke in legalese and in the process dotted endless

70. Sir Frederick Smith MP, the Attorney General, 1917, later, 1st Earl of Birkenhead. *(Internet source)*

i's as well as crossing a multitude of t's. In part, he reiterated what Bonar Law had said the previous day.

He was representing a government that had instituted the MC and had determined its composition. A deficiency of the Commission to have emerged was that it did not number a lawyer among its members and, accordingly, the taking of evidence, while satisfactory for an inquiry, was not sufficiently well founded to be used in a court of law. It follows that the nub of Smith's early remarks was to advise that no evidence given to the MC could be used in the later prosecution of that witness. Smith then commented, perhaps 'speculated' is more accurate, upon the wishes of Parliament in establishing the MC by saying:

> It said to them [the witnesses] in effect: 'Throw yourselves practically and amply upon this Commission, and upon the protection given by this Act of Parliament, and we, on our part, give our assurance to you in return that nothing which you say at this Commission shall be used against you subsequently until it is supported and proved.'
>
> As I have said in the House of Commons, there was not … one single voice raised against it, and if there had been a single voice raised against it, the answer would have been immediate. Such were the circumstances under which these officers appeared before the Mesopotamia Commission. I say frankly that I think the Act contemplated that the Commission would take evidence judicially; that is to say … take evidence according to legal rules. I remember making the observation at the time the Commission was appointed that there was not a single lawyer upon it.

Smith went on to say that the rules of evidence had not suddenly evolved as the result of some caprice. Rather were they the product of long deliberations and the experience of wise men. Their chief preoccupation was to see that an innocent man should not be found guilty. None could argue with that. Smith added that although the MC had not laid formal charges at anyone's door, nevertheless the Press had insisted that Parliament and the Government should act as though charges *had* been laid and, what is more, *had been proved*. He then quoted from evidence taken by the MC and was immediately challenged by Sir Henry Dalziel, not on the evidence but his access to it.

This disagreement occupied valuable time and Mr James Hogge added his weight to the protest. The Speaker ruled that the Attorney General could not quote directly from the evidence but could summarise it. After this small spat, the debate moved on. Sir Frederick spoke of the procedure for the taking of evidence and said that as an officer gave his evidence any members of the

Commission could ask him questions in the form of a cross-examination. He alleged that the witness was then dismissed and in many cases was never recalled. In the meantime, any number of other witnesses were called and may well have laid blame on the earlier witness and his conduct in the matter in question. The original witness was 'never given the slightest opportunity of making any reply to the allegations.' Smith claimed, incorrectly as it happens, that this happened frequently and then posed the question:

> Can anyone suggest that you can properly punish on the strength of evidence taken in this way? Is there anyone in the House who will go so far as to say that you can inflict a most grave punishment upon a man when the evidence has been taken in this manner?

The Attorney General reminded the House of how serious some of these 'charges' were. Against Sir Beauchamp Duff it was of suppressing the truth, failure to communicate to Sir John Nixon information received as to the possible concentration of 60,000 Turks at Baghdad, and censuring General Cowper in respect of his demand for river transport. The principal charge made against Sir John Nixon was of suppressing the truth of the medical breakdown at Ctesiphon. The charge against General Hathaway was of not exhibiting due care and diligence in estimating and considering the medical provision that was necessary.

He pointed out that every one of these charges was against a general officer and, if asked to advise the military authorities as to whether a case could be brought against these officers at a court martial, he would undoubtedly reply in the affirmative. Smith then speculated that the unsought and unconfirmed opinion of the Judge Advocate General established the fundamental distinction between the case made against the officers and the case made against the civilians.

The Attorney General opined that no one would wish, in any way, to attenuate the gravity of some of the conclusions of the Commission, so far as civilians go. However, if a just and fair balance of the situation was to be maintained, it was essential to remember that the charges made against the officers were charges that in a court martial could be made the subject of proceedings, whereas the charges against civilians were of an entirely different character.

Smith underscored Bonar Law's suggestion of the previous day that a tribunal be formed, partly composed of generals and partly of judges, with those involved represented by counsel, and those who presented the facts also with counsel. He considered that this tribunal would fit the bill.

Sir John Jardine, the MP for Roxburghshire, asked:

> Will the Right Honourable Gentleman explain what are to be the powers of
> this Court? Does he mean that it shall deal with matters of errors of
> judgment, which are not criminal offences or misdemeanors? May it deal
> with cases of deficiency of intellect, for instance?

Smith explained the manner in which the proposed inquiry might conduct
its business, at which Commander Wedgwood asked, 'Would the Report
come within the purview of the court of inquiry?' To which Smith replied,
'the Minority Report will be handed over with the rest of the Report.'
Wedgwood persevered, saying, 'Will Lord Hardinge come before the
inquiry?' Crushingly, Smith answered, 'I think that is obvious.' Undeterred,
Commander Wedgwood raised a key issue when he commented, 'I made a
charge against Lord Hardinge and will that come before the tribunal?' Smith
responded by saying:

> That will be entirely for the tribunal to decide after they have read the
> Minority Report. The whole of the Report will be read by the tribunal, and
> the tribunal will act, and they will have Lord Hardinge before them. I may
> point out that when Lord Hardinge came before the Commission my
> honourable and gallant friend did not cross-examine him.

'No,' replied Wedgwood, 'that is to his advantage and not mine.' Smith did
not agree and forced Wedgwood onto the back foot by riposting:

> I am not so sure about that. I think that is a very strange doctrine. My
> Honourable and Gallant Friend in the Minority Report has made reflections
> of a very grave character upon Lord Hardinge's discharge of his official
> duties. Lord Hardinge goes before that Commission, he is compelled to
> attend for the purpose of being cross-examined, but my Honourable and
> Gallant friend did not cross-examine him when he was there. In fact, he
> made no effort at all to get Lord Hardinge there to cross-examine him, and
> then he made his Minority Report.

The debate raged on, conducted in the most civilised tones, with great
attention paid to the possible means by which those named in the Report
might be called to judicial account. The different status and conditions of
service between military and civilian was an issue discussed in mind-
numbing detail. Colonel Sir Mark Sykes interjected to say:

It is difficult for one who has little or no legal experience at all to follow the speeches which have just been made. One thought that passed through my mind … during the two hours and a quarter which have been occupied in the speeches we have heard was, how many men have been killed at the front and how much we have done towards preventing them being killed or towards helping on the War? If the result of these Debates is to set up permanent Courts which go on inquiring … into one scandal after another, with fresh questions raised, with further depreciation of our prestige in the eyes of our Allies, I do not see how we are helping on the War in any way whatever.

Sykes had a point; the debate thus far had been entirely focused on legal procedure and had yet to reach any sort of conclusion. The time was fast approaching 1900 hrs when Sir Henry Craik rose to speak. Refreshingly, unlike many of those who had preceded him he wanted to talk in specific terms about the principal issue. That is to say, the medical debacle and the suffering of British and Indian soldiers, and the manner in which that was reported. He said:

I cannot find, after carefully studying the Report, anything in their conclusions that are not vague and indiscriminate, and even contradictory. I would like to illustrate my point by quoting some of the contradictory references from the Report. In paragraph 111 they say: *'There are passages in the evidence of Lord Hardinge, Surgeon General Hathaway and other responsible witnesses which might lead to the inference that the medical breakdown in Mesopotamia was due to the shortage of ordinary river transport, for which, of course, the medical authorities were not responsible.'* If this were true, it would follow that the medical authorities must be relieved of blame for the results of the breakdown. One would have thought that, but how do they go on? They say: *'We cannot agree with such a contention.'* On page 113 of the same Report they say: *'The defects of medical provision caused avoidable suffering to the sick and wounded, and during the breakdown in the winter of 1915–16 this suffering was most lamentably severe. The deficiencies, which were the main causes of the avoidable suffering of the sick and wounded, were in the provision of the following: River hospital steamers, medical personnel, river transport, ambulance land transport.'*

In the other part of the Report they point out that if the medical authorities were not responsible for the ordinary river transport they must be relieved of all blame, and in another part of the Report they say: *'In our opinion the known shortage of ordinary river transport, if anything, aggravates rather than palliates the omissions of the medical authorities.'*

Surely we have a right to ask how are we to reconcile these ridiculous contradictions between different parts of the Report. The real fact is that there seems to be a sort of determination to find some scapegoat for that which has attracted more attention than any other part of the Report in the public minds – the lamentable, scandalous, and dreadful way in which our sick were treated during that campaign.

Although Sir Henry had identified contradictions that damaged the veracity of the MC Report, none of the following speakers expanded or challenged Sir Henry's thrust. Later in the day, Mr Austen Chamberlain, the Secretary of State for India, made his contribution and conceded that, as he was named, his conduct might be called into question by any future tribunal. He continued:

Accordingly, Sir, my resignation, my final resignation, is in the hands of my Right Honourable Friend the Prime Minister, and I only speak from this bench at this moment because, owing to His Majesty's absence from London on public work, it has been impossible to take His Majesty's pleasure upon it. With that personal explanation of my position, I will proceed at once to deal with some of the matters on which I think the House has a right to call for a statement from me.

He then went on to make his statement, in which he defended General Sir Edmund Barrow, Sir John Nixon and Sir William Meyer and poured scorn on the MC Report for its selection of information and the emphasis it put on an incomplete picture. Chamberlain was speaking in his own defence and of those who answered to him. He was fluent and persuasive, but he was obliged to concede that the arrangements in Mesopotamia were severely flawed.

He sought to defend the system of 'private' correspondence, saying that if it had been classified as 'secret' instead, the result would have been the same. This was misleading and untrue. A 'secret' document can be seen by anyone with the appropriate security clearance, and 'secret' is the lowest secrecy grading, with only 'confidential' and 'restricted' gradings below. A 'private' document is what it says – privy only to the person addressed. Chamberlain then admitted:

Quite frankly when I used this so-called 'private' form of telegram I was not aware that it was the practice of the India Office and of India that private telegrams should be regarded as the personal property of the official who sent or received them, and could be carried away by him when he left. We constantly use private telegrams to convey secret information directly one to the other, and then make them official afterwards, by which means they are placed on record. It is always within the competence of the Viceroy at the other end, or myself at this end, to place any private telegram on public record if we wish, but I was not aware of that particular procedure, and I only discovered it by accident on the day Lord Hardinge was leaving India. Had I been aware of it I should have made a number of these telegrams official after they had been sent as private.

Chamberlain still had points to make and turned to the perceived villain of the piece, Lord Hardinge. This was a man for whom he had worked over an extended period. It was Hardinge who misled the India Office in general and Chamberlain in particular with his concealed ambition to annex the whole of Mesopotamia. It would not have been unreasonable if Chamberlain had thrown Hardinge to the wolves. He did not do so. Instead, he had this to say:

I hope that the temper of the House today and the speeches which have been made will have done something to bring our countrymen outside to a juster [sic] appreciation of the great character and the great services of Lord Hardinge. The Viceroyalty of India is not the only office that he has held. He has spent a life in the service of his country. He has rendered great and exceptional services in the high posts, which he has filled. He was taken out of a career that he had made his own and, at the request of the Government of the day, was appointed Viceroy of India.

He went there at a time of difficulty, of disturbance and of danger, and he very nearly paid with his life for his acceptance of the post. He piloted India through these stormy years; he piloted her through the dark early months of the War. He stripped the country. He and Sir Beauchamp Duff stripped their own resources to make good our deficiencies here at home. They gave of their troops more than it had ever been supposed they could have parted with. They reduced the British garrison to a lower point than safety had always been held to demand. They gave rifles, guns, military equipment of every kind, and at one fell swoop over 500 of the officers of their army were taken to officer our new armies here. Then, Sir, because, there has been a breakdown in military administration, Lord Hardinge is to be held up to public odium and contempt, his great services forgotten, and the most popular viceroy that India has ever had – one who won not merely the respect, but the affection of her princes and peoples in a measure that had never been accorded to any of his predecessors – is to be denounced and hounded down, and you hear people say that in no other capacity during his life is he fit to serve his country or his king.

This is a generous statement by any yardstick, but it should be noted that the giving of Indian assets to the national cause did not cause either Hardinge or Duff any personal inconvenience. It was nothing other than their bounden duty to deploy public assets to best advantage. To describe the debacle of Mesopotamia over the period September 1914 to April 1916 as a 'breakdown in military administration' is a masterly and misleading understatement. It appeared that the party line was to defend Hardinge, and Chamberlain had just aligned his toes along that line.

Colonel Sir Mathew Wilson followed Chamberlain and offered his regrets at the latter's resignation, and then suggested that the House:

> will agree with me in feeling that he bears little or no blame. These commissions are very dangerous things to have started. I believe you will never get a military officer in a high position to take on his shoulders any initiative if you elect to try men by court martial because they have failed to obtain the success which was hoped for at first.

The clock was striking nine o'clock when Sir John Jardine rose to speak at great length. He ranged widely over the MC Report. He reviewed the case for a new judicial tribunal and commented on the probable cost to the public purse. Turning to the performance of Lord Hardinge, he offered the view that:

> The Commission's findings absolve him from crime and misdemeanour, but point only to lack of judgment, lack of energy, or lack of grip. The House of Lords, in a judgment, once said negligence is often extremely like fraud, and a learned judge of long experience said it was sometimes difficult to tell whether a man was a knave or a fool, and I repeat that we do not find anything but lack of judgment and error, except it might be as to the private letters amongst friends, which, I should think, could be disposed of right away.

Sir John Rees did not agree, allied himself with the Minority Report and struck a very straightforward note when he said that the findings of the MC should be recognised and that the Viceroy should be held responsible for civilian failures and General Sir Beauchamp Duff for military failures. Sir Henry Craik spoke with some passion in defence of the Indian Medical Service and the Royal Army Medical Corps, then utterly damned Sir William Meyer by saying with heavy irony:

> We are not deprived of the services of Sir William Meyer, a man who has risen in the service by constantly ingratiating himself with the financial

authorities through cheese-paring, who must not be taken – I say this with all careful consideration – as a specimen of the Indian Civil Service of the better type, a man who has in every case injured and done his best to injure and curtail the usefulness of the Medical Service. We are not deprived of Sir William Meyer's services because of any reflection cast upon him by this Report – indeed, I think he is appointed to some new, higher, and more important post.

The MC Report had commented upon the management of public finances in India and its tone was generally negative, but Meyer was not singled out for censure. The cautious parochial and pedestrian attitude of the Indian Government towards its finances was a corporate matter and responsibility. Meyer was a leading member of that government. Craik's acid attack was made despite Sir William being completely exonerated by the MC Report. However, like most of the vast volume of words spoken in the House, the personal attack did nothing to change anything. Meyer, incidentally and justifiably, did go on to greater things.

Despite the absence of any censure or any support for Craik's view, Chamberlain chose to defend Meyer in these words:

I have dealt mainly with my own office and with myself, but I cannot leave the subject without saying something also about the high officials of the Indian Government who have been the mark for every kind of attack, and even for most scurrilous abuse in the campaign of invective which has followed upon the publication of the Commission's Report. Among them is Sir William Meyer, the Finance Minister of India, a man who has given long years of service to the Crown, who was trusted by the late Viceroy and is trusted by the present Viceroy, who has piloted the finances of India so far with success through times the anxiety and the difficulty of which I think few Members of this House probably realise, and who is now held up to public odium and contempt. Why? Because when the construction of a railway was suggested to him on political, commercial, and military grounds, he said that he did not believe in the commercial success of the railway. He left the Government of India to decide upon the political grounds, and he said that if the Commander-in-Chief thought it necessary for military reasons it must be referred home for the decision of His Majesty's Government. What else could he have done? If it were a military necessity it was not for him, but for the military authorities, to say so, and to put it forward on that ground. If it were recommended as a commercial speculation, then I agree with Sir William Meyer. He was right. I do not think that it was a good speculation, and, at any rate, it was not the time for building commercial railways in Mesopotamia or elsewhere.

Mr Joseph King rose to take another bite at the Government's cherry and made the point that the MC Report had provided 'a number of revelations, and established a large number of facts which are in direct contravention and contradiction to the statements made by ministers, on their solemn faith – I might almost say on their solemn oath – as being facts'.

He recalled that during 1915 and up to May 1917, the House had complained about the dearth of information provided on the Mesopotamia operations. King then struck a telling blow at the Prime Minister's veracity, saying that it was not until 2 November 1915 that the Prime Minister eventually made a statement. King remembered that statement on Mesopotamia, which used the unfortunate words:

> General Nixon's force is now within measurable distance of Baghdad. I do not think that in the whole course of the war there has been a series of operations more carefully contrived, more brilliantly conducted, and with a better prospect of final success.

King, with forensic precision, then pointed out at the time the actuality was that Nixon's force was well advanced on its passage to destruction. King then inflicted further wounds when he quoted Chamberlain, who, having been asked about the medical arrangements for the Mesopotamian expedition, answered that, 'The condition of the wounded is very satisfactory, and the medical arrangements have worked well under difficult conditions.' Adding a little later, when asked to give more information to the House on the expeditions generally, 'I am unwilling to give the House any information as to the accuracy of which I cannot absolutely vouch.'

King was scathing and berated Chamberlain for giving assurances when the wounded and the sick were suffering such trials and horrible conditions. King said dismissively, 'That is one episode of this miserable story which I think the House and the country ought to bear in mind. We have been misled, we have been shamefully misled.'

As the evening wore on it was evident that there was no clear consensus in the House. Mr Joseph King resumed his seat and the Speaker called the Secretary of State for Foreign Affairs, Mr Arthur Balfour, who made what was perhaps the most telling contribution of the day. He certainly enlivened the debate after a gentle beginning. First he supported the Attorney General, who had fully explained to the House the broad principles on which the Government proposed to act and principles from which it could not depart. He said that he felt sure that the House and the country would agree that to condemn, punish or remove anyone 'merely on the strength of the

71. Arthur Balfour, the Foreign Secretary, December 1916–October 1919. Previously, Prime Minister 1902–1905. *(Internet source)*

Mesopotamia Commission Report, might be to inflict a grave injustice upon individuals, and we do not propose to do that under any temptation or pressure'.

Arthur Balfour recognised that the country was responding to the horrors revealed in the MC Report and it was 'natural and unavoidable' to try to find somebody who was responsible and to punish them. However, it was the responsibility of the House to see that 'this natural desire never exceeds the bounds of strict justice'.

He went on to say that there were two alternatives before the House and, since the speech by the Attorney General, His Majesty's Government had sought to find the general feeling of the House and the direction in which it wanted the Government to move. The Foreign Secretary said that HMG was comfortable to proceed with either of the alternative tribunals and he commented that some members seemed to regard both alternatives as 'a means of bringing criminals to justice or meting out a deserved punishment. I do not regard them in that light at all.' He accepted that that might be one of the outcomes of a tribunal and speculated that 'another result would be to show that some men have been most unjustly attacked by the Commission, and it would give them a much-needed opportunity of vindicating their character before the public.' He continued by saying:

> I must frankly admit that I am in many respects very little moved by the Report of the Commission. Nothing can exceed the feelings of horror with which everybody must read of the tragic events, which followed the retirement of the British force, but the general character and the manner in which the Commission has approached this question is not the proper method of dealing with these great state affairs. Anybody who listened with attention, as I am sure most Honourable Members of the House did, to the speech of my Right Honourable Friend the Secretary for India must have felt that <u>the Commission, after that speech, is quite as much on its trial as any of the gentlemen whom it has arraigned</u>. [Author's emphasis]
>
> I must frankly add that I profoundly dissent from the expediency of the course which my Right Honourable Friend [Chamberlain] has thought it right to pursue. I believe it to have been wrong, although right in intention, in my opinion, in substance. I do not believe, personally … merely on the ground that this Commission has casually imputed some share of responsibility to my Right Honourable Friend or anybody else for their share in these transactions, that they are right in withdrawing themselves from the service of the country. Something has been said by the honourable gentleman who has just sat down [Mr King] and by others about the case of Lord Hardinge. Lord Hardinge, as soon as the Commission reported, tendered his resignation to me. I did not accept it.

> **Mr Joseph King:** I beg the Right Honourable Gentleman's pardon. I never said a word in my speech about Lord Hardinge.

> **Mr Arthur Balfour:** I apologise. The Honourable Member was indulging in general invective, and I confess that I thought he included Lord Hardinge.

> **Mr Joseph King:** Might I ask the Right Honourable Gentleman whether he reads the despatches in the Foreign Office as carelessly as he listens to my speeches?

248

Mr Arthur Balfour: I read them with quite as much care and much less interest. The Honourable Gentleman will hardly deny that Lord Hardinge has been made the target of the most virulent and persistent attacks, reflected perhaps more in questions which have been asked by honourable gentlemen, including, I think, the Honourable Gentleman himself, but I am glad to see that they have sensibly diminished in virulence since we entered upon this debate this afternoon. I wanted to tell the House, and I think it is fair that I should state it, that Lord Hardinge offered his resignation to me quite early in the stages of this controversy, and I declined to accept it. He offered it again and pressed it on me in a letter, which I received yesterday, and I again refused to accept it. I refused to accept it on the broad ground, which I think ought to move everybody who really feels what the country requires of its citizens in a time of war. Those who want Lord Hardinge to resign or want him to leave his present place want him at this crisis in this nation's history to give up all efforts towards carrying on the great struggle in which we are engaged. That is a liberty, which we do not give to anybody in this country. Many of the civil servants in my department have desired to go to the front and take their part in the fighting line. They have been refused, and they have been told that their duty to their country requires them to stay in the Foreign Office. Am I to be told that the head, permanent, civil servant at the Foreign Office …

Mr Swift MacNeill: He has no right to be!

Mr Arthur Balfour: Am I to be told that he is to have a liberty, which is denied to his subordinates?

Colonel Collins: Twenty-one generals were sent home from Mesopotamia as failures. Why should not the same law apply to the Viceroy of India?

Mr Arthur Balfour: I do not know what the Honourable and Gallant Gentleman means. I wholly fail to follow his reasoning. Does anybody suggest that Lord Hardinge is incompetent to carry out the duties on which he is now engaged?

Mr MacNeill: I suggest it. It is an outrage.

Mr Arthur Balfour: If a Permanent Under-Secretary at the Foreign Office is to be dismissed from his place because his superiors pursue a particular policy, how are you going to carry on the Civil Service of this country? Why is Lord Hardinge responsible for Lord Grey's policy? He is not responsible. Nobody knows better than the two Honourable Gentlemen who interrupted me just now that if you were to accept these principles your so-called permanent civil servants would go out of office as often as your political heads of departments. [**Hon. Members**: 'No!'] Of course they would. If they were to be made responsible for all that the heads of their departments do, how can it be otherwise?

Mr MacNeill: May I for one moment courteously interrupt the Right Honourable Gentleman? He knows perfectly well that Lord Hardinge was responsible for foreign policy when he went with the King as the King's Minister to Kiel to hold a *conversazione* with the Czar.

Mr Arthur Balfour: I know nothing of that kind.

Mr MacNeill: It was in June, 1908.

Mr Arthur Balfour: Although I was not in office at that time but was a member of the Opposition, I am perfectly certain that if the Honourable Gentleman cares to inquire of the many distinguished persons who were Lord Grey's colleagues at that time, they will confirm my statement that the Honourable Gentleman is labouring under a profound delusion.

Mr MacNeill: Oh, no!

Mr Arthur Balfour: Those are, broadly speaking, the grounds on which I do not propose to accept Lord Hardinge's resignation, the ground being that Lord Hardinge is an excellent permanent head of the Foreign Office. Therefore, even if he did not do his duty in India, in my opinion that is no reason at all for telling him that he is not to do something else that has nothing to do with India.

Commander Josiah Wedgwood: Then do not dismiss the other people.

Mr Arthur Balfour: What?

Commander Josiah Wedgwood: Do not dismiss the generals.

Mr J. MacVeagh: Why allow Chamberlain to resign?

Mr Arthur Balfour: If the generals are occupied in some service to their country quite unconnected with the military profession, I do not see why they should not do it, simply because as military men they have failed.

Sir Henry Craik: You have suspended Sir William Babtie.

Mr Arthur Balfour: Does not the Honourable Gentleman see that he is suspended from doing the kind of work in which he is supposed to have failed? That is the point. Why should you suspend a man who is supposed to have failed in India from doing work which has nothing to do with India, and which is connected with a wholly different sphere of public activities? I do not think that Lord Hardinge has been fairly treated by the Commission. Even if he had been I should refuse to accept his resignation, but he has not been fairly treated. I do not suggest for a moment that the Commission, whatever blunders and mistakes they have made in the course of their investigations [author's emphasis] ever intended to do anything but strict justice, but their method of dealing with these great questions makes, in my opinion, strict and fair justice almost impossible. What did we want from the verdict of such a commission? We wanted, if possible, to anticipate the views, which an impartial historian, fully acquainted with the facts, would take of recent transactions. That is not the way they looked at this question. Would any historian, trying to estimate Lord Hardinge's services to India in general during his administration there, or his services to India and the Empire during the War, occupy himself, as the Commission have very much occupied themselves, with matters of such relative triviality, such as whether the telegram was an official or a private telegram? [Author's emphasis]

* * *

Arthur Balfour was naive. The campaign in Mesopotamia, and specifically the period September 1914 to April 1916, has been the subject of study by a host of historians as the bibliography at the end of this book reveals. Many of those believe that Hardinge and others had a case to answer, and if sympathy was to be dispensed it was owed to the soldiers who fought an implacable foe in ghastly conditions, handicapped by the complete incompetency of their leadership, both military and political. That said, it is true that no crime had been committed and the offences, if there were any, were 'administrative' in genre.

Balfour, by dint of his appointment, was in a position of enormous influence and as the superior of Hardinge in the Foreign Office he was in a position to arbitrate on the latter's employment unless or until the Prime Minister or a body created by the House of Commons overruled him. His defence of Hardinge was not yet complete, and he continued:

The chief cause of a private telegram being sent to Lord Hardinge and not used by him has been entirely disposed of by my Right Honourable Friend [Mr Chamberlain], and the criminals there, are not Lord Hardinge nor the

Secretary of State for India. They are the Commission. [Author's emphasis] Does anybody doubt that statement? Can anyone doubt it after what my Right Honourable Friend has said? Then it is alleged that Lord Hardinge did not consult his Council sufficiently and that all the work was done by him and the Commander-in-Chief.

For Balfour to suggest that the members of the MC were 'criminals' was excessive. Not in the least abashed, he refuted absolutely the suggestion that the Council for India was not consulted, saying that it was furnished with all the relevant documents at its weekly meeting; not, he claimed darkly, the practice of previous viceroys.

Balfour's position was unvarnished, Hardinge had wide responsibility for a vast country with an enormous population and accordingly he could not be held to answer for the detailed travails in Mesopotamia. The Viceroy did 'advise' the advance on Baghdad, but in Balfour's view that matter had already been disposed of. Nevertheless, he asserted:

> If Lord Hardinge is called into question for that, if he is to be hauled before a tribunal, if he is to be prevented from serving his country in the office which he now holds, because he advised the advance on Baghdad, all the most important gentlemen on the Front Bench opposite and on this Front Bench also deserve precisely the same treatment.

Balfour's argument is difficult to follow. Quite what responsibility the opposition front bench had to do with the advance on Baghdad is unclear. Balfour then addressed the general lack of adequate medical equipment. He did not suggest that there was sufficient explanation or excuse for the general deficiency of medical stores other than to say that England and India entered the war unprepared.

Balfour added, quite reasonably, that it was not Lord Hardinge's fault that India entered the war unprepared. This statement was unlikely to be challenged; indeed it was not the cause of his censure and the parlous funding of the Indian Army was agreed to be the responsibility, ultimately, of the House of Commons.

Balfour then suggested, in the face of all the evidence, that Hardinge made every possible effort to support the Home Country despite the threat of outside aggression, frontier warfare, and internal dissension. Balfour pointed out that, under Hardinge's leadership, India reduced her white troops at one moment to 15,000. Balfour believed that was evidence of Hardinge's commitment to the war.

Lord Hugh Cecil remarked that the Council was 'never officially consulted about Mesopotamia'. On the matter of the provision of troops for Mesopotamia, Commander Josiah Wedgwood then interjected: 'Under explicit orders from home, they were relieved of all responsibility.'

Mr Arthur Balfour: And that was done under Lord Hardinge's administration. India was bled white for war purposes before the Mesopotamia Expedition began; and then are you going to look with too critical, too microscopic an eye upon the fact that a country which had sent men, guns, officers, medical stores, and rifles was not fully equipped for dealing with the situation in Mesopotamia? You may hunt through the pages of the Report of the Commission and you will never find there broad considerations brought in.

Lord Hugh Cecil: My Right Honourable Friend evidently has not read the Report. He discusses these matters with only an indolent attention to fact. My Right Honourable Friend can see, if he looks, that these facts which he has himself stated, most properly, as important facts, all appear in the Report.

Arthur Balfour was not going to let that go, and said that Lord Hugh Cecil had done him an injustice. He suggested that the Report did not deal fairly with Lord Hardinge and his great efforts in connection with the war. He claimed that, 'The Commission enumerated a lot of facts, not all correctly,' and then at the end of the Report said that, 'so and so is more responsible for this or that transaction.'

He again brought the 'impartial historians' of the future into his dissertation, arguing that they would say the war came as a great surprise to both India and the UK and that, as a result, mistakes, errors and human losses came at the beginning of the war because of imperfect preparation. He drew attention to the undisputed fact that the defects were gradually corrected, although the unhappy losses that they caused would never be repaired.

Balfour's thrust was that in war there are always difficulties, and invited the House to imagine another commission of the same type appointed to look at every letter and study every telegram since August 1914 down to the end of 1915. He concluded that there was no defence for deficiencies in preparation. But, he predicted, at war's end and in the future, what the Commission called 'an atmosphere of economy' would prevail. After an overly long and poorly argued speech, he finished by saying:

The deficiency of medical stores during the whole period of the Mesopotamia Expedition, and the great horrors which make one's blood run cold, were largely due to a different set of causes. General Nixon was making a great invasion of a barbarous land and thought to gain a great and relatively easy success. He was wrong in his opinion, and he met with a great reverse. Where you have a great reverse in the course of a war in a savage country, where your wounded cannot be left behind for proper medical treatment, these horrors must occur with an army which is in retirement.

Commander Wedgwood: If they have not got sufficient transport.

Mr Arthur Balfour: My Honourable and Gallant Friend does not see the point. It is perfectly true that at the time his means of communication were on a very low scale, but on a scale that might have been sufficient, and I suppose would have been, if General Nixon had had the success he anticipated. It proved to be quite inadequate when a disaster occurred which compelled his retreat. But that he was going through, he thought, and the number of casualties he would have to provide for would be somewhere about 500, while it was 3,500. So that an army, which had it been successful, would have had ample means of carrying back the wounded through all these hundreds of miles to the base had not got them when the number of wounded was multiplied manifold, and when they had to be carried back in the face of a triumphant enemy.

This convoluted response by Balfour has to be read slowly for it to make any sort of sense, even though the argument is weak. He would have convinced no one, and certainly not Wedgwood, because Hansard recorded his immediate reply.

Commander Josiah Wedgwood: 'There was no hospital ship – not one.'

Balfour took this as his cue, once more, to speak at length and in detail. He returned to the defence of Hardinge and in that process explained to Wedgwood the difficulty of recovering wounded men in a hostile land. This was more than a little patronising of Balfour, as Wedgwood had not only seen active service in two wars but had been decorated and had first-hand experience of recovering the wounded. To Wedgwood's credit, he showed remarkable restraint and did not rise in protest.

Balfour conceded that 'there was great miscalculation' but denied that it was the responsibility of the Viceroy. He explained the vast burden of responsibility borne by Hardinge and emphasised that as soon as news of the breakdown of the medical service came to his notice he took action. Balfour asserted, 'The idea that this inquiry was very greatly delayed is really untrue. In the middle of September [1916] Lord Hardinge had word of the matter and, by the end of the month, the inquiry was started.' Balfour gave a brief résumé of the career of Lord Hardinge and lauded his diligence, experience and diplomatic skills. He remarked:

> Let me, in conclusion, say this: Lord Hardinge is now engaged on matters which have nothing whatever to do with Indian administration – the work of the Foreign Office. That is a continuation of what, after all, is his life's work. His Indian experience was merely an episode.
>
> Lord Hardinge has the confidence of the Office. He has the confidence of the Diplomatic Service. He is useful to his chiefs. He is not, of course, responsible for policy. He is responsible, and has great responsibility, like the permanent heads of other offices. This responsibility he carries out quite admirably.
>
> I do not think that I should be serving the best interests of the country in a great crisis when the country has need of all that her sons can do in every sphere, because, forsooth, of some comments described in the Report of the Commission, or because those comments are going to be revised and reviewed by a tribunal that has yet to be appointed, to agree that Lord Hardinge should retire into private life and give up that admirable work that he is carrying on, that he, by training and ability, is most excellently suited for, and so deprive the country of the services that I can assure the House at this moment we can ill spare.

Balfour had dominated the debate in his all-embracing defence of Hardinge and casual denigration of the MC and its Report. By so doing and by ruling categorically on the continued employment of Harding, he had, effectively, reduced the likelihood of there being any future action against any of those censured.

Sir Archibald Williamson: It seems to me that it is the Commission that is on its trial tonight. We have listened to a series of very eloquent defences of the various gentlemen associated in this matter. I have every sympathy with the Foreign Secretary, who naturally does not wish to lose a colleague who is valuable to him. We have much sympathy with the Secretary of State for India when he complains of the difference between what the Commissioners say and what the newspapers have said they say. There is no doubt whatever that if the public read the Report of the Commissioners they will come to very different conclusions. One must have every sympathy with the Secretary for India and others on that account, and one has also sympathy with the Right Honourable Gentleman in regard to the telegrams, which have had to be paraphrased, and the omissions in those telegrams.

No doubt these were causes of difficulty to the Secretary for India. But I would remind the House that the paraphrasing of telegrams was not done by the Commission, but by the India Office itself. With reference to the omissions in those cables and telegrams, we were instructed by the India Office and the Government that reference to complications in Persia, and matters connected with Russia, must be omitted from any telegrams quoted by the Commission. Consequently the Commission were unable to do otherwise than they did.

* * *

Williamson's mild and dignified response to an accusation of criminality reflected well on him and brought the parliamentary day to a close. The House rose at 2300 hrs and the members went to their respective beds in the knowledge that, come the morrow, they would go around the same roundabout again.

It had been a very significant debate, not least because of the extraordinary accusation of criminal behaviour on behalf of the MC and the total and repeated exoneration of Hardinge by his political masters of anything and everything. By this speech, and his remarks about Hardinge, Arthur Balfour had effectively emasculated the MC. The effect would be seen in the next few weeks.

The following day, 13 July 1917, the House assembled for the second day of the debate. The House was called to order and Sir Archibald Williamson, the member for Elginshire, was first to catch the Speaker's eye. Having served on the MC, he had spent the previous sitting listening to any number of members criticising the MC and its entire works. He was aggrieved, and it showed. Once on his feet he got off to a frank start by saying:

> I find myself today placed unexpectedly in a position of some responsibility. Having been one of those who took part in an investigation of a long and arduous character, the Report of which has now been presented to this House, I must ask the indulgence of the House if I discharge the responsibility which is cast upon me today of defending the Commission against some of the attacks which I think have somewhat wantonly been made against it.

Williamson pointed out that the Commission, brought into being by the House with its membership appointed by the House, found itself in the position of a criminal in the dock rather than in the position of a body investigating and reporting upon occurrences at the request of the House. He reminded the House that the Foreign Secretary, no less, had actually stated that the Commission was on trial rather than those who had been referred to in the Report.

He made mention that he and his fellow Commissioners had spent eight months taking evidence and that they had distilled their findings into a document running to 188 pages. He questioned the ability of the House to do justice to the Report in the brief time allocated for debate and without the evidence before it. He averred that the MC would have no objection to the evidence being printed; in fact, it would be very pleased that the evidence should be published. He said that when, and if, the evidence was published it would but serve to deepen the sad impression that was left upon the minds of the Commissioners themselves. Williamson then observed:

> There has been, yesterday, in the debate an effort to discredit the Commission. Apparently from what we heard, nothing very much occurred, and no one is to blame. While passing eulogies, most of which I do not deny were well deserved, on the distinguished services of statesmen and soldiers, we must not forget the grief of the parents who have lost their sons in Mesopotamia, of the widows and fatherless children who have suffered for the sins of omission as well of commission of those who were referred to.

The member then turned to the matter of the Vincent-Bingley Report, which he reminded the House was in the hands of the Government before it appointed the Mesopotamia Commission. That report apparently did not give the Government satisfaction, for it did not publish the Report and instead it took the further step of appointing this Mesopotamia Commission to go into the whole matter anew. HMG added wider terms of reference, which gave the Commission power to inquire into other matters as well as those relating to the breakdown of the medical service. The Mesopotamia Commission found that the circumstances described by the Vincent-Bingley Commission were fully confirmed by independent evidence. Not only that, but it was found that exactly the same persons were responsible for the medical part of the inquiry, as those which the Mesopotamia Commission found to be responsible.

Williamson commented on the attendance of individual witnesses and their lawyers and observed that the witnesses numbered in the hundreds, and he claimed that it was inconceivable that all these witnesses could come to make their statements accompanied by lawyers. It just was not practical.

He continued by saying that he was quite certain that the House of Commons, when appointing the Commission, never thought it was appointing a court of law. The House of Commons appointed the Commission, as men of 'ordinary intelligence and common sense', to inquire into what had happened, and make a report to the House. On the basis of the Report, the House of Commons, in its wisdom, could take such action as it deemed appropriate.

Williamson, not unreasonably, remarked that it was only right that the Government should defend the Commission that had been brought into being by the House of Commons. No charges were framed because it was not the business of such a commission to frame charges.

He turned again to the management of witness statements and refuted the allegation that the witnesses had no opportunity of replying, and added that most of the findings were based on the words of the witnesses themselves. It appeared that there was a rule in the Commission that when one witness made a serious reflection on another, that 'other' witness was informed. Some of those 'other' witnesses were recalled; others could have been recalled if they had requested to do so. Williamson insisted that the Commission did not refuse to recall any witness who asked to be recalled. He referred specifically to the Commander-in-Chief in India and to the Secretary of State, and said that they were both supplied with the whole of the evidence as and when it came out. General Nixon, Surgeon General Sir William Babtie, Surgeon General Hathaway and Surgeon General MacNeece had all evidence that appeared to be relevant supplied to them.

The member reminded the House that the MC was to investigate what happened in the Mesopotamian campaign, and it was not in its remit to draw attention to Lord Hardinge's illustrious services to the Crown. The bestowal of accolades was not for the MC, for that was the prerogative of the House of Commons and the Government.

Williamson raised the standard of reporting and comment in the newspapers and said that the conclusions of the Report and the conclusions of the newspapers were entirely and totally different. He defied any man with balanced judgment to read the Report carefully and then to read what was reported by the newspapers and to find the same result from the two readings. Regretfully, the country was taking its impression of the Report from what they read in the newspapers.

The Secretary of State for India, Mr Chamberlain, raised the topic of Sir John Biles and the design and provision of river craft for the Tigris.

Williamson responded with a host of facts. This subject has been briefly ventilated elsewhere in the text, so the lengthy discussion that followed is not reiterated here.

River craft having been disposed of, Williamson brought his speech to a close by regretting that the Commission was unable to bring in a whitewashing report. He averred that he knew that that was expected, certainly by an element of the Press. He said that it was unfortunate and he very much regretted that the Commission was unable to come to such conclusions.

Presumably, this was said tongue-in-cheek. He concluded his speech by saying:

> The gravamen of the findings of the Commission, I think, is really unshaken by yesterday's debate, although there has been a great deal of defence of individuals. As for asking for trials, the Commission has certainly no objection, on principle, to trials. It was not a tribunal to inflict punishment; it was only requested by this House to ascertain to the best of its judgment the correct facts. It is for the House to follow up these facts if it sees fit to do so.
>
> I do feel that the blame, the individual responsibility, which is brought out in this report is very serious. I admit it is very serious, especially to the individuals concerned. But, however serious and however grave it is, it is an ephemeral thing compared, as I hope, with the permanent results of the investigation.
>
> A great deal will have been achieved if the Report of the Commission draws attention to the need for reform of Indian administration. That is what the Commissioners kept always before them, that they might leave behind them not alone a record of mismanagement and a record of blame, but might leave behind them a record that they found the condition of administration in India unsatisfactory. I think it is high time the Government, the country, and the House took this matter in hand and brought the Government of India up to modern standards.

Captain Aubrey Herbert initially struck a pragmatic note when he said that he had concluded that if the House had to decide between retribution or salvation, by introducing much needed reforms, the House would choose salvation.

He agreed with Colonel Sir Mark Sykes, who the previous evening had asked, 'What are we doing by this debate to help the war effort?' He nailed his colours to the metaphorical mast by declaring that he would welcome any inquiry, which he hoped, at the very least, would 'get rid of Sir William

Meyer and Sir Beauchamp Duff'. He did not end there, and sought punishment for Surgeon General Hathaway and Sir William Babtie. Having accepted at face value the conclusions of the MC in respect of the four men named, Herbert then said that he would welcome any inquiry that would restore Chamberlain to office because, he claimed with some justification, the House knew that Chamberlain's only fault was loyalty to his colleagues and subordinates.

He pleaded for mercy for Sir John Nixon on the basis that he was 'a very gallant, fighting Englishman', but did not acknowledge those many other gallant, fighting Englishmen who had died at the whim of Nixon.

Finally, he expressed the hope that Lord Hardinge would be 'returned to that career for which his training and qualifications suited him so admirably'. Herbert saw nothing in the MC Report that gave cause for the censure of Hardinge. It was an unbalanced contribution to the debate, and Herbert was not alone in this respect. However, Mr Joseph King, who spoke later, balanced Herbert's contribution initially by reiterating, in large measure, his early observations. Then he continued:

> There is one other point to which I wish to call the attention of the House in connection with this report, which seems to me to be rather misunderstood, or placed in the wrong light. Honourable Members on both sides have referred to the delinquencies of officials and ministers as if they were crimes and misdemeanours, and as if they were capable of being brought to a court of law, and being established there as crimes, misdemeanours or offences according to the criminal law of the land.
>
> As I take it, no criminal charge has been brought or been imagined by anybody. It is not a question of whether a man has been guilty of a crime; it is a question of whether the men we have entrusted with enormous powers, who have had immense confidence placed in them, have proved worthy. Have they proved capable, have they done their best, have they used the ability and imagination, the industry and the courage, which we expected of them? I believe on those points these men stand convicted. The evidence indeed has not been published, but extracts of it have been published. There is the story as put together by such unprejudiced men as Lord George Hamilton – a man who, having lived so much in official life, is certain not to have taken an unfair view towards the officials, a man who has been Secretary of State for India himself, and naturally from Conservative instincts and record might naturally be expected to be exceedingly kind to the traditional methods and achievements of the English Government. From that point of view we ought to consider that we have a right to complain.

These men have been judged by their equals. They have been judged by men sympathetic to them. It has been no hostile court before whom they have been brought, and these are the men who have condemned them.

Lord Portsmouth, writing to *The Morning Post* on 12 July 1917, had been unimpressed by what he had heard so far. He concluded that the debate 'exhibits the most degrading of spectacles – an official bureaucracy, whether aristocratic or democratic, acting as a kind of trade union in its worst aspect to defeat the ends of justice and the responsibility of public servants to the public.'

Chapter notes

297 Mr Bonar Law (1858–1923). He is the only British Prime Minister to be born outside the UK and was also the one with the shortest term in office (October 1922 to May 1923). He died in office. In 1917 he was Leader of the House of Commons and Chancellor of the Exchequer, having been previously Secretary of State for the Colonies (May 1915 to December 1916).

Chapter 18

Responsibility – the Reckoning

'Responsibility is the test of a man's courage.'
(Admiral Lord St Vincent, 1735–1833)

The debate was at an end and the consensus seemed to suggest that something should be done, but quite what and to whom and in what degree was not clear. The committee formed by Lloyd George and consisting of Lord Curzon, Austen Chamberlain (censored by the Mesopotamia Commission), G.N. Barnes[298] and Lord Derby[299] was tasked with making recommendations to consider what form of disciplinary action could and should be taken. When Hardinge had sight of Curzon's recommendations, he commented that they were 'worthy of him, drastic and cruel'. [300]

71. David Lloyd George.
(Internet source)

Curzon was of a mind to apply draconian sanctions at the senior level but he was thwarted when five of the six officers insisted on their right to be tried by court martial. The MC Report was not, of itself, proof of either criminality or even malfeasance, and the disciplinary proceedings were quietly dropped.

The *Manchester Guardian* encapsulated the position in which His Majesty's Government found itself. It recorded:

> But after all, does the public servant have the right to have the benefit of all legal rules of evidence like the burglar? We are not sure. The burglar, if convicted, loses his civil rights; not so the politician or the public servant who is censured for incompetence or bad judgment. The one is innocent until he is convicted; the other has to be above suspicion. In the one case the issue is one of guilt in the eye of the law; in the other it is one of political fitness or unfitness. The true analogy is not with the criminal but with the employee, who often loses his position on evidence that would be

insufficient to convict a man on a criminal charge. All that can be reasonably expected of an employer who has grounds for suspicion is that he should act without haste and without prejudice; he need not observe all the legal rules of evidence. We confess that for the Government, after appointing a commission, to appoint a judicial court of inquiry strikes one as an evasion of executive responsibility.[301]

The *Manchester Guardian* had hit the nail on the head. In London there was this unfinished business. What to do about the MC and its Report? The House of Commons had made noises about forming a tribunal/court of inquiry to take further evidence in accordance with judges' rules, but there was corporate inertia in Whitehall. No one initiated further action and so, by default, London took the easy way out and decided to do ... absolutely nothing. It 'evaded executive responsibility', mentioned by the *Guardian,* to a heroic degree.

The MC Report was ignored and allowed to wither on the vine. Its pages were left unturned in public libraries and this heart-rending chronicle of abject misery and suffering was just quietly shelved and forgotten.

* * *

The cyclic nature of history and military history in particular is evidenced by the American/British invasion of Iraq (Mesopotamia) in 2003. This was, ostensibly, on the premise of seeking out the 'Weapons of Mass Destruction' (WMD) held by the Iraqi Government. Eighty-nine years earlier, the aim of the invasion was to secure a source of oil, swiftly changed to an endeavour to annex the entire country.

In both cases the public were misled as to the validity of the action that subsequently led to massive loss of life. The most recent campaign left chaos in its wake and gross instability in the country. At the time of writing, that murderous instability still persists.

In the face of increasing public clamour, it was in 2009 that the Prime Minister (Brown) instituted an inquiry to be headed by Sir John Chilcot GCB PC, a senior civil servant.

Decades earlier, the MC (see pages 223–226) consisted of five members who were elected politicians; one was a member of the House of Lords and three were military men. Chilcot's team was made up, initially, of two historians, a diplomat and a crossbench member of the House of Lords – none were elected individuals, none have a military background and none are lawyers, a deficiency shared with their forbears. Chilcot does, however,

263

have two ex-officio individuals – a QC and a general – to give legal and military advice when required.

Predictably, the composition of the Chilcot team drew cross-party criticism. Sir Martin Gilbert, a historian and member of the inquiry, and hopefully open-minded, wrote in 2004 that George W. Bush and Tony Blair 'may well, with the passage of time and the opening of the archives, join the ranks of Roosevelt and Churchill'. He may have been right, but he died in February 2015 and his contribution to the Chilcot Report, whenever it is made public, remains to be seen.

Amid rising public disquiet, the Chilcot Inquiry went about its business with a notable lack of urgency and made it clear that it did not intend to report until 2016, at the earliest. The *Daily Telegraph* commented:

> Sir John Chilcot's public inquiry into the causes of Britain's war in Iraq inspires little confidence. The inquiry itself was born of Gordon Brown's political calculation, a transparent ploy to distance himself from his predecessor Tony Blair. … Whenever that the inquiry reports, it seems unlikely to change many minds: Britain's opinions of that bloody and costly war are too deeply entrenched for any analysis, no matter how authoritative, to change them.
>
> The extraordinary duration of the inquiry is a further cause for despair. Sir John's decision to allow those criticised in his report to respond to that criticism may have had honourable motivations, but its practical effect has been disastrous: six years on there is still no date for publication. As the process drags on, lawyers on generous fees are the only beneficiaries.[302]

It may well be that the Chilcot Inquiry, or one of its historian members, recognised the criticism of the MC in its dealings with witnesses and has accordingly made every effort to avoid that pitfall of a hundred years before.

Although acknowledging the traditional 'right of centre' position of the newspaper, nevertheless its comment is germane. The public perception, in early 2016, is that the report of the Chilcot Inquiry will be less than satisfactory, although the members are unlikely to be accused of 'criminality', as their predecessors were. Nevertheless, the possibility of a transparent report that might lead any individual to face legal action is remote in the extreme and the nine caveats that limit the information to be published and available to the public will be a factor.

The high probability is that, just as in 1917, the findings of the Chilcot Inquiry will lead nowhere, but at great expense.

In mid-July 1917, the debate was over; in the desert wastes of

Mesopotamia the mercury hovered between 110°F and 120°F, and so there was nothing new there. What was new was that the only sound was that of the wind as it found its way through the thorn bush.

The guns were silent; Baghdad had fallen to the thrusting Lieutenant General Maude and his vast army on 11 March. The war had moved much further on, and the trials and tribulations of an earlier generation of soldiers who had failed to reach Baghdad had faded slightly in memory.

The cemeteries were being reorganised and where possible some of the bodies of men who had drowned, died of exposure, shock or bullet wounds were being identified and given a burial appropriate to their faith. Basra now looked like the base of a large army; from utter chaos had come order, and September 1914 seemed like a hundred years ago.

There was general public anticipation that there would be retribution for the failures in Mesopotamia, but in reality, only two individuals suffered the least inconvenience.

The publication of the MC Report in June 1917 had hit the Army Council like a bombshell. It was expecting there to be criticism, but not of this gravity. On 6 July, and notwithstanding the performance of Hardinge in the House of Lords only a few days before, it directed that charges should be framed and court martial proceedings started against Duff, Nixon, MacNeese, Babtie and Hathaway.[303] Barrow was ignored. The following day, after some further thought, it was decided to allow the 'accused' the opportunity to defend themselves at a public inquiry.

A minor glitch to be overcome was that, if a court martial was to be the tool for retribution, then Section 161 of the Army Act 1916, which applied specifically to courts of inquiry, would have to be waived. This section, inconveniently, debarred the trial of any soldier after three years from the commission of the offence.

The military arrangements hit another, and more serious, stumbling block on 11 July, when the inadmissibility of the evidence obtained by the MC became evident. By 19 July, any thoughts of conducting trial by court martial had been abandoned, but despite this, the 'accused' (not yet formally charged with any offence) were ordered to provide written explanations for their conduct and legal advice was made available to them. General Sir Edwin Barrow was excluded from the process and was cleared, tacitly, of any malfeasance.

Paul Davis[304] had researched the matter in considerable detail but was unable to find these explanations on file; however, he did find that, 'On 5 September Sir William Babtie's statement was accepted as satisfactory.'[305] Surgeon General Hathaway's was not considered until 20 March 1918, and at that meeting the council decided that he should be called upon to retire. Hathaway was well towards the end of his service and his anticipated retirement age anyway. He left with his pension intact and, hurt pride apart, was unscathed. MacNeese was exonerated that same day.[306]

Nixon's explanation was reviewed on 4 September 1918, seventeen months on – the Army Council then 'excused him'.[307] Duff did not respond to the order for an explanation. He was not pursued, the matter was dropped and so he too was, in effect, exonerated by default.

The senior officers responsible, in one form or another, for the debacle in the desert had walked free. Curzon had alleged in a memo to the Cabinet on 17 June 1917 that:

> the publication of the Report would – in such a case as that of the ex-Viceroy – in itself be a punishment to those whose conduct had been thus exposed and that it would be very damaging to their reputations and future careers.[308]

To a point he was right; they did indeed, albeit briefly, carry the taint of censure, but there was no discernible impact on future careers. The public

72. Commonwealth War Grave Commission Cemetery in Basra, now Iraq.

memory is short; the war would soon be won and then the campaign in the Middle East would slip into its correct perspective as just a 'side show' to the main event.

In 1917, the Government progressively exculpated those responsible for the disastrous events in the desert. For the men of the Tigris Corps, and the 6th Division in particular, this was the final and most insulting betrayal.

Initially, their elected political masters and their military leaders had betrayed them. Now, the House of Commons, at whose behest they had gone to war and which had the capacity to provide redress, had betrayed them. Frederick Smith, Arthur Balfour and David Lloyd George figured high on the list of these, the most recent betrayers.

The sequence of events outlined here begs the question, was justice served?

Emphatically, it was not!

Was it a public disgrace?

Of course it was, and a hundred years later, the events that gave rise to the Mesopotamia Commission remain an immovable, dark blot on Britain's military history. The hope is that the men who died will not be forgotten and the men who indirectly caused their deaths will not be forgiven.

Chapter notes
298 George Nicoll Barnes CH PC (1859–1940), Labour politician.
299 Edward George Villiers Stanley, 17th Earl of Derby KG, GCB, GCVO, TD, PC, KGStJ, JP (1865–1948). From July 1916 Under-Secretary of State for War, later, Secretary of State. Ambassador to France 1918–20.
300 Busch, B.C., *Hardinge of Penshurst*, p.218.
301 *Manchester Guardian*, 13 July 1917, p.4.
302 The *Daily Telegraph*, 14 August 2015.
303 Army Council meeting, 216, 6 July 1917, WO/163/22.
304 Davis, P.K., *Ends and Means*, p.221.
305 Army Council meeting, 230, 5 September 1917, WO/163/22.
306 Army Council informal meeting, 20 March 1918, WO/163/23.
307 Army Council informal meeting, 4 September 1918, WO/163/23.
308 Busch, B.C., *Hardinge of Penshurst*, p.218.

Appendix A

What Happened to Old ...?

'How softly but how swiftly they have sidled back to power
by the favour and contrivance of their kind.'
(Rudyard Kipling, *Mesopotamia*, 11 July 1917)

Tens of thousands of people played a part in the desert campaign between September 1914 and April 1916. The overwhelming majority did as they were bidden, and many paid with their lives. Apart from Charles Townshend, none of those who ordered affairs in Mesopotamia were ever at any physical risk.

It would be appropriate to tie up some loose ends and determine just what effect, if any, the MC Report had on some of the main players.

* * *

Austen Chamberlain KG
Secretary of State for India, 25 May 1915–17 July 1917

His resignation raised his profile, attracted many plaudits for his high principles and did him no harm at all. He was quickly back at the centre of public life. Chamberlain, possibly the least culpable of those censured, was guilty of being misled. His resignation brought a wave of support and his principled action added to his reputation. The India Office was no great loss and, although out of high office, he was quickly re-employed. He became Chancellor of the Exchequer in 1919, a post he held until 1921, by which time he was the leader of the Conservative Party and Lord Privy Seal.

His career flourished and in 1924 he became Foreign Secretary. In this post he excelled, and his skilled negotiations in 1925 established the 'Locarno Pact'. In an effort to maintain the post-war status quo in the West, Chamberlain was prepared to assist the German Foreign Minister in seeking a British guarantee of Germany's western borders.

Chamberlain actively supported the cause of Franco-German reconciliation and his aim was to create a situation where Germany could pursue its territorial revisionism in Eastern Europe 'peacefully'. Chamberlain believed that if Franco–German relations improved, France would abandon its *cordon sanitaire*, and as soon as France had traded off its relations with eastern allies, closer relations with Germany would be the beneficial result, although Poland and Czechoslovakia would be obliged to adjust to German demands.

With hindsight it is glaringly obvious that this was an incredibly dangerous policy, depending as it did on German goodwill in which, we now know, that nation was manifestly hugely deficient. Chamberlain, by his actions, was a contributory factor to the outbreak of the Second World War.

His success in driving through this flawed plan resulted in his being awarded the Nobel Peace Prize. In addition, he was created a Knight of the Order of the Garter.

Chamberlain died on 17 March 1937, aged seventy-three, just as the German war machine was limbering up. Less than three months later, his half-brother Neville became Prime Minister and fell victim to that war machine, in part, created by Austen.

* * *

General Sir Beauchamp Duff GCB GCSI KCVO CIE KStJ
Commander-in-Chief of the Indian Army, 8 March 1914, replaced in June 1917

Duff may have ignored the Army Council, but the censure of the MC and the accusation that he (and Hardinge) '*showed little desire to help and some desire actually to obstruct the energetic prosecution of the war*' caused him distress. He was, for practical purposes, removed from his post as soon as he returned to the UK to give evidence to the MC. He was, of course, at the time the incumbent Commander-in-Chief of the Indian Army and a person of considerable substance. The indignity added to his pain and apparently he was the one individual to be filled with remorse. He was found dead in his bed on 20 January 1920. Allegedly, he had committed suicide by taking an overdose. He was sixty-two.

* * *

Lieutenant General Sir John Nixon GCMG KCB
Commander, Indian Expeditionary Force 'F',
1 April 1915–19 January 1916

Although Nixon was censured by the MC and later exonerated by the Army Council, he was nevertheless removed from the active list of the Army and retired in late 1918. In 1975, Nixon attracted the attention of Norman Dixon, who coupled Nixon's name with others when he wrote of a group:

> whose besetting sin was overweening ambition coupled with terrifying insensitivity to the suffering of others. These men like Haig, Townshend, Walpole, Nixon and Joffre seemed dedicated to one goal – self-advancement. Vain, devious, scheming and dishonest, they were certainly not inactive in the courses they pursued, nor, of course, were they without military talents.[309]

Be that as it may, the following year Nixon was decorated as Knight Grand Cross of the order of St Michael and St George (GCMG). This is a very high honour and its award to Nixon was a powerful indication of his absolution by His Majesty's Government.

In 1921, Nixon and his wife went to the Côte d'Azur to spend the winter. On 15 December, Nixon died at St Raphael, aged sixty-four. His career had been exemplary until those fateful few months (April 1915–January 1916) in which he commanded in Mesopotamia.

* * *

Lieutenant Sir Edmund Barrow GCB KCMG
Military Secretary to the India Office, 1914–1917

He was sixty-two when he took up the job of Military Secretary to the India Office. After his censure by the MC in 1917, he moved smoothly on and was appointed to be a member of the autocratic Council of India. He retired in 1919 and died in 1934.

* * *

Lieutenant General Sir William Babtie VC KCB KCMG
Director, Medical Services India, 22 March 1914–5 June 1915
Principal Director, Army Medical Services, Mediterranean,
15 June 1915–10 March 1916

He was an officer whose personal qualities were never in doubt, but the MC questioned his competence. In September 1917, he provided the written explanation demanded of him. Then he too moved smoothly onward. On 1 March 1918, he was promoted to lieutenant general and appointed Inspector of Medical Services. The following year he was decorated as Knight Commander of the Order of the Bath (KCB) but he did not have long to enjoy his enhanced status because he died on 11 September 1920, aged sixty.

* * *

Major General Harold G. Hathaway CB
Principal Medical Officer Mesopotamia, April 1915 to about 6 July 1916

Hathaway was obviously over-promoted and out of his depth, but it took time for his inadequacy to be noted. He was 'mentioned in despatches' for his services up to September 1915 and the taking of Kut. This was not gazetted until 4 April 1916, by which time the dire medical situation in Mesopotamia was well reported. On 6 July 1916, after a month's sick leave, he was posted 'home', and that implies back to the UK.

On 24 February 1917, his name was 'brought to the notice of the Secretary of State for War for valuable services rendered in connection with the war'. The Army Council gave thought to his 'explanation' on 20 March 1918, and barely two weeks later, on 7 April, his retirement was recorded. Hathaway, who had been born on 30 June 1860, enjoyed a lengthy retirement until his death on 3 September 1942, aged eighty-two.[310] No photograph of Hathaway could be found.

* * *

Major General Sir Charles Townshend KCB DSO
GOC 6th (Poona) Division, Indian Army, 23rd April 1915–29 April 1916

After the surrender of Kut, it was thought that, had Townshend insisted that he and his officers would stay with their men, some of the horrors of the

271

ensuing death march would have been avoided. However, marching 1,000 miles with his men was not on Charlie's agenda and, from April 1916, Charles Townshend went into very comfortable captivity.

He was the recipient of guards of honour and a pleasing degree of Turkish adulation. Enver Pasha, the Turkish War Minister, who knew full well the conditions his people were inflicting on their prisoners, condoned it. He was an unmitigated swine, and Townshend had the opportunity to influence him when he visited, but failed to do so.

Charles Townshend lived in considerable style in a handsome house on the island of Halki. He was comfortable in captivity and was able to swim and walk about the island at will. Once settled, Townshend started to lobby the British Government to allow his wife to join him in 'captivity'. The Turks had no objection but H.H. Asquith wrote to Mrs Townshend on 1 August 1916[311] refusing permission.

Charlie's next ploy was to ask the Turks to give him parole so that he could go and live quietly in Spain. This approach came to nothing but it had afforded Charlie the chance to partake of generous lunches during the negotiations.

As winter approached, Townshend and his entourage were moved to Prinkipo, a larger island with a more sheltered aspect. The new prison was the former home of the British Consul; 'It looked like a country vicarage with a charming garden,' reported Errol Sherson, his cousin and the first of his biographers.

The bad news was that, back in England, the Marchioness of Townshend, despite eleven years of childless marriage to the 6th Marquess, had given birth to a son. This small boy would be the 7th Marquess and Charles Townshend would now never be Lord Townshend – he was not going to be a lieutenant general soon either.

In October 1916, his disappointment was slightly ameliorated when he was notified that he had been promoted to Knight Commander of the Order of the Bath (KCB). With marked lack of grace, he grunted at Boggis that it was 'not before time', adding, 'I don't suppose anyone will begrudge me my KCB after thirty-five years' service in nine campaigns and nine mentions in despatches. It has not been awarded *too* soon.'[312]

It has to be said that, based on his record of success, he could reasonably have expected to be decorated back in September 1915, after he took Kut. Townshend's regular contact with senior Turks and the manner in which they entertained him started to affect the setting of his moral compass, and increasingly he identified with the Turkish cause. An amateur psychologist might wonder if he was an early example of the 'Stockholm syndrome'.[313]

As the war ran to its end, Townshend sought to play a part in the peace negotiations. He was rejected by HMG. Similarly, on his return to the UK, via Paris, where he spent time with his wife, he was invited coldly to explain, 'in writing', why he had given an unauthorised press conference to *The Times*.

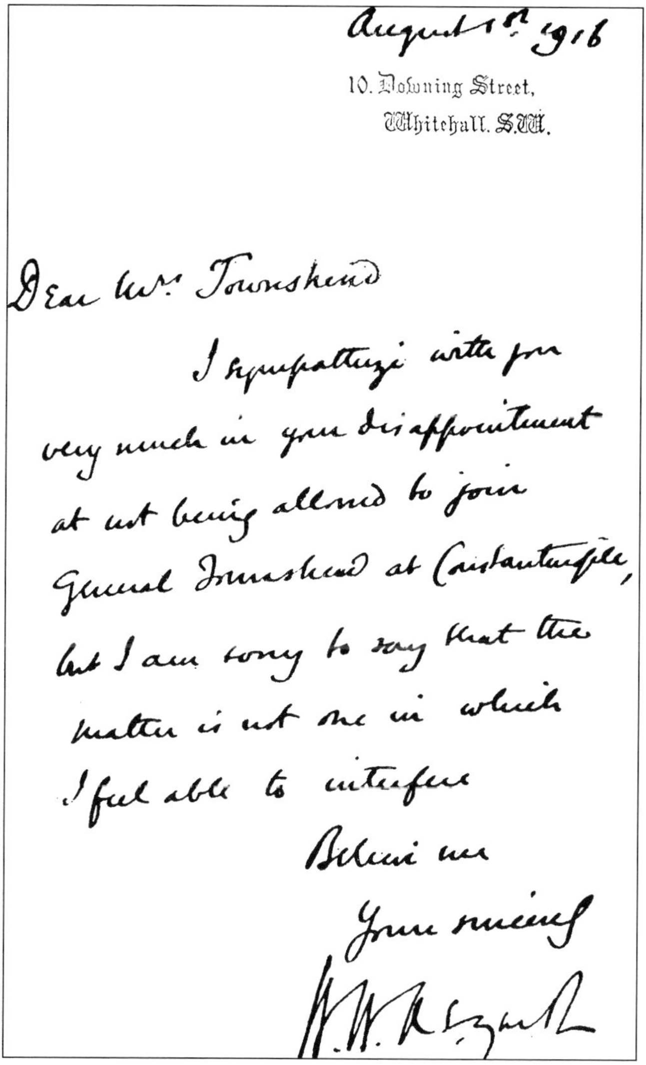

August 1st 1916

10. Downing Street,
Whitehall. S.W.

Dear Mrs Townshend

I sympathize with you very much in your disappointment at not being allowed to join General Townshend at Constantinople, but I am sorry to say that the matter is not one in which I feel able to interfere

Believe me

Yours sincerely

H. H. Asquith

73. The Prime Minister's reply to Mrs Townshend. *(A.J. Barker)*

74. Townshend in captivity with his personal staff. From the left. LCpl J. Boggis, Tewfic Bey (Turkish ADC) General Townshend, Captain Morland ADC. *(Braddon)*

Townshend lobbied for further employment but had by now attracted the disfavour of Field Marshals Haig and Robertson. To be held in low esteem by one field marshal would be career limiting, but the disfavour of two is terminal. To cap that degree of disfavour, the icing on the career cake was when King George V expressed the view that Charles Townshend should have stayed with his men.

Townshend wrote his book *My Campaign in Mesopotamia*, which was published in February 1920. It did him no good and was seen as an apologia.

He stood for election to the House of Commons when the member for The Wrekin died suddenly; his retirement was brought forward three months to allow him to stand. Townshend was duly elected as MP for The Wrekin in 1921, but he was not a successful politician. He spoke rarely and then only on military topics. He was in the company of men who were his intellectual equal or superior, with a wider experience of worldly matters. Nevertheless, he entertained ambitions to be the ambassador to Turkey and meddled in the affairs of that part of the world, to the intense irritation of the Foreign Office.

In October 1922, there was a general election and Townshend sought a seat closer to the family home in Norfolk. He was distracted by his only daughter's wedding, failed to find a seat and his political career spluttered to a close.

It is alleged that General Mellis had sought to have Townshend indicted for neglecting his soldiers. That sounds entirely likely but no evidence has been found to substantiate the claim. Townshend spent more time in Paris and, after a good lunch at The Ritz on 17 May 1924, he was taken ill. He died just before midnight on that day.

He is buried at East Raynham in Norfolk. His grave bears a simple, lichen-covered slab, upon which is engraved 'Townshend of Kut'. Mellis, Delamain et al were notably absent from the funeral. The obituaries were muted. *The Times* implied, accurately as it happened, that he was a seeker after glory. The *Daily Telegraph* carried a more generous obituary by Colonel Repington, but even he commented adversely on the separation of the officers and men after the surrender of Kut.

* * *

Lieutenant General Sir George Gorringe KCB KCMG DSO
GOC 12th Indian Division, April 1915–29 January 1916
Chief of Staff, Tigris Corps,
30 January 1916–12 March 1916
Commander, Tigris Corps, 12 March 1916 – ?? July 1916

Gorringe was a direct contemporary of Townshend but did not share the gregarious nature of Charlie. He is described in negative terms by all contemporary sources. 'Bully', 'rude', 'aggressive' and 'domineering' are usually the words used. He was not popular at any level.

In Cockney rhyming slang, he was known as 'bloody orange'.[314] He was an officer who demonstrated little innovative flair and formations under his command suffered high casualty rates. He was removed from command of the Tigris Corps in July 1916, but went on (as major general) to command 47th Division in France, a post he held until March 1919.

During his period with 47th Division, his chief of staff, the senior of his staff officers, was Lieutenant Colonel B.L. Montgomery, Royal Warwickshire Regiment, who said later of Gorringe, 'All the corps commanders under whom he served were junior to him in service but he was very unpopular and Haig would not give him a corps.'

The influence of the bachelor general on the aspiring Montgomery was considerable, and as the GOC liked and trusted his 30-year-old Chief of Staff, so he delegated enormous responsibility to him, 'Thus despite his young age Monty now assumed complete responsibility, under General Gorringe, for the running of a division – involving 15,000 troops including infantry, machine gunners, field gunners, heavy artillery, tanks, engineers and cavalrymen.'[315]

Montgomery was a bombastic and unpleasant man; to what extent he took his cue from Gorringe, one can only surmise.

Post-war, Gorringe commanded the 10th Division in Egypt. In 1921, he was promoted to lieutenant general and retired in 1924. He went to live and farm near Shoreham-by-Sea, and died there, aged seventy-seven, on 24 October 1945, having lived to see the accomplishments of his protégé.

* * *

Lieutenant General Sir Walter Delamain KCB KCMG DSO
Commander, 16th Brigade Indian Army, 27 September 1914–29 April 1916

Delamain survived his capture at Kut. After his release he was given command of a division and was subsequently promoted to lieutenant general in April 1920. In that rank he served as Adjutant General of the Indian Army until his retirement in March 1923. Delamain died in 1932.

* * *

Lieutenant General Sir Fenton Aylmer VC KCB,
13th Baronet of Donadea
Commander, the Tigris Corps, 10th December 1915–12 March 1916

Aylmer was a contemporary of Townshend and, like so many others mentioned in this book, had served in the relief of Chitrál. He was a brave man but by most accounts a weak personality who was dominated by Nixon for the first critical five weeks of his command of the Tigris Corps. It was Nixon who made all the strategic decisions, but also greatly influenced the tactical battle from 9 December 1915 until he left the theatre in mid-January

1916. General Lake, who replaced Nixon, was similarly assertive and Aylmer found himself fighting battles with plans not of his making.

He was relieved of command and replaced by Gorringe. When he gave his evidence to the MC, he emphasised that on operations all of his plans had been overruled. He retired from the Army in 1919, having conducted himself with admirable dignity. Fenton Aylmer died in Wimbledon, Surrey, on 3 September 1935, aged seventy-three.

* * *

Major General Sir Charles Mellis VC KCB KCMG
GOC 6th Indian Division at the Battle of Shaiba, 12–14 April 1915, Commander of the Cavalry column at the Battle of Ctesiphon and, thereafter, 30 Brigade

Mellis was the very epitome of the soldier's general. He was as brave as a lion and his soldiers venerated him. The enemy, too, held him in great respect.

He was captured at Kut but was in poor health, so he travelled upriver to Baghdad by steamship. From choice he would have remained with his men, but his health in the short term precluded that. However, as soon as he recovered, he joined the survivors of the dreadful march as they trudged towards Anatolia.

He was given assistance and rather better rations on his journey, but was enraged by the plight of his soldiers he encountered on the march. Mellis collected up survivors and berated the Turkish guards on behalf of his men. He insisted that some men be accommodated in hospitals.

He was a tower of strength and an inspiration to all who saw him. Charles Mellis was eventually imprisoned at Broussa, in north-west Anatolia, and, while there, continued to be a thorn in the side to the Turks and Enver Pasha, the War Minister, in particular.

After his release, he returned to the Indian Army, from which he retired on 24 February 1920. He died on 6 June 1936, aged seventy-six, and is buried in St Peter's Churchyard, Frimley, Surrey.

* * *

Charles Hardinge, 1st Baron Hardinge of Penshurst
KG GCB GCSI GCMG GCVO ISO PC
Viceroy of India, 1910–1916, Permanent Secretary,
the Foreign Office, 1916–1920, Ambassador to France,
1920–1922

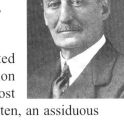

Charles Hardinge is, arguably, the most highly decorated British subject and, on the basis of government approbation over many years, must surely be considered to be the most capable and talented public servant ever. Lord Mountbatten, an assiduous collector of 'honours', pales into insignificance in comparison.

Hardinge had been lionised throughout his distinguished career. It was three years after his death, in 1944, that his autobiography was published. In this book, Hardinge devoted a little over two pages to the Mesopotamia Commission. In his text he listed the membership of that commission and then commented in these words:

> It should be observed that not one of these gentlemen had ever been to India except General Lyttelton when a subaltern, nor had any of them any knowledge of Indian administration except Lord Hamilton, who had, many years earlier, been Secretary of State for India.
>
> The Report when published was regarded by all those who knew anything of Indian affairs as unfair and narrow-minded, and as a travesty of fact and justice … while 132 pages of closely printed matter was given to the Report, only eight lines were given to the dangerous and anxious situation in the interior of India and on the frontier, after India had sent no less than 300,000 troops across the seas to France, Egypt, China, and East Africa.
>
> Everybody was blamed all round, beginning with Austen Chamberlain and myself and ending with many distinguished military officers. To achieve this end important official telegrams bearing on the issue were omitted and some mutilated, while private letters were turned to mean the reverse of what was intended and important portions omitted. It was really an inexplicable performance.[316]

Thirty years after the event, in 1947, the MC was no more than a footnote to history, and Hardinge was too. He could not be challenged. From beyond the grave he went on to say that after the publication of the Report he tendered his resignation, on 30 June 1917, to Balfour, the Foreign Secretary and his superior. Balfour 'refused to accept it'. He referred to his statement to the House of Lords on 3 July and recorded that, 'It was enthusiastically received in India and received commendation from the moderate opinion in the Press and elsewhere.' That is an overstatement not borne out by the headlines of the day.

It appears that although Hardinge had the support of Balfour, he did not enjoy the same degree of approbation from Lloyd George, the Prime Minister. Hardinge recalled the sequence of events and wrote:

> It was on 9 July that Lord Curzon came to see me at the Foreign Office and told me at some length that, as an old friend, he was the bearer of a message from the War Cabinet to the effect that the Government would not ask me to resign but they made the suggestion to me to do so in order to 'ease the situation and to avoid hostile criticism of the Foreign Office in the future which my position there might provoke.'[317]
>
> He spoke without interruption for about twenty minutes while I was growing angrier every minute. When he stopped, I let fly and told him that his action was hardly that which could be described as that of a friend when he came as an emissary of a craven cabinet to ask me to 'ease the situation' for them.

Hardinge drew Curzon's attention to his thirty-seven years of exemplary public service at the highest levels and, by his account, lambasted Curzon to such effect that, 'he slunk from my room like a whipped hound.' It is worth noting that Curzon had an unfortunate manner at the best of times, with an unusual capacity to spread discord, and was not the best choice of an emissary. The meeting between the two men was unlikely to be amiable, and although Curzon and Hardinge had once been close associates, they had not been friends for a decade or more.

Following this meeting, Harding wrote another letter of resignation, which was in Balfour's hands on 11 July. Balfour's speech in the House of Commons on the 12th clearly rejected the gesture.

About a week later, Hardinge realised that Balfour was putting himself at risk by defending him. By his account, he selflessly and in the public good offered his resignation a third time, pending the verdict of a judicial tribunal. The War Cabinet considered a statement to this effect, written by Balfour, in which he said that Hardinge 'could not devote his whole energies to the work of his laborious and difficult office … until the result of the inquiry is known.'

The War Cabinet reconsidered its position and on 18 July, Bonar Law announced in the House that, 'The Government has decided that it would be detrimental to the public interest if the Foreign Office were deprived, at the present juncture, of the services of Lord Hardinge.'

Hardinge noted, 'Thus ended a very unpleasant interlude in my work but thanks to Mr Balfour's chivalrous championship, *I came out on top in the fight for my reputation, which was dearer to me than life.*' (Author's italics) In his autobiography, Hardinge expresses no remorse for any of the tens of thousands of Indian Army soldiers killed in pursuit of his aims, and far from refuting the criticism of him, he merely ignores it. He emerges from the pages of his autobiography as an arrogant, vain, pompous and mean-minded person.

The freeing of Hardinge from blame now made it all the more difficult for HMG to deal with the military officers. Hardinge's biographer, B.C. Busch, made the judgement that:

> Hardinge had supported the parsimonious, pre-war attitude which served soldiers ill in Mesopotamia; he did not intervene effectively enough to cure the medical problems, he was blind to Duff's faults; he failed to consult his council, and circumvented the meaning if not the law of India's constitution. But his guilt was hardly the sort for which he could be tried and his contribution … far outweighed his faults in listening too willingly to his military advisors.[318]

The final accolade for Hardinge was his appointment as Ambassador to France in November 1920. He served in Paris for two years but during this period he had to deal with the difficult Lord Curzon, who had urged his resignation in 1917. Anglo-French relations deteriorated to such a degree that he decided to retire to Kent in 1922. Unexpectedly, Lord Curzon wrote a generous valedictory letter to Hardinge on his retirement. The impact of the letter on the recipient was such that it was reproduced in his autobiography twenty-five years later.

He was a cold, reserved personality with a well-developed sense of self-worth, and had very few close friends. His work had been everything to him and, after his retirement, he never filled the gap in his later life. He served as a Special Constable during the General Strike of 1926 and revisited India at the invitation of Lord Irwin, the Viceroy, in 1933. He was a reclusive individual and in the twilight of his life he was lonely. He died on 2 August 1944 and is buried at Fordcombe, Kent.

Chapter notes

309 Dixon, N.E., *On the Psychology of Military Incompetence*, p.155.

310 From the service record of Major General Hathaway provided by Becks Skinner, Director, the Army Medical Services Museum, Ash Vale, Surrey.

311 Barker, A.J., *Townshend of Kut*, p.210.

312 Sherson, E., *Townshend of Chitrál and Kut*, p.337. Sherson's italics.

313 Stockholm syndrome is not a medical term, but is a phenomenon in which captives begin to identify with their captors. At first this seems to be a defensive response generated by fear of violence. Insignificant acts of kindness by the captor are magnified out of proportion in the captive's mind, not least because in a hostage situation the captive will have lost all sense of perspective. All the key factors appear to be in place to induce Stockholm syndrome in Sir Charles Townshend.

314 University of Birmingham for First World War Studies (General's Nicknames).

315 Hamilton, N., *The Full Monty*, Allen Lane, London, 2002, p.117.

316 Hardinge, Lord, *Old Diplomacy – The reminiscences of Lord Hardinge of Penshurst*, J. Murray, London, 1947, p.215.

317 Hardinge incorporated a footnote, which said that he recorded the precise form of words used at this interview immediately after the meeting, p.216.

318 Busch, B.C., *Hardinge of Penshurst*, p.274.

Appendix B

Witnesses Called to Give Evidence

The Mesopotamia Commission took evidence from 118 witnesses who testified on oath. In the Report it listed the names of those whose evidence it judged to be the most significant. These are tabulated below.

The Marquess of Crewe KG PC MA FSA	Late, Secretary of State for India
Rt Hon Austen Chamberlain PC MP	Secretary of State for India
Lord Hardinge PC GCB GCMG ISO	Former, Viceroy of India
Lord Inchcape GCMG KCSI KCIE	Director, Anglo-Persian Oil Co
Sir Thomas Holderness KCSI KCB LCS BA	Under Secretary of State for India
Gen Sir Beauchamp Duff GCB KCVO KCSI CB CIE	Former, C-in-C, India
Gen Sir O'Moore Creagh VC GCB GCSI KCB	Former, C-in-C, India
Gen Sir Edmund Barrow GCB	Military Secretary at the India Office
Gen Sir John Nixon KCB ADC	Late, GOC IEF'D'
Maj Gen Sir George Gorringe KCB CMG DSO	Late, GOC Tigris Corps
Lieut Gen Sir Percy Lake KCB KCMG	Chief of General Staff, GOC IEF'D'
Lieut Gen Sir Fenton Aylmer VC KCB	Late, GOC Tigris Corps
Maj Gen M. Cowper CB CIE	Late, Deputy Adjutant & Quarter Master General (DAQMG) IEF'D'
Maj Gen K.S. Davison CB	Late, Inspector of Communications IEF'D'
Maj Gen G.V. Kemball CB DSO	Late, Chief of General Staff, IEF'D'

Maj Gen Sir George Younghusband
KCMG KCIE CB
Brevet Col S.H. Climo CB DSO

GOC 7th Division
Late, Commander 30th Brigade

The following officers of the Royal Indian Marine

Capt W. Lumsden CVO CIE RN
Comdr A. Hamilton

Capt W.B. Huddleston

Director, RIM
Late, Principal Marine
Transport Officer
Late Principal Marine
Transport Officer

Representing the War Office

Maj Gen F.B. Maurice CB
Brig Gen The Hon R. Stuart-Wortley
Lieut Col H.F.P. Percival DSO

Director Military Operations
Director of Movements
Assistant Director of Supplies

Medical Witnesses

Sir Alfred Keogh GCB

Surg Gen Sir William Babtie VC KCMG
CB MB KHS
Surg Gen H.G. Hathaway CB

Surg Gen J.G. MacNeece CB

Col P. Hehir CB MD IMS

Maj R. Markham Carter FRCS IMS

Director General, Army
Medical Services
Late, Director of Medica
Services, India
Late, Assistant Director of
Medical Services, India
Late, Director Medical
Services, India
Late, Assistant Director of
Medical Services   IEF'D'.
Later, PMO 6th Division
Commanding Officer of
HMHS *Varala*

Civilian Witnesses

Mr E.A. Ridsdale FGS

Sir Robert Carlyle KCSI CIE

Sir Mackenzie Chalmers KCB CSI

Sir John Hewett GSCI

Member, Vincent-Bingley
Commission, Red Cross
Late, Member, Council of the
Viceroy of India
Late, Member, Council of the
Viceroy of India
Late, Member, Council of the
Viceroy of India

	Chairman, Indian Soldiers' Fund Joint War Committee of the British Red Cross
Sir William Clark KCSI	Late, Member, Council of the Viceroy of India
Mr J.B. Brunyate CIE CSI ICS	Financial Secretary to the Indian Government

Appendix C

An Analysis of *Mesopotamia*

Rudyard Kipling (1865–1936)

75. Rudyard Kipling. *(The Kipling Society)*

Mesopotamia
1917

They shall not return to us, the resolute, the young,
The eager and whole-hearted whom we gave:
But the men who left them thriftily to die in their own dung,
Shall they come with years and honour to the grave?

They shall not return to us, the strong men coldly slain
In sight of help denied from day to day:
But the men who edged their agonies and chid them in their pain,
Are they too strong and wise to put away?

Our dead shall not return to us while Day and Night divide –
Never while the bars of sunset hold.
But the idle-minded overlings who quibbled while they died,
Shall they thrust for high employments as of old?

Shall we only threaten and be angry for an hour?
When the storm is ended shall we find
How softly but how swiftly they have sidled back to power
By the favour and contrivance of their kind?

Even while they soothe us, while they promise large amends,
Even while they make a show of fear,
Do they call upon their debtors, and take counsel with their friends,
To conform and re-establish each career?

Their lives cannot repay us – their death could not undo –
The shame that they have laid upon our race.
But the slothfulness that wasted and the arrogance that slew,
Shall we leave it unabated in its place?

Kipling was a well-established literary figure by the outbreak of the First World War and, in 1907, won the Nobel Peace Prize for literature, the first English-language recipient, and the youngest. He was a great admirer of the British soldier and a shrewd observer, as evidenced by his well-known *Barrack Room Tales.*

At the beginning of the First World War, Kipling was too old to serve in uniform, so he had to settle for contributing to the cause by writing pamphlets and poems in support of the UK's war aims. Not the least of these was the restoration of Belgium after that country had been occupied by Germany. In September 1914, Kipling was asked by the British Government to write propaganda, an offer that he immediately accepted.

Kipling's penmanship was not only popular, but was also effective. The main thrust of his work was to extol the virtues of the British military, but in addition, he wrote vividly about German atrocities against Belgian civilians – not all based on fact. But then, that is the nature of propaganda.

The sinking of the RMS *Lusitania* in 1915 enraged Kipling, who judged it to be a deeply inhumane act. He characterised the war as a crusade for civilization against barbarism. In a 1915 speech, Kipling declared, somewhat excessively, that, 'There was no crime, no cruelty, no abomination that the mind of men can conceive of which the German has not perpetrated, is not perpetrating, and will not perpetrate if he is allowed to go on. … Today, there are only two divisions in the world … human beings and Germans.'[319]

The heavy loss of life that the BEF had taken by the autumn of 1914 shocked Kipling, who laid the blame at the doors of the entire pre-war generation of British politicians. He argued that they had failed to learn the lessons of the Boer War and, as a result, thousands of British soldiers were now paying with their lives for their failure in the fields of France and Belgium.[320]

Kipling's son, John, died in the First World War, at the Battle of Loos in September 1915, aged just eighteen. John had volunteered for the Royal Navy, but after a failed medical examination due to his poor eyesight, he then applied for military service as an army officer. His eyesight remained an obstacle and he was, once more, rejected. His father was a lifelong friend of Lord Roberts, Commander-in-Chief of the British Army and Colonel of the Irish Guards. At his father's request, John was accepted into the Irish Guards, notwithstanding his failure to meet the medical criteria.[321]

John was sent to his battalion at Loos in a reinforcement contingent. He was last seen badly wounded by shrapnel. An unsuccessful search for the boy's body became Kipling's post-war mission. A corpse identified as his was found in 1992, although that identification has since been challenged. The death of his son was a burden Kipling carried for the rest of his life.

Rudyard Kipling's *Mesopotamia* was published on 11 July 1917, when the Report of the Mesopotamia Commission was being hotly debated. The poem appeared simultaneously in the London *Morning Post* and the *New York Times*. It was masterly timing, designed to gain maximum exposure. Kipling's earlier propaganda work had already drawn him into the political scene and such was his standing that his anger at events in Mesopotamia expressed in his poetry demanded attention and struck a chord with the general public. Julian Moore wrote a paper in 2006 analysing *Mesopotamia,* and this commentary, especially its structure, owes much to his work, which is acknowledged.

Kipling wanted there to be retribution for those whose culpable incompetence had led to so many avoidable deaths. The preceding text in this book makes only too clear that the campaign was notable for the failures in every facet of the expedition. Strategically it was flawed; however, tactically, due to Townshend, it was effective. That is until the already flawed balance between operations and the logistic support became evident. The medical drum needs no further banging here.

Kipling presumes the reader will be aware of the specific aspects that he addresses, and so he rails against the political and military leadership responsible for the debacle in the desert, bringing to bear all of his formidable rhetoric. 'In six quatrains of ballad-like rhyme and metre',[322] Moore avers that Kipling 'has aimed volleys on behalf of the common soldier at':

> the men who edged their agonies and chid them in their pain

and

> the idle-minded overlings who quibbled while they died.

The poet was not alone in being outraged that those responsible were not subject to trial and punishment. Some just walked way into genteel retirement; others, like Duff, Nixon and Townshend, were exonerated. Some might take the view that, had Townshend not been a prisoner of war and been interrogated, he might have been found wanting. Hardinge, who never expressed regret or remorse, gave events in Mesopotamia scant cover in his autobiography. He went on to be Ambassador to France, no less. Kipling poses the question:

> Shall they thrust for high employment as of old?

He continues with a clear reference to Hardinge by writing:

> How softly but how swiftly they have sidled back to power
> By the favour and contrivance of their kind?

Another question:

> Do they call upon their debtors, and take counsel with their friends,
> to confirm and re-establish each career?

Kipling, ever the patriot, disassociates himself from:

> The shame that they have laid upon our race.

Moore, seeking to be even-handed, makes the valid point that Nixon was only part of a very complicated chain of command. He observed that,

> Nixon was directly responsible to the Commander-in-Chief, Indian Army, who answered to the Viceroy, who received orders from the Secretary of State for India, who was advised by the Military Secretary for India, who was responsible to the War Council, which was commanded by the Imperial Staff, which answered, finally, to the Cabinet. Since half of this chain was in India, and half in London, problems in administration and military command were virtually insurmountable, and gave rise to Kipling's bitter resentment of:

the idle-minded overlings who quibbled while they died.

The Indian Army was the epitome of bureaucratic inefficiency, and as a result, officers of the British Army had little time for the organisation, chain of command and customs of the Indian Army. The Mutiny of 1857 by sepoys in the Army of the East India Company was still within living memory, and there was an unreasonable question mark over the discipline of the Indian Army and the competence of its Anglo-Indian officers. Townshend, who was an officer of the Indian Army, held his soldiers in low regard and had done so since the siege of Chitral in 1895. Kipling observed this attitude and, knowing that half the expedition had been killed and the survivors had suffered the most dreadful neglect and deprivation, it is little wonder that he wrote of:

the slothfulness that wasted and the arrogance that slew.

The public response to the disaster of the campaign was to call for an investigation; Kipling was entirely at ease with that, and so he wrote:

Shall we only threaten and be angry for an hour?

Kipling made no bones about his view of the multiple administrative nonsenses, reminding his readers that:

They shall not return to us, the strong men coldly slain
In sight of help denied from day to day:
But the men who edged their agonies and chid them in their pain,
Are they too strong and wise to put away?

Hardinge and Duff were the targets and specifically the,

idle-minded overlings who quibbled while they died.

The *Morning Post* took a very strong line and used the Mesopotamia Commission as a weapon to attack Hardinge, who because of his recent appointment as Permanent Secretary at the Foreign Office was seen as an instrument of the Prime Minister, Lloyd George. The reintroduction of Hardinge to the centre of government also offended the poet and gave rise to the bitter lines:

How softly but how swiftly they have sidled back to power
By the favour and contrivance of their kind?

Kipling was not alone in his anger. This was shared by most of the Press, and his indictment of those involved and of the British Government attracted general support. The fact that the culprits were apparently to walk away, not only unpunished but also rewarded, was the trigger for the following:

Even while they soothe us, while they promise large amends,
Even while they make a show of fear,
Do they call upon their debtors, and take counsel with their friends,
To confirm and re-establish each career?

Kipling posed the question, and the answer was highly unsatisfactory. The foregoing text has dealt with the manner in which the main players in this drama had been quietly exculpated 'and the whitewash that so appalled Kipling was complete', so Julian Moore summed up, and he has the last word, saying:

> For the modern reader, the verses have a power that transcends their specific political origin. They embody all the frustrated outbursts of a civilian public watching a generation of soldiers die at the behest of incompetent generals, and at the insidious command of self-interested politicians. This is Kipling at his most stentorian. The imperial trumpeter had become the public herald. [323]

Chapter notes

319 Gilmour, D., *The Long Recessional: The Imperial Life of Rudyard Kipling*, p.250.
320 Ibid, p.251.
321 Bilsing, T., 'The Process Of Manufacture of Rudyard Kipling's Private Propaganda', *War Literature and The Arts*, Summer 2000, retrieved 15 August 2013.
322 Moore, J., *Mesopotamia*, 2006.
323 Ibid.

Bibliography

Barker, A.J., *Townshend of Kut*, Cassel, London, 1967.

Barker, A.J., *The First Iraq War 1914–1918: Britain's Mesopotamian Campaign*, 2007 (originally published 1967 as *The Neglected War* (UK) and *The Bastard War* (USA)).

Bilsing, T., 'The Process of Manufacture of Rudyard Kipling's Private Propaganda', *War Literature and The Arts* (Summer 2000), retrieved 15 August 2013.

Braddon, R., *The Siege*, Jonathan Cape, London, 1969.

Busch, B.C., *Hardinge of Penshurst: A study in Diplomacy*, Archon Books, Hamden CT, 1980.

Churchill, W.S., *The World Crisis*, Vol. 1 Scribner's New York, 1923.

Crewe Papers, Cambridge University Library, I/13(9).

Corrigan, G., *Mud Blood and Poppycock*, Cassell, London, 2003.

Dahl, E.J., 'From Coal to Oil', *Joint Force Quarterly*, Gen. H.H. Shelton, Washington DC, USA, April 2001.

Davis, P.K., *Ends and Means: The British Mesopotamia Campaign and Commission*, Associated University Press, Delaware, USA, 1994.

Dixon, N., *On the Psychology of Military Incompetence*, Jonathon Cape, London, 1976.

French, D., 'The Dardanelles, Mecca and Kut: Prestige as a Factor in British Eastern Strategy, 1914–16', *War and Society*, 5(1) 1987, p.54.

Gilmour, D., *The Long Recessional: The Imperial Life of Rudyard Kipling*, Pimlico, London, 2003.

Gould, D., 'Lord Hardinge and the Mesopotamia Expedition and Inquiry', 1914–1917, *The Historical Journal*, Vol. 19, No. 4, 1976.

Hansard, 12–13 July 1917, HM Stationery Office, 1917, Vol. 95, London.

Hardinge papers, Cambridge University Library.

Hardinge papers, Kent County Record Office.

Hunter, C., *Eight Lives Down*, Transworld Publishers, London, 2007.

Kipling, R., *Mesopotamia 1917.*

Laffin, J., *British Butchers & Bunglers of World War 1*, Sutton Publishing, Stroud, 1988.

Lake, Sir P., Commanding IEF'D', *Report on the fall of Kut,* National Archives, WO32/5199.

Mesopotamia Commission Report, HM Stationery Office, London, 1917.

Millar, R., *Kut: The Death of an Army*, Secker & Warburg, London, 1969.

Moberly, F.J., *History of the Great War: The Campaign in Mesopotamia 1914–1918,* Vol. 2, HM Stationery Office, London, 1924.

Moore, J., *Mesopotamia*, The Kipling Society, Billericay, Essex, 2006.

Mousley, E.O., *The Secrets of a Kuttite*, 1921, reprinted by Naval & Military Press, Uckfield.

Nash, N.S., *Chitrál Charlie*, Pen & Sword, Barnsley, 2010.

Nunn, W., *Tigris Gunboats*, Andrew Melrose, London, 1921.

Sandes, E.W.C., *In Kut and Captivity*, Murray, London, 1919.

Sherson, E., *Townshend of Chitrál and Kut*, William Heinemann, London, 1928.

Sumner, I., *The Indian Army 1914–1947*, Osprey Publishing, Oxford, 2001.

Sykes, Sir Mark, The *Daily Telegraph*, 22 November 1915.

Townshend, C.V.F., *My Campaign in Mesopotamia*, Thornton Butterworth, London, 1920.

Townshend. C., *When God made Hell*: *The British Invasion of Mesopotamia and the Creation of Iraq*, Faber & Faber, London, 2010.

Vincent-Bingley Report, HM Stationery Office, London, 1916.

Whalley-Kelly, H., *Ich Dien: The Prince of Wales's Volunteers*, Regimental History, published privately.

Wilcox, R., *Battles on the Tigris*, Pen & Sword, Barnsley, 2006.

Wilson, A., *Loyalties: Mesopotamia 1914–1917*, Oxford University Press, 1931.

Index

295